First World War
and Army of Occupation
War Diary
France, Belgium and Germany

8 DIVISION
2 Battalion Rifle Brigade.
Rifle Brigade (The Prince Consort's Own)
2nd Battalion
5 November 1914 - 30 April 1919

WO95/1731

The Naval & Military Press Ltd
www.nmarchive.com
Published in association with The National Archives

Published by

The Naval & Military Press Ltd

Unit 10 Ridgewood Industrial Park,

Uckfield, East Sussex,

TN22 5QE England

Tel: +44 (0) 1825 749494

www.naval-military-press.com

www.nmarchive.com

This diary has been reprinted in facsimile from the original. Any imperfections are inevitably reproduced and the quality may fall short of modern type and cartographic standards.

© **Crown Copyright**
Images reproduced by permission of The National Archives, London, England, 2015.

Contents

Document type	Place/Title	Date From	Date To
Heading	6th Division 25th Infy Bde 2nd Bn Rifle Brigade Nov 1914-May 1919		
Heading	8th, Division. 25th, Brigade. 2nd, Rifle Brigade.		
Heading	2nd Rifle Brigade. 25th Private 8th Division. Vol I 5-29.11.14		
War Diary		05/11/1914	30/11/1914
Heading	25th Brigade 2nd Rifle Brigade. Vol II 1-31.12.14		
War Diary		01/12/1914	31/12/1914
Miscellaneous			
Heading	8th, Division. 25th, Brigade. 2. Rifle Brigade. January, 1915		
Heading	25th. Brigade 2nd Rifle Brigade Vol III 1-31.1.15		
War Diary		01/01/1915	31/01/1915
Miscellaneous			
Heading	8th, Division. 25th, Brigade. 2nd, Rifle Brigade. February, 1915.		
Heading	25th Brigade 2nd Rifle Brigade Vol IV 1-28.2.15		
War Diary		01/02/1915	28/02/1915
Heading	8th, Division. 25th, Brigade, 2nd, Rifle Brigade. March, 1915.		
Heading	25/8 Brigade 2nd Rifle Brigade Vol V 1-31.3.15		
War Diary		01/03/1915	30/03/1915
Miscellaneous	13th Kensingtons London Reg		
Miscellaneous	2nd Bn. The Rifle Brigade R B/s	18/03/1915	18/03/1915
Miscellaneous	Instructions For Operation On March 10th 1915. App A		
Miscellaneous	Battalion Order By Lieut Colonel R.B. Stephens Comdg 2nd Bn The Rifle Bde. App B.	09/03/1915	09/03/1915
Miscellaneous			
Heading	8th, Division. 25th, Brigade. 2nd, Rifle Brigade. April, 1915.		
Heading	25th Brigade 2nd Rifle Brigade Vol VI 1-30.4.15		
War Diary		01/04/1915	30/04/1915
Heading	8th, Division. 25th, Brigade. 2nd, Rifle Brigade. May, 1915.		
Heading	8th Division 25th Brigade 2nd Rifle Brigade Vol VII 1-31-5-15		
War Diary		01/05/1915	31/05/1915
Heading	8th Division 2nd Rifle Brigade Vol VIII 1-30.6.15		
War Diary		01/06/1915	30/06/1915
Heading	8th, Division. 25th, Brigade. 2nd, Rifle Brigade. July, 1915.		
Heading	8th Division 2nd Rifle Brigade VOL IX 1-31.7.15		
War Diary		01/07/1915	31/07/1915
Heading	8th, Division. 25th, Brigade. 2nd, Rifle Brigade. August, 1915.		
Heading	8th Division 2nd Rifle Bde Vol X August 15		
War Diary		01/08/1915	31/08/1915
Heading	8th, Division. 25th, Brigade. 2nd, Rifle Brigade. September, 1915.		
Heading	8th Division 2nd Rifle Brigade Vol XI Sep 15		

War Diary		01/09/1915	30/09/1915
Heading	8th, Division. 25th, Brigade. 2nd, Rifle Brigade. October, 1915.		
Heading	8th Division 2nd R.B. Oct 15 Vol XII		
War Diary		01/10/1915	31/10/1915
Heading	8th Division 2/R.B. Nov Vol XIII		
War Diary		01/11/1915	30/11/1915
Heading	8th, Division. 25th, Brigade. 2nd, Rifle Brigade. December 1915.		
Heading	2/R.B. Dec Vol XIV		
War Diary		01/12/1915	30/12/1915
Heading	8th. Division. 25th, Brigade. 2nd, Rifle Brigade. January, 1916.		
Heading	2 Rifle Bde Jan Vol XV		
War Diary	Rest Billets Boseghem.	01/01/1916	08/01/1916
War Diary	Sine of March	09/01/1916	10/01/1916
War Diary	Fleurbaix	11/01/1916	15/01/1916
War Diary	Trenches	16/01/1916	18/01/1916
War Diary	Bac St Maur	19/01/1916	31/01/1916
Heading	8th, Division. 25th, Brigade. 2nd, Rifle Brigade. February, 1916.		
War Diary		01/02/1916	29/02/1916
Heading	8th, Division. 25th, Brigade. 2nd, Rifle Brigade. March, 1916.		
War Diary		01/03/1916	31/03/1916
Heading	8th, Division. 25th. Brigade. 2nd, Rifle Brigade. April, 1916.		
War Diary		01/04/1916	30/04/1916
Heading	8th, Division. 25th, Brigade. 2nd, Rifle Brigade. May, 1916.		
War Diary	Henencourt Wood	01/05/1916	03/05/1916
War Diary	Albert Trenches Left Sub Section	04/05/1916	11/05/1916
War Diary	Millencourt	12/05/1916	19/05/1916
War Diary	Albert	20/05/1916	23/05/1916
War Diary	Millencourt	24/05/1916	24/05/1916
War Diary	Albert Trenches Left. Sub-Sector	25/05/1916	27/05/1916
War Diary	Henencourt	28/05/1916	31/05/1916
Heading	25th, Brigade. 2nd, Rifle Brigade. June, 1916.		
War Diary	Henencourt Wood	01/06/1916	04/06/1916
War Diary	Albert	05/06/1916	11/06/1916
War Diary	Trenches	12/06/1916	16/06/1916
War Diary	Long Valley	17/06/1916	20/06/1916
War Diary	Millencourt	21/06/1916	23/06/1916
War Diary	Trenches	24/06/1916	26/06/1916
War Diary	Long Valley	27/06/1916	29/06/1916
War Diary	Trenches.	30/06/1916	30/06/1916
Miscellaneous	D.A.G. G.H.Q. 3rd Echelon. Here With War Diary of This Battalion For Month of June.		
Miscellaneous	2nd Rifle Bde.	24/06/1916	24/06/1916
Miscellaneous Map	A Form Messages And Signals.		
Miscellaneous	2nd Bn. The Rifle Brigade.	24/06/1916	24/06/1916
Miscellaneous	2nd. Bn. The Rifle Brigade. Preliminary Operation Orders.	23/06/1916	23/06/1916
Miscellaneous	Report On Raid Carried Out By 2nd Bn Rifle Brigade On 25th June Against Trenches x 7 L 9.6-X 7-b 9.9.	26/06/1916	26/06/1916

Type	Description	From	To
Miscellaneous	Headquarters, 3rd Corps.	26/06/1916	26/06/1916
Heading	25th Inf. Bde. 8th Div War Diary. 2nd Battn. The Rifle Brigade. July 1916		
War Diary	Ovillers La Boiselle	01/07/1916	01/07/1916
War Diary	Song Valley (Bivouac)	02/07/1916	07/07/1916
War Diary	Allouagne	08/07/1916	19/07/1916
War Diary	Annequin	20/07/1916	23/07/1916
War Diary	Trenches Hohenzollern	24/07/1916	31/07/1916
Heading	8th, Division. 25th, Brigade. 2nd, Rifle Brigade. August, 1916.		
Heading	To D.A.G 3rd Echelon Base Herewith War Diary For Month of August 1916		
War Diary	Reserve Trenches.	01/08/1916	02/08/1916
War Diary	Trenches.	03/08/1916	07/08/1916
War Diary	Fouquieres	08/08/1916	14/08/1916
War Diary	Brigade Reserve Trenches	15/08/1916	21/08/1916
War Diary	Front Line	22/08/1916	24/08/1916
War Diary	Trenches.	26/08/1916	31/08/1916
Miscellaneous			
Miscellaneous	Raid By 2nd Rifle Brigade		
Miscellaneous	H Q S 25th Bde C.R.A. (For Information)	17/08/1916	17/08/1916
Miscellaneous	8th Division	19/08/1916	19/08/1916
Miscellaneous	Div Ra 25th Bde	19/08/1916	19/08/1916
Miscellaneous	H Q 8th Division	19/08/1916	19/08/1916
Miscellaneous	Reference Map Attached.	19/08/1916	19/08/1916
Map			
Miscellaneous	8th D.A. 0/82/4	21/08/1916	21/08/1916
Miscellaneous	Artillery Time Table		
Miscellaneous	Artillery Time Table Feint G 5.		
Miscellaneous	Artillery Time Table.		
Miscellaneous	8th D.A. O/82/4/1. Reference 8th D.A. O/84/4. dated 21-8-16	22/08/1916	22/08/1916
Miscellaneous	8. Division	18/08/1916	18/08/1916
Miscellaneous	Headquarters, I Corps.	21/08/1916	21/08/1916
Miscellaneous	A Form Messages And Signals.	23/08/1916	23/08/1916
Miscellaneous	Div. R.A.	22/08/1916	22/08/1916
Miscellaneous	16th Division 40th Division	24/08/1916	24/08/1916
Operation(al) Order(s)	25th Infantry Brigade. Operation Order No. 116.	24/08/1916	24/08/1916
Miscellaneous	16th Div	24/08/1916	24/08/1916
Miscellaneous	Left Group, 16th D.A. Centre Group, 16th D.A.	22/08/1916	22/08/1916
Miscellaneous	Time Table Bombardment Night of 24th/25th Aug.		
Map	Phase "A" Scale 1/10,000		
Map	Phase "B" Scale 1/10,000		
Miscellaneous	Central Registry. 8 Div 25 Bde		
Miscellaneous	First Army. No. 854/129 (Ga). 25th August, 1916.		
Miscellaneous	Preliminary Report On Attempted raid By 2nd Battn. Rifle Brigade North And South of Hulluch Road of 24/25th August, 1916.		
Miscellaneous	First Army. No. 854/129 (Ga). 25th August, 1916.		
Miscellaneous	Preliminary Report On Attempted Raid By 2nd Battn. Rifle Brigade North and South of Hulluch Road Between H.18.b. 7. 1/2 7. And G. 12.b. 7.5. On Night of 24/25th August, 1916.		
Miscellaneous			
Miscellaneous	Not To Be Written On		

Heading	8th, Division. 25th, Brigade. 2nd, Rifle Brigade. September, 1916.		
Miscellaneous	To The D.A.G 3rd Echelon Base.		
War Diary	La Bourse	01/09/1916	30/09/1916
Heading	8th, Division. 25th, Brigade. 2nd, Rifle Brigade. October, 1916.		
Miscellaneous	To The D.A.G G. H.Q. 3rd Echelon Base		
War Diary	Hohenzollern Reserve Trench.	01/10/1916	03/10/1916
War Diary	Front Line	04/10/1916	26/10/1916
War Diary	Trones Wood	27/10/1916	31/10/1916
Heading	8th Division. 25th Brigade 2nd Rifle Brigade November 1916		
Miscellaneous	To The D.A.G. 3rd Echelon		
War Diary	Citadel Camp (Somme)	01/11/1916	03/11/1916
War Diary	Meaulte	04/11/1916	07/11/1916
War Diary	On-March	08/11/1916	08/11/1916
War Diary	Carnoy To Trenches	09/11/1916	09/11/1916
War Diary	Trenches	10/11/1916	14/11/1916
War Diary	Guillemont Camp	15/11/1916	16/11/1916
War Diary	Sandpits.	17/11/1916	19/11/1916
War Diary	Warlus	20/11/1916	30/11/1916
Heading	8th, Division. 25th, Brigade. 2nd, Rifle Brigade. December, 1916.		
War Diary	Warlus (Rest Billets)	01/12/1916	12/12/1916
War Diary	Wireless	13/12/1916	25/12/1916
War Diary	Warlus (Rest Billets)	26/12/1916	31/12/1916
Heading	2nd Bn Rifle Bde. Jan-Dec 1917		
War Diary	Maurepas Fregicourt.	01/01/1917	03/01/1917
War Diary	Camp 14	04/01/1917	09/01/1917
War Diary	Warlus	10/01/1917	30/01/1917
War Diary	Camp Maurepas.	31/01/1917	31/01/1917
War Diary	Maurepas Ravine	01/02/1917	08/02/1917
War Diary	Maurepas Camp	09/02/1917	11/02/1917
War Diary	Camp 13 Bray-Corbie Rd	12/02/1917	18/02/1917
War Diary	Camp 13 Bray-Carbie Road	19/02/1917	21/02/1917
War Diary	Camp 17 Suzanne	22/02/1917	22/02/1917
War Diary	Quarry Farm Sector Bouchavesnes	23/02/1917	25/02/1917
War Diary	Bouchavesnes Junction Wood	26/02/1917	28/02/1917
Miscellaneous	To D.A.G. 3rd Echelon Base		
War Diary	Curlu	01/03/1917	01/03/1917
War Diary	Junction Wood	02/03/1917	03/03/1917
War Diary	Bouchavesnes Sector.	04/03/1917	15/03/1917
War Diary	Junction Wood. Nrclery	16/03/1917	18/03/1917
War Diary	Moislains	19/03/1917	19/03/1917
War Diary	Bouchavesnes	20/03/1917	24/03/1917
War Diary	Moislains	25/03/1917	26/03/1917
War Diary	Equancourt	27/03/1917	29/03/1917
War Diary	Fins-Nurlu Dessart Wood Fins-Equancourt.	30/03/1917	30/03/1917
War Diary	Dessart Wood Fins. Equancourt.	30/03/1917	30/03/1917
War Diary	Nr Moislains Riverside Wood	31/03/1917	31/03/1917
War Diary	Riverside Wood Manancourt	01/04/1917	02/04/1917
War Diary	Sorel-Le-Grand	03/04/1917	03/04/1917
War Diary	Fins-Gouzeaucourt.	04/04/1917	06/04/1917
War Diary	Lieramont	07/04/1917	11/04/1917
War Diary	Aizecourt-Le-Bas	12/04/1917	15/04/1917
War Diary	Heudicourt	16/04/1917	20/04/1917

War Diary	Gouzeaucourt-Gonnelieu	21/04/1917	28/04/1917
War Diary	Gouzeaucourt	29/04/1917	30/04/1917
War Diary	Sorel-Fins Gouzeaucourt	01/05/1917	08/05/1917
War Diary	Villers Guislains	09/05/1917	13/05/1917
War Diary	Nurlu	14/05/1917	28/05/1917
War Diary	Nurlu Aizecourt-Le Haut	29/05/1917	31/05/1917
War Diary	Aizecourt-Le Haut	01/06/1917	01/06/1917
War Diary	Vaux Sur-Somme	02/06/1917	03/06/1917
War Diary	Croix Rouge	04/06/1917	10/06/1917
War Diary	Rouge Croix	11/06/1917	12/06/1917
War Diary	S.W. of Caestre	13/06/1917	13/06/1917
War Diary	S.E. Poperinghe	14/06/1917	18/06/1917
War Diary	E of Steenvoorde	19/06/1917	28/06/1917
War Diary	Poperinghe	29/06/1917	29/06/1917
War Diary	Dominion Camp. Ypres-Poperinghe	30/06/1917	30/06/1917
Miscellaneous	D.A.G 3rd Echelon		
War Diary	Reninghelst-Poperinghe	01/07/1917	10/07/1917
War Diary	Bonningues	11/07/1917	11/07/1917
War Diary	Bonningues	12/07/1917	23/07/1917
War Diary	Reninghelst-Poperinghe	24/07/1917	30/07/1917
War Diary	Ouderdom Vlamertinghe	01/08/1917	04/08/1917
War Diary	Steenvoorde	05/08/1917	09/08/1917
War Diary	Ypres Ouderdom Vlamertinghe Westhoek	10/08/1917	16/08/1917
War Diary	East of Ypres	17/08/1917	18/08/1917
War Diary	Ouderdom Amertinghe	19/08/1917	19/08/1917
War Diary	Borre Caestre Area	20/08/1917	26/08/1917
War Diary	Kortepyp Camp NR Nieppe	27/08/1917	31/08/1917
War Diary	Kortepyp Camp. Near Neuve-Eglise	01/09/1917	10/09/1917
War Diary	Red Lodge Near Ploegsteert Wood	11/09/1917	18/09/1917
War Diary	St. Yves. Warneton Sector. Ploegsteert	19/09/1917	24/09/1917
War Diary	St. Yves. Warneton Sector	25/09/1917	26/09/1917
War Diary	De Seule Camp Bailleul-Armentieres Road	27/09/1917	30/09/1917
War Diary	De Seule Camp Bailleul-Nieppe Road	01/10/1917	12/10/1917
War Diary	Romarin Camp. Near Ploegsteert.	13/10/1917	20/10/1917
War Diary	Front Line Warneton Sector	21/10/1917	29/10/1917
War Diary	De Seule Camp Bailleul-Nieppe Road	30/10/1917	31/10/1917
Map	Message Map.		
Miscellaneous	Message Form		
Miscellaneous	D.A.G 3rd Echelon Base		
War Diary	De Seule Camp Bailleul-Armentieres Road	01/11/1917	11/11/1917
War Diary	Near Vieux-Berquin	12/11/1917	15/11/1917
War Diary	Wieltje Near Ypres.	16/11/1917	16/11/1917
War Diary	Passchendaele Sector Ypres Front	17/11/1917	19/11/1917
War Diary	Brandhoek Poperinghe Vlamertinghe Road.	20/11/1917	28/11/1917
War Diary	St Jean Area Near Ypres.	29/11/1917	30/11/1917
War Diary	N.E. Passchendaele St Jean (Nr Ypres)	01/12/1917	02/12/1917
War Diary	St Jean-Wizernes-Acquin	03/12/1917	03/12/1917
War Diary	Acquin (Training Area.)	04/12/1917	24/12/1917
War Diary	Junction Camp St Jean Nr Ypres	25/12/1917	29/12/1917
War Diary	Nr Passchen Daele	30/12/1917	31/12/1917
Miscellaneous	Report of the Past played by the 2nd Battn The Rifle Brigade in the recent Operations at Passchendaele	06/12/1917	06/12/1917
Miscellaneous	Headquarters 25th Infantry Brigade	06/12/1917	06/12/1917
Miscellaneous	4th Copy.		
War Diary	Bellevue Passchendaele Sector.	01/01/1918	02/01/1918
War Diary	B Camp Brandhoek Poperinghe-Vlamertinghe Road	03/01/1918	06/01/1918

War Diary	Wieltje St Jean	07/01/1918	07/01/1918
War Diary	Wieltje-St Jean Area	08/01/1918	14/01/1918
War Diary	Bellevue Passchendaele Sector.	15/01/1918	16/01/1918
War Diary	Passchendaele Sector	17/01/1918	17/01/1918
War Diary	E. of. Steenvoorde	18/01/1918	18/01/1918
War Diary	East of Steenvoorde	19/01/1918	31/01/1918
War Diary	Steenvoorde Area	31/01/1918	31/01/1918
War Diary	Sh. 27. K. 28 K. 29 K. 34 K. 35	01/02/1918	02/02/1918
War Diary	Poperinghe	03/02/1918	12/02/1918
War Diary	B Camp Brandhoek	13/02/1918	15/02/1918
War Diary	Near Passchendaele (Front Line)	16/02/1918	18/02/1918
War Diary	Near Passchendaele Front Support Lines)	19/02/1918	19/02/1918
War Diary	B Camp Brandhoek	20/02/1918	22/02/1918
War Diary	Passchendaele Sector	23/02/1918	26/02/1918
War Diary	Near Passchendaele	27/02/1918	27/02/1918
War Diary	B Camp Brandhoek	28/02/1918	28/02/1918
Heading	25th Inf. Bde. 8th Div. War Diary 2nd Battn. The Rifle Brigade. March 1918		
War Diary	Brandhoek	01/03/1918	02/03/1918
War Diary	Passchendaele	03/03/1918	06/03/1918
War Diary	Steenvoorde	07/03/1918	10/03/1918
War Diary	Tilques	11/03/1918	31/03/1918
Miscellaneous			
Heading	25th Brigade. 8th Division. 2nd Battalion The Rifle Brigade April 1918.		
War Diary	Thennes-Cottenchy-Le Mesge	01/04/1918	11/04/1918
War Diary	Le Mesge-Camon	12/04/1918	18/04/1918
War Diary	Camon-Blaney Fronville-Villers-Bretonneux	19/04/1918	23/04/1918
War Diary	Villers-Bretonneux	23/04/1918	26/04/1918
War Diary	Boutillerie Huchennville	28/04/1918	30/04/1918
War Diary	Lhuys-Salouel-Huchenneville	01/05/1918	09/05/1918
War Diary	Berry-Au-Bac-Ventelay-Courlan-Don	10/05/1918	19/05/1918
War Diary	Guyencourt-Berry-Au-Bac.	20/05/1918	27/05/1918
War Diary	Chundry-Sarcy-Champlat	28/05/1918	31/05/1918
War Diary	Hocquincourt-Bannes-Grauves-Soullieres	01/06/1918	16/06/1918
War Diary	Woignarue-Buigny-Hocquincourt	17/06/1918	17/06/1918
War Diary	Woignarue	26/06/1918	30/06/1918
Heading	War Diary July 1918 2nd Bn The Rifle Brigade		
War Diary	Woignarue	01/07/1918	07/07/1918
War Diary	Woincourt	08/07/1918	31/07/1918
War Diary	Mont St Eloi Ottawa Camp	31/07/1918	01/08/1918
War Diary	Map 44 A S. W.	02/08/1918	05/08/1918
War Diary	Vimy	06/08/1918	11/08/1918
War Diary	Sheet 44 A S.W.	12/08/1918	12/08/1918
War Diary	Vimy	13/08/1918	26/08/1918
War Diary	Oppy Sector	27/08/1918	31/08/1918
Miscellaneous	2nd. Battalion The Rifle Brigade Operation Order Ref. Map. LA Targette.		
Miscellaneous	Headquarters, 25th Infantry Brigade	05/10/1918	05/10/1918
War Diary		01/09/1918	30/09/1918
Operation(al) Order(s)	2nd Battalion The Rifle Brigade Order No. 121	21/09/1918	21/09/1918
Heading	25th Bde. 8th Division. War Diary. 2nd Bn. The Rifle Brigade October 1918.		
War Diary		01/10/1918	31/10/1918
War Diary	Baudour-Pommeroeul-Cattelet	01/11/1918	12/11/1918
War Diary	Rumes-Esplechin-Baudour	13/11/1918	27/11/1918

War Diary	Rumes	28/11/1918	30/11/1918
War Diary	Rumes	01/12/1918	14/12/1918
War Diary	Rumes-Barry-Ath-Enghien	15/12/1918	27/12/1918
War Diary	Enghien	28/12/1918	31/12/1918
War Diary		01/01/1919	31/01/1919
War Diary	Enghien	01/02/1919	28/02/1919
War Diary	Enghien	01/03/1919	11/03/1919
War Diary	Enghien Ath	12/03/1919	25/03/1919
War Diary	Ath	26/03/1919	31/03/1919
War Diary	Ath	01/04/1919	30/04/1919
War Diary	Ath	00/05/1919	00/05/1919
Miscellaneous	Special Order of The Day Major-General Sir William C.G. Heneker, K.C.B. D.S.O., Commanding 8th Division.	25/01/1919	25/01/1919

6TH DIVISION
25TH INFY BDE

2ND BN RIFLE BRIGADE
NOV 1914 - MAY 1919

8th, Division.

25th, Brigade.

2nd, Rifle Brigade.

25/8

Battn. ordered home
home from
England 7.11.14

121/2625

2nd Rifle Brigade. 25th Brigade.
8th Division.

Vol I. 5–29.11.14

~~Confidential~~

2

War Diary of 2 Bn Rifle Brigade

(AF (2118 not available)

from Nov 5th to Nov 29th

Nov 5th Bn embarked at SOUTHAMPTON on
SS VICTORIAN 29 officers 983 other ranks

Nov 6th Sailed 2am

Nov 7th Disembarked at HAVRE 10.30 am
Marched to Rest Camp No 1.

Nov 8th In Camp

Nov 9th In camp.

Nov 10th Bn Entrained at midnight at GARE
MARITIME, HAVRE

Nov 11th Bn detrained at STRAZEELE 6am
Marched to billets at VIEUX BERQUIN
2 miles from railway station.

Nov 12th Bn rested in billets

Nov 13th Bn rested in billets

3

Nov 14th Bn marched with rest of Brigade at 1 pm from VIEUX BERQUIN to LA FLINQUE FARM, 1 mile SE of LAVENTIE. Went into billets there in reserve at 9 pm. Headquarters, Band & ½ C Coy in the Farm, A and D Coys at Cross Road 200x to the SE. ½ C Coy in supporting trench 300x in rear of our advanced line. Intermittent firing along the front.

Nov 15th Bn remained in billets all day – At 6 pm heavy firing in front line – Bn paraded in readiness to move – and fell out at 8 pm. Slight sniping round billets during the night – ½ C Coy withdrawn to billets from trenches –

Nov 16th Shell fire during morning and afternoon. 5 pm B Coy moved out to supporting trench in rear of Lincoln Regt – D Coy to supporting trench in rear of R.I. Rifles, on right and left respectively of Brigade line –
Casualties – one a/Cpl. killed –

Nov 17th 6 PM Battalion relieved Lincolns in trenches on right of Brigade line

Nov 18th Battalion closed in to its left to make room for 23rd Bde on right

4

Nov 18th (cont) Handing over of right section of our trench to Devon Regt completed. Casualties – one Rfn wounded

Nov 19th Enemy sapping up at several points towards our trenches –
Patrols sent out at various points reported enemy's trenches occupied in uncertain numbers, and rumble of transport was heard in AUBERS village – The latter was reported by a patrol led by Lt Col Constable & Colonel of SA Pauly – One Rfn wounded and missing.

JMB –

Nov 20th In the trenches – work continued at improving parapets, communication trenches, &c – One rifleman wounded –

Nov 21st In the trenches – enemy very quiet – occasional shots from snipers and considerable movement of transport in the enemy's lines –
6 pm. Relieved by BERKSHIRE Regt and went back into billets near LAVENTIE. Two Companies (A. D) up in support of firing line

JMB.

Nov 22nd   Rested in billets at LAVENTIE - 5

44 men sent to Field Ambulance suffering from frost bite in the feet - When the Batt'n went into the trenches on the 17" Nov" the trenches were full of mud and water - A heavy fall of snow on the 18th made matters worse - On the night of the 18th a very hard frost set in, freezing the men's wet boots with the result that almost all ranks suffered badly from swollen feet - The worst cases were unable to walk and were evacuated by the Field Ambulance - Tallow and Vaseline have now been provided to help matters - Warm under vests and sheepskin coats were issued today - Sandbags with straw in them for the men's feet are now up in the trenches -

Enemy quiet all day - except for intermittent howitzer shelling which does no damage - many of the shells do not burst -

The snow makes patrol work difficult as men show up so on it -

White sheets are being provided for this work -

One Rfn wounded by a stray bullet -

6

Nov 23rd Rested in LAVENTIE Billets all ~~monday~~ day - Made fascines - cleaning up &c

Nov 24th Rested in Billets -
6 PM relieved the R. Berkshires in the trenches - all quiet 9PM -

Nov 25th All quiet except for intermittent sniping - A few shells along the trench lines in the afternoon - Work continued of improving parapets of fire trenches, making supporting trenches, communication trenches shelters &c - Party of 15 Field Coy RE to assist - Casualties one killed one wounded - Usual patrols to enemy's trench line and ~~Ke 2~~ forward saps point to the line being lightly held - Observation post in FAUQUISSART CHURCH noticed some half dozen civilians at work digging - The work was continued at night -
9PM -

Nov 26th - Trench work continued all day Sniping on the increase

Nov 27th 1 am. Lt Durham and 24 men of B Coy under Sgt Davis and Corporal Thompson went out to surprise a sap of the enemy's about 120 yds from our trenches - The sap was successfully charged, the enemy's piquet post of about 6 men fired a few shots and fled. Our party occupied the trench and opened fire on the enemy's lines. Unfortunately L. Durham was nowhere to be found. After 30 minutes the party were ordered to return to our own trench as the enemy were returning in large numbers. Casualties L. Durham missing, Pt Robinson killed. It is feared L. Durham pursued right down the enemy's trench beyond reach of help. The result of the enterprise was to show that the enemy's saphead was merely an advanced post occupied for observation purposes and from which to run parallels. No sign of any mining operations could be found.

The enemy's troops opposed to us would appear to be more numerous than was supposed. It took them some 30 minutes to man their main trench and they appeared to have there some 200 rifles —

They reoccupied their advanced sap and continued the sniping —

8am Our observation post at FAUQUISSART church was heavily shelled —

6pm Relief by R. Berkshire Regt —
Batt. marched into Div. Reserve
Billets at LAVENTIE —

JHB.

8

Nov 28th Rested in billets. Cleared up
11am Major Harman DSO ~~Left~~
~~Co. Powell~~ killed by a shell and
Capt E B Powell wounded while
walking in billets. Heavy rain at
night.

Nov 29th Quiet day in billets. The men's
feet from the cold and wet are
still very bad.
JWB.

J W Brockholes Lt & Adjt

for OC 2"B" Rifle Brigade
25th Infantry Bde
8th Division
Expeditionary Force

9

Nov 30th Billets in LEVANTIE heavily
shelled at 11am, 1pm, and 4pm.
Casualties Nil.
6pm relieved R. Berkshire Regt in
the trenches. A quiet night but snipers
active. JWB.
Capt Whitaker walking out beyond
the wire was fired on by enemy. He
did not return and two parties who
went out failed to find his body.
JWB.

25th Brigade.

2nd Rifle Brigade.

Vol II. 1 – 31.12.14

121/3888.

2nd Battn. The Rifle Brigade.

December 1914.

Dec 1st Continued work on communication trenches and support trenches —

12 noon — Our artillery shelled with effect the house of TRIVELET on our left front, known to be occupied by the enemy —

6 pm Capt Whitaker's body recovered — He was lying dead up against the German wire entanglements — JMR—

Dec 2nd A quiet day — occasional sniping —
The Division are very anxious for exact information as to what Corps is in our front — All efforts to take a prisoner were unsuccessful as the enemy keep to their lines and don't appear to be pushing any patrols beyond their trenches — JMR—

10

Dec 3rd: Work on communication and support trenches continued —
6 pm Relieved by R. Berkshire Regt in trenches and marched to billets at F' DESQUN Two Coys in advance supporting firing line at PICANTIN and RUE MASSELOT.
JWB —

Dec 4th: Rested in billets — Quiet day except for continuous shelling between hqrs and LAVENTIE.

Dec 5th: Heavy rain most of the day — Rested in billets — Large issue from ordnance of great coats, service dress &c — JWB —

Dec 6th: 6 pm Relieved R. Berkshire Regt in the trenches — 10 p.m. Message received from Corps Commander that there was a rumour that the Germans intended attacking tonight All quiet — JWB —

Dec 7th: Work on support trenches — Heavy rain — The trenches a sea of mud.

Dec 8th: Continuous rain — Three casualties through the holes of loopholes — JWB —

Dec 9th: Continuous rain — Relieved by R. Berks at 6 pm and marched into

11

billets in ESTAIRES where the Battn
[were] in Divisional reserve

Dec 10th. Rested in billets. JWP.

Dec 11th. Rested in billets. The whole Battn had hot baths and a complete issue of clean underclothing from the Divisional Bath House. JWP.

Dec 12th. 4.15pm Marched to the trenches and relieved R. Berks" Regt. JWP.

Dec 13th. All quiet. Continued work on communication trenches which are almost all under water. Fire trench very bad in places. JWP.

Dec 14th. Confidential orders received to adopt an aggressive attitude from midnight 14/15th. Our artillery kept up a heavy bombardment all day. Major CW Percival killed, directing a working party. JWP.

Dec 15th – Heavy bombardment from artillery supported by infantry fire – Practically no movement on part of enemy who only replied with a few shells. C McGregor and 12 men went out with to sap head 200 yards from our lines and found it unoccupied. Enemy's main trench appeared to be more lightly held than usual.   JM

4 pm – Redistribution of line consequent on withdrawal of 26' Inf Bde – Our line increased to about 800 yards, and one coy. withdrawn to Brigade reserve at LA FLINQUE – 3 Coys to be in trenches 9 days and 1 Coy in reserve for 3 days. JM

Dec 16th: Our artillery shelled enemy all day at intervals – Two patrols under C Mansel and Bulkeley Johnson visited saps in front of our line and found them unoccupied. Very wet and muddy and apparently abandoned for some days – Patrols reached German wire, but could find no signs of enemy moving out beyond his main trench which appeared occupied in usual strength –   JM Major

Dec 17: Our trenches on the left of our section were shelled in the morning – Our artillery replied and kept it up at intervals all day
JM Major

13

At dusk Lt Pilcher took a patrol onto the right of our line to visit enemy's advanced trench in front of the section the Battn. took over yesterday. It was unoccupied and only a shallow work. A dead German was found stripped of all badges and a copy of a German newspaper — JW Capt

Dec 18th. 2am order received to keep quiet and abandon all enterprises.

2pm verbal orders received to be ready to demonstrate in front of our own lines

4pm operation orders received to harass the enemy and prevent him to our front while the 23rd Bde attacked NEUVE CHAPPELLE on our right at 4.15pm —

At 4.20pm 1 platoon from C Coy, 1 from D Coy and 2 from A Coy advanced and occupied enemy's saps and advanced trenches in front of our line — The enemy's fire was drawn and

Dec 19th he was kept engaged till 2am when the order was received from Bde to abandon active operations and withdraw — JW Capt

14

withdrawal carried out successfully — and normal line of trenches re-occupied at 7am — Casualties R. McGinck slightly wounded, other ranks 1 killed two wounded — Capt Hon E Coke and 2/Lt Mason and 91 other ranks joined the Battⁿ Kept quiet all day — JMB Capt

Dec 20th: 5am Enemy shelled vigorously just behind our line of trenches — and at daylight opened a heavy rifle and machine gun fire from their main trench, which was kept up throughout the day —
4pm message received from hqrs that 23rd Inf Bde expected attack — Night passed off quietly —
Our right Coy (A Coy) was relieved by SCOTTISH RIFLES and went into billets at LAVENTIE
Orders received from Bde to resume normal line of trench on night of 21st
JMB Capt

Dec 21st Orders received to continue bursts of rifle and machine gun fire — Little reply from enemy —
4pm Battⁿ resumed original line of trench A & C Coy returning from billets — All four coys in the firing line, one platoon from each in support —
JMB Capt

Dec 22ⁿᵈ 9am Message received from Bde fr all
units to stand to arms until further orders,
an aviator having reported large bodies of
the enemy behind AUBERS. The Batt-
awaited attack for 24 hours but the enemy
showed no signs of moving – on the contrary
our patrols reported him as busy mending
his wire –

JWBCapt

Dec 23ʳᵈ All quiet.
4pm Relieved by P. Berks Regt and
marched into billets in LEVANTIE after
11 days consecutively in the trenches –

Dec 24ᵗʰ Rested in billets – Hard frost

Dec 25ᵗʰ Xmas day – Rested in billets.

JWBCapt

Dec 26ᵗʰ Rested in billets during the morning. 4pm Relieved R. Berks in trenches
where an informal truce reigned – No
firing on either side. The opportunity was
taken to do a lot of work in the open and
mending wire –

11pm Order received from Brigade to
stand to arms and expect an attack at
12.15am – This was based on information
brought in by a deserter –

11.40pm our artillery opened heavy

shell fire - No reply from the enemy and the night passed off quietly -

JMcM

Dec 27th At day break both sides fired a few shots in the air, but little notice was taken of it, and a state of quiet continued - The Germans made no effort to take cover.

2.30pm Reported this curious state of affairs to Brigade - The opportunity was again seized to push forward a bit of work in the open -

7 p.m. One platoon from B Coy and one platoon from D Coy, covered by parties, dug out two communication trenches from our lines to the enemy's advanced trenches - about 80' - 100' each - The enemy made no sign of moving or interfering with our working parties who had nearly completed their task when bursts of fire from our artillery stopped all work - Heavy rain all night made the firing trenches worse than they have ever been yet -

JMcM

Dec 28th 10am The enemy reopened sniping after an absolute silence since Xmas Eve - Orders received from Divn to permit no truce either formal or informal and to fire vigorously on any one exposing themselves -

Dec 28th (Cont'd) Enemy's fire slackened off at dusk and our working parties on the wire and in front of our trenches were undisturbed. Heavy rain fell. JWB Capt

Dec 29th The result of the heavy rain and thaw was that the parapet in the fire trench fell in in a number of places. Water rose steadily all day in the fire trench and communications trenches. The state of affairs was reported to the Divn who replied that our present forward line of fire trench was to be held at all costs. JWB Capt

4.30pm Relieved by R. Berks Regt in the trenches - and marched into billets, HQrs, C & D Coys at FT D'ESQUIN, A Cy at RUE MASSELOT, B Cy at RUE DU BOIS. JWB Capt

Dec 30th Rested in billets.

Dec 31st Rested in billets. JWB Capt

2/RB.

8th, Division.

25th, Brigade.

2nd, Rifle Brigade.

January, 1915.

25th Brigade

2nd Rifle Brigade.

Vol III. 1 – 31.1.15

121/4262

2nd Battalion The Rifle Brigade.

January 1915

1915

Jan 1st. Rested in billets —
4 pm relieved Royal Berks Regt in Trenches. Owing to rising floods in our fire trench new breastworks were started on ground level, immediately in rear of the flooded portions of fire trench. Doubtless the enemy is having equal difficulty over the water as he makes no effort to disturb our working parties. His advanced saps appear never to be occupied now a days and sniping is intermittent. Rain fell most of the night. JMB Col

Jan 2nd No movement on either side all day — Towards evening the enemy on our right attempted to open conversation — They are not for fighting at present —
Work carried on all night on new breastworks — A fatigue party of 75th RA worked on a new communicating trench for us — Enemy opened frequently with machine guns but did no damage. Our artillery shelled the enemy's trenches to our right port heavily —

Jan 3rd Quiet day except for half an hours heavy bombardment by our Divl Artillery of the enemy's trenches and TRIVELET. Work continued at night on new breastworks and communicating trench — JMB Col

19

Jan 4th   More rain – Relieved at 4 pm by R.
Berkshire Regt and marched in Div' Reserve
billets at LEVANTIE JMcC Capt

Jan 5th   Rested in billet

Jan 6th   Batt'n marched by Coy's into ESTAIRES
to the Divisional Baths – JMcC Capt

Jan 7th   Rested in billet in the morning –
   4 pm Relieved R. Berks R. in the trenches –
At the end of the relief enemy shelled FAU-
QUISSART cross roads – doing no damage

Jan 8th   1 am – Continued work on breastworks and
new communication trenches – water rising
rapidly – an effort to capture a patrol of the
enemy's was foiled by the water – A number of
the enemy were out at 4.30 am on their parapet bailing – fire was opened on them by
a machine gun and "D" coy – it is thought
with some effect.
   2.30 pm our 6 in howitzers shelled TRIVELET
and bolted some 30 Germans who were caught
by F.A. shrapnel, rifle & machine gun fire.
[The heavy rain of the day cleared up towards night] The fire trench is now so bad
that it is only possible to keep one platoon
per coy in the trench by day –   JMcC

20

Jan 8th (cont'd) Heavy rain fell towards night —
JMcC/ft

Jan 9th. 1am Continued work on new communicating trenches, breastworks, and shelters. Enemy sniped vigorously till dawn in return for their surprise of the previous night — Water rose continuously and work was terribly slow and heavy in the sodden clay —
4am Heavy rain put a stop to all work —
By midday all communicating trenches were impassable and the water still rising.
Our artillery shelled the enemy's trenches vigorously all day at intervals — Germans replied in spasms, principally on the FAUQUISSART cross roads — Rain continued to fall and water to rise —
10pm. D Coy again surprised a party of the enemy at work on their parapet and opened fire — The Germans replied at once with rifle fire, 3 maxims and shell fire, but did no damage —
JMcC/ft

Jan 10th. 1am Rain stopped and work was continued on breastworks — The water however still rose and no communicating trench is now available —
3pm Our artillery opened a very heavy fire on a NEUVE CHAPELLE to our right — No reply from the enemy —
4pm Relieved by R. Berks. Regt in the trenches and marched into Bde reserve —

Hqrs, C & B Coys at F¹ D'ESQUIN, A Coy on RUE BACQUEROT, D Coy at PICANTIN.

Jan 11ᵗʰ Rested in billets — A. Reinforcement arrived — 3 NCO's 97 R/f/emen —
D and A Coys found two fatigues of 50 men each for work in the trenches

Jan 12ᵗʰ Rested in billets
4 pm Draft inspected by G.O.C. Bde —

Jan 13ᵗʰ Morning rested in billets
4 pm Relieved R. Berks Regt in the trenches. A dry night but very dark — No moon — work
Jan 14ᵗʰ on breastwork continued from 3 am till dawn — enemy's snipers were very active on our right front — L̃ Pilcher took out a patrol to the enemy's advanced trench N. of FAUQUISSART RD near the ruined house and found it full of water and unoccupied — 3 M.G.45

Jan 15ᵗʰ Up to 2 am we replied at two hour intervals to enemy's snipers with heavy bursts of rifle and machine gun fire. From 3 am till dawn work continued on breastwork. A/Cpl. Harvey and two men went through enemy's wire and reached his trench 100ˣ to right (S.W.) of TRIVELET and found about 250ˣ of trench unoccupied with three feet of water in it. They returned unobserved by enemy. This unoccupied length of trench accounts for the fact that nearly all enemy's sniping is done opposite our two right companies. A very dark night but no rain. Work was also done on communication trench leading to B and D coys so that all coys are now accessible in daylight except C whose communication trench is very wet and shallow. Enemy fired a few shells during the morning near FAUQUISSART CROSS ROADS but without doing any damage.

16th Jan. Digging on breastwork was to have started at 3 a.m. but owing to darkness no work could be begun until 4.30 a.m.
4.30 a.m. to dawn. All companies thickening and heightening breastwork especially traverses. As there has been less rain during last few days coys. were able to work on the flooring of breastwork in dug-outs putting down wire, straw and gratings which make a great improvement.
3 p.m. Enemy shelled pavé road across muddy field behind H.qrs. but without doing any damage although there were a lot of men about at the time.
5 p.m. Relieved by R. Berkshire Regt. in trenches and marched into Bn'. Reserve billets at L'AVANTIE.

17th Jan: Rested in billets.

23

18th Jan: Rested in billets.
2 p.m. 1st Line transport inspected by G.O.C. Bde.
Captain R.C. Buxton posted to A coy.

19th Jan Relieved 2nd R. Berkshire Regiment in trenches at
5 p.m.
6.30 p.m. B, C & D coys commenced work on breastwork
and continued until midnight. A coy commenced work
at 2 a.m. 20th. The enemy opened bursts of machine gun
fire now and did a little shelling at intervals up till 2a.m.
on 20th.

20th Jan: 1.30 a.m. A coy carried out a practice alarm before
commencing work, taking the support platoon from
RUE TILLELOY to fire trench. It was ½ hour
before the trench was fully manned.
Patrol reported enemy bailing water out of gap in
their trench S.W. (our right) of TRIVELET.
5.45 a.m. other companies practised alarm. B taking
13½ mins; C six mins; D seven mins. to man
fire trench. Reserve platoons took 25 mins to
reach Hqrs. from Line. Runners went out and
only 58 men were present out of four platoons,
the remainder (at least 60) being away on
carrying & ration fatigues.
5.30 p.m. All coys commenced work and up
to 10 p.m. patrol reported that enemy were
in the open behind their parapet bailing and
pumping water in the same place as before i.e.

between right corner of TRIVELET (S.W.) and tall chimney. By a pre-arranged plan the 1st Battery R.F.A. opened fire on them at 10.30 which was the signal for a heavy burst of rifle and M.G. fire from our trenches. There was very little reply from the German Rifles.

21st Jan: 2 A.M. Patrols reported enemy had stopped working but saw an enemy patrol of about 12 men who were fired on by our left machine gun. All quiet till stand to arms 5.45 a.m. Another practice alarm.
Germans seen working to the our left of tall chimney during morning. Heavy rain during day and night which interfered with work. Frost in the early morning. Rifles.

22nd Jan:
A quiet day — Bright and dry — Some shelling about midday by the enemy at RE and civilian working parties working on redoubt near Trust Ard Post.

4.45 p.m. relieved by R. Berkshire Regt in the trenches — and marched into billets at F' DESCOUIN C Coy at PICANTIN, B/ A Coy at RUE MASSELOT —
5 men/gas

23. Jan: Frost continued — rested in billets.

24 Jan: Rested in billets.

25ᵗʰ Janʸ Relieved R. Berks Regᵗ in trenches at
5pm. after standing ready since 9am on
account of attack on 1ˢᵗ Division. Enemy
to our front very active with sniping and
machine gun fire which they kept up till
dawn. Worked from 8pm to midnight
on new parapet and redoubt. JM Capt
Reinforcement of 40 N.C.O's & Pᵗᵉˢ joined Bⁿ

26ᵗʰ Janʸ Enemy continued sniping all day & if
anyone appeared -
4pm Wire from G.H.Q. that fresh Corps are reported on the British front and that attacks on
various parts of the line are to be expected &
watched for —
Work carried on as usual from
8pm to midnight, and enemy's sniping answered
back. Enemy fired some shrapnel into 'A' Coy
wounding a man — JWB Capt

27ᵗʰ Janʸ Hard frost continued — a quiet day
in spite of its being the Kaiser's birthday.
3 pm a few shells fell perilously near
Bⁿ Hqrs — Enemy remained very quiet all
night except for occasional outbursts of
sniping. Work continued on new parapet
till midnight — a very bright moon till
4 am. JM Capt

28ᵗʰ Janʸ 4pm Relieved by R. Berks Regᵗ in trenches

and marched into Divl Reserve at LAVENTIE.

Jan 29th Rested in billets

Jan 30th Rested in billets - Battn marched into Divisional Baths at ESTAIRES.

Jan 31st LAVENTIE shelled again -
5pm Relieved R Berks Regt in the trenches. A 4 in howitzer shell burst in A Coys billets killing one man and wounding 3 more - later the enemy fired shrapnel into A Coys parapet killing one and wounding one - Sniping in the early part of the night was heavy but kept it under - Casualties 2 killed, 3 wounded - work continued on breastwork - A full moon helped work but interfered with patrolling work - Cpl Wayoff and Cpl Harvey awarded DCM for good patrol work on various occasions and for bringing in Capt Whitaker's body on Dec 1st.

JMB/LtCol

8th, Division.

25th, Brigade.

2nd, Rifle Brigade.

February, 1915.

121/4657

25th Brigade

2nd Rifle Brigade.

Vol IV 1–28.2.15

2nd Battalion The Rifle Brigade.

February 1915

Feb 1st Fine weather continued - Enemy sniped heavily from dusk till midnight, to which we replied. Work continued on new breastwork and parados from 2am till dawn. Lt. Pilcher took out a patrol on the left of our lines and reported the enemy's advanced trenches still full of water and unoccupied. The Union Jack which he planted the previous night on the enemy's barricade in front of TRIVELET was still flying.

Feb 2nd Rain fell - a very quiet night, work continued - Casualties this day only two men wounded - A draft of 30 NCOs and Rfn joined the Battn.

Feb 3rd Fine weather again -
10 am Enemy shelled the centre of our lines with shrapnel -
1 pm Enemy shelled our parapet and in rear of here - one man wounded - German observation and sniping post was spotted at the top of a house opposite the centre of our lines. Our artillery silenced it -
5 pm Relieved by R. Berks Regt in the trenches and marched into Bde reserve. H.Qrs, C, D, Coys and 1 M Gun to Fe DESQUIN and SE End of LAVENTIE, B Coy and 1 M. Gun to RUE DU BOIS, A Coy to PICANTIN - the latter new billets

During the relief the Germans shelled occasionally between Hqrs and the trenches. This is the first time they have done this during a relief. There were no casualties from this shelling, but during the three days in the trenches the Batt: lost 4 men killed and 18 wounded, the heaviest casualties to date for a single tour of duty.

Feb 4: Rested in billets. (A Coy's new billets at PICANTIN were found to be in a most unwholesome state.) Major C E HARRISON joined the Batt: and took over command from Capt R VERNEY (Lt Col R B STEPHENS having proceeded on leave to England on the 1st inst.) J M...

Feb 5: [Rested in billets - C.O. inspected new draft of 30 men.] Enemy shelled the billets from 1pm - 3pm. Quality of shells was poor and no damage was done. J M...

Feb 6: Rested in billets.
5.45pm Relieved R. Berks Regt in the trenches. Work continued on parapet. Patrols reported enemy working on their wire and we fired on them. Otherwise a quiet night. J M...

Feb 7: Enemy shelled trenches on TILELOY RD just to the N of headquarters between 1 & 3pm. No damage done.

30

Feb 11th. Rested in billets. Battn. marched by Coys into ESTAIRES to the Divl. Baths.
JMB/wr

Feb 12th. Rested in billets.
5.45 pm Relieved R Berks Regt in the trenches. No moon, and work brought almost to a standstill. Patrols went out as usual and reported Germans working on their parapet and wire. Fire was opened on them as usual. Work continued on our own wire. JMB/wr

Feb 13th. Heavy rain all morning which blew off later. Germans shelled FAUQUISSART at intervals — otherwise a very quiet day and night. Still too dark to do much work. JMB/wr

Feb 14th. A quiet day & night.

Feb 15th. A quiet morning except for intermittent shelling along the RUE TILLELOY — which included 6 shells at H.qrs. No damage done.
5.30 pm Relieved by R Berks Regt and marched into Bde Reserve [A to R PICANTIN D 15 RUE DU BOIS, C and B to F. DESQUIN. JMB/wr]

Feb 16th. Rested in billets. Draft of 62 NCO's and Riflemen joined the Bn., about 20 of them men who had left the Bn. sick.
JMB/wr

Feb 17th. Rested in billets. Weather awful — water rising all round again.
JMB/wr

Feb 7:- (cont:) Lt Col R.B. STEPHENS returned of 29
leave and resumed command of the Battn.
A quiet night - German working parties
located and fired on - Work continued on
own parapet and wire -

Feb 8th. Enemy shelled farm near 1st Aid post
and set it on fire, and shelled at intervals all day without doing any damage -
Patrols from all companies reported the
Germans working on their wire - We opened
from our trenches with machine gun and
rifle fire - Otherwise the Germans seem
to show no great activity and hardly ever
seen to come out beyond their wire -
Their fire trench appears to be fully
manned throughout the length in front,
as if they had overcome the water difficulty -

Feb 9th. A quiet day -
5.45 pm Relieved by the R Berks in the
trenches and marched into Divl Reserve
in LAVENTIE. Casualties this time in the
trenches were only 3 killed 5 wounded, as
against a total of 22 the previous time

Feb 10th Rested in billets -

Feb 18th Morning rested in billets —
5.45 pm Relieved R Berks Regt in the trenches.
A quiet night — work continued as usual
on parapet &c — Enemy opened fire with a
Machine Gun from TRIVELET, a thing they
have not done for a long time — 1 "B" cas"

Feb 19th — Goc Bde went round the lines —
A quiet day — At dusk saw about one company and some waggons moving behind enemy's
lines — evidently relief taking place as that
evening the Germans sniped very actively.
0 "M" cas"

Feb 20th Sniping very active all day — At night
work continued on parapets &c 2 "B" cas" —

Feb 21st Thick fog all morning — Cleared up at 10 a.m
6 pm Relieved by R Berkshire Regt in the trenches
and marched into Div: Reserve at LEVANTIE —

Feb 22d Rested in billets — Batt" marched
into ESTAIRES for the funeral of Gen! JE GOUGH
mortally wounded in our lines on the the 20th.
"A" Coy, his old company, found the firing party.

Feb 23d Rested in billets —

Feb 24th 6 pm Relieved by R Berks Regt in the
trenches — A very quiet night, and a good deal
of snow fell —

Feb 25th. About 2 inches of snow – Germans shelled about FAUQUISSART CHURCH as usual – Siege guns flattened out the big chimney and factory of LES MOTTES – Very bright moonlight night hampered patrolling, but a lot of work was done –
JMcyK

Feb 26th. Thick fog in the morning – Cleared later – 2pm Saw a party of Germans working on a stack about HAUT POMMEREAU – 1st Battery opened on them and scattered them – A very quiet night
JMcyK

Feb 27th – A very quiet day – 4 pm – A gun of 1st Battery was brought up in the dark to the Aid post and opened direct fire on enemy's wire opposite No 1 lines – 30 shots were fired in 11 minutes and considerable damage was done to parapet and wire. The Germans made no reply –
6 pm Relieved by R Berks Regt and marched into Bde reserve, [A, D, Coys, Hqrs and M. guns to Fr DESQUIN, B Coy to PICANTIN, C Coy to RUE DU BOIS –]
JMcyK

Feb 28th. Rested in billets –
JMcyK

8th, Division.

25th, Brigade,

2nd, Rifle Brigade.

March, 1915.

25th Brigade
1/8
2nd Rifle Brigade
Int V 1 – 31.3.15

121/4871

2nd Battalion The Rifle Brigade.

March 1915

March 1st. Rested in billets all day - Bitter wind and snow - JMCpt

March 2nd. 25th Inf Bde handed over its trenches to the 22nd Bde of the 7th Division and marched into reserve - 6pm Battn was relieved by 2nd R. Warwicks and marched into billets about LA CORGUE SOUTH - Billets very dirty and insanitary
JMCpt

March 3rd. 7am - 8am Company Parades -
Spent the day cleaning billets
6pm. Found four working parties of 100 men each for work on B Lines - Casualties 3 wounded JMCpt

March 4th. 7am - 8am Company Parades - Musketry, Physical Drill, Bayonet fighting
9.45 am Battn Route march, attack formations
2.30 pm - 3.30 pm Training of Trench Blocking parties
JMCpt

March 5th. 7am - 8am Company Parades
9.30 am Route March
2.30 pm Training of Trench blocking parties.
JMCpt

March 6th. 7am Company Parades
Pouring rain all morning -
Orders received to dispose of all surplus kit and move into close billets
10pm working party of 550 men on B lines
Casualties 1 wounded JMCpt

March 7th: Batt's day for Div: Baths —
Found a fatigue party of 250 N.C.O.s & men
on B Lines — Casualties one Rfn. Killed

March 8th: Before dinner parades under OC Coys
2.30pm Batt'n Parade Attack formations
Small working party on Assembly Trenches
B Lines laying out tools, ammunition, clearing
wire and making bridges

March 9th: Parades under OC Coys —
Confidential instructions for attack on NEUVE
CHAPPELLE issued to Coys. (Copy marked A attached)

Battalion paraded 10.30pm &
marched with the brigade to the
assembly trenches. A hot meal
was provided en route at CROIX
BARBÉE.

The day of the 10th March 1915.

1. Instructions and orders for the operations were issued and were accurately carried out.

2. At 8.25 a.m. the Battalion was lying down behind the firing line of the Royal Berkshire Regt ready for the second advance. Formations. Four lines of small columns each of half a platoon. At 8.35 a.m. the order was given to ... for the front line to advance. Rapidity was insisted upon. At 8.50 a.m. the first line had reached the village street & the Smith Dorrien trench was occupied by scouts & bombers. A message to this effect was sent to Brigade Headquarters at 8.57 a.m. A few of the enemy were killed & about 50 prisoners taken during the advance through the village. Most of these were got out of cellars by the second line. The first line was ordered not to stop for prisoners but to get to the far end of the village

as quickly as possible. Touch was at once obtained with the Indians who were level with us on our right & with the R.I. Rifles slightly behind us on our left.

3. The Bn was now on the line given to it as its objective & a position to entrench was at once chosen & work commenced. This is the position now held. During the morning a message was sent to Bde headquarters saying that there seemed to be very few of the enemy in front of us & asking if a further advance was to be made. I was told that our left was held up & we could not go on till they got through. The battalion continued to dig all day but lost a good many men from the fire of two field guns posted near ⑰ & ⑳ & from a maxim ⑲ which moved up & down the road in front of the wood. At 5.30 pm the Indians on our right advanced to a—

38

position was the R des LAYES a good bit in front of our line. The night passed quietly. Our casualties on this day were 4 officers + 112 men killed + wounded.

11th March
1. The enemy began to shell the village early in the morning. He also had commenced during the night a new trench parallel to the edge of the BOIS DE BIEZ which joined the other trenches about (P.5). This trench is about half way between the wood & the R DES LAYES + is now their main trench.
2. During the morning orders were received to withdraw when relieved by W. Yorkshire Regt & to form up with the rest of the Brigade behind the line (26) – (43). In order to become a reserve to the advance of the 24th Brigade. The W. Yorks never took over our trenches and the battalion remained

where it was. About midday the CO received a message from Bde HQ saying that if the enemy counter-attacked he was to attack him in turn & follow him up. He replied proposing to attack (97) & (93) + asking for the support of the rest of the Brigade; he said there was no sign of a counter-attack by the enemy. To this a reply was received saying the attack could not be sanctioned at present. Shortly afterwards a Staff officer of the DEHRA DUN brigade came to the CO saying they were about to attack. The message received from the Brigade was shown to him & he was told that the battalion was not moving forward.
(A draft of 1 officer + 20 others arrived).

12th March.

1. About 1 am orders were received to be formed up ready to attack at 7 am. The objective was to be the line (97) (93) + the CO proposed to move his left until it rested on the water ditch bounding the Chateau garden on its northern side. The CO wanted to advance in a direction parallel to the water ditches & perpendicular to the R. DES LAYES + not at an angle to these obstacles, as we afterwards did.

2. About 2.50 am the Indians reported that they were leaving

40

their forward trench & would hold the line of the Smith Dorrien trench & nothing to the left of the Brewery road.

3. The battalion was getting ready for the above move when, about 4.45 a.m., the enemy made a counter attack against the whole front: this was easily repulsed. When daylight came the ground in front of us was strewn with their dead and there was a great number close to the enemy's new trench showing that we had caught his supports & reserves as they were forming up.

4. At 7.30 a.m the time of the attack was altered to 10.30 a.m & at 10.30 it was again altered to 12.30 pm to be preceded by a bombardment from 12 noon. The CO endeavoured to co-operate with the Indians but they had orders to bombard from 12.30 to 1 pm & attack at 1 pm.

5. About 9 a.m the enemy attempted a second counter-attack

which was dispersed before he
could get far from his trenches.

6. At 12.30 pm our leading line
advanced + was immediately met
by a cross-fire of machine guns
& rifles from the neighbourhood of
93 94 & from the new enemy
trench parallel to the R. DES LAYES.
These trenches are 400 - 500 yds.
from our position, the intervening
ground being open plough
intersected by dykes. Only a
small percentage of our leading
line reached the Smith Dorrien
trench about pt 56. The
remainder were all killed or
wounded. The C.O. ordered the
attack to stop as it was obviously
impossible to cross this ground
under heavy machine gun & rifle
fire from front & flank.

7. At 4.45 pm orders were
received to attack again at
5.15 & to rush these trenches
regardless of loss. The guns were
to bombard until 5.15 pm. This
bombardment did not in any
way lessen the amount of

42

rifle & machine gun fire from the enemy. The second attack failed in exactly the same way as the first, but with even more casualties.

B. In the opinion of the CO the attacks failed for the following reasons:-
① Because of the nature of the ground, heavy plough & ditches running obliquely to the line of advance.
② The distance was too great for any possibility of rushing the enemy's trench.
③ The enemy had been strongly reinforced, was well dug in & had many machine guns.
④ The artillery bombardment was ineffective, probably from want of knowledge of the exact position of these said enemy trenches.

Under these conditions it was impossible for infantry to succeed however large numbers were thrown into the attack.

(A draft of 1 off & 72 others arrived)
13th & 14th March
1. Work was continued on our line ~~who~~. The enemy's shelling

43

was very heavy.

2. The total casualties in the battalion from 10th to 14th both dates included were 12 officers + 365 other ranks killed + wounded. (A draft of 1 off + 95 men arrived)

15th March.

Enemy's shelling continued. During the night 14th/15th parties continued to collect wounded + bury the dead. Work was also carried on in the trench.

16 March. Enemy's shelling abated considerably. Work on the trenches was handicapped by a shortage of R.E. stores. All dead buried in tr. and clestio br?

17. March. Enemy shelled rather more heavily today. A large amount of R.E. stores were collected during the day also numerous spare rifles + a great quantity of ammunition. In the evening a coy of the 1st Londons arrived + were attached to the battalion, 40 men being posted to each coy. Took over the Smith Dorrien trench in front of the Brewery from the Indians + extended our line accordingly. A lot of work was got through in the trenches

44

during the night, the parapet being now from 4 to 8 feet thick in most places at the top. There are still a few gaps but the ground is very dry & firm. B Coys reserve platoon moved to Bn HQ.

18 March. Enemy's snipers very active in the early morning. Shelling very spasmodic & comparatively rare. [Enemy sent over numerous blind shells of large calibre during the afternoon.] Work in the trenches handicapped by the darkness, however a lot of work was got through on the wire & trench. A very quiet night

~~19 March~~ Snow fell at 1 a.m. & continued the rest of the night.

19 March. An exceptionally quiet morning. A few small shells about 10.30 a.m in area in rear of trenches. Snow falling all the morning. Bitterly cold day. Shell pitching in parapet killed two wounded two riflemen. A draft of 3 officers & 205 riflemen arrived. Work in the trenches at night progressed, a lot of chevaux de frise being put out. A very quiet night. Snow fell again.

45

March 20th. Quiet all day. Two men wounded in fire trench by snipers. Occasional shelling behind our lines. Relieved by Royal Berks in the evening — A & B Coys to support trenches at (27) C & D to H.Q. & machine gun to billets at CROIX BARBÉE.

March 21st. Rested in billets. A & B Coys found working parties for Royal Berks during night. Support trenches were shelled slightly by enemy.

March 22. Rested in billets. A & B Coys were relieved in support trenches by C & D Coys. Roads round support trenches were shelled by enemy.

March 23. Rested in billets. C & D Coys in support trenches. Slight shelling in neighbourhood of billets. A lovely day. Rain at night. A German bomb accidentally exploded when being moved, by support trenches & wounded one man. A draft of six officers arrived.

March 24th [Rested in billets. Some rain during the day. C & D coys shelled throughout the day at intervals.] Marched at 6pm to billets at La Gorgue. C & D coys were shelled as they left support trenches — no casualties. Marched as a brigade from PONT DU HEM.
2 Lt. Watney & 5 r/fn proceeded to St VENANT for a course of instruction in trench mortars.

March 25th. Marched at 10.30 a.m. to billets between Estaires and Sailly. [A dull rainy day. Not enough accomodation in billets.]

March 26th. Rested in billets. Marched at 6.45 pm to billets NE of SAILLY. Hargreaves, Warner & Pearce joined in the morning from home, having been posted to the Battalion.

March 27th. Rested in billets.
March 28th. Rested in billets
March 29th. Battalion parade 10.30 a.m. route march. Coys paraded from 7 – 8 a.m. & last drafts for musketry etc at 2 pm.
Watney & 5 r/fn returned from 1ST VENANT.
Lt. Col Lord Henniker, cmdg 3rd Bn,

47

& Major W. Seymour, cmdg 1st Bn. called on the Bn. this afternoon thus bringing three commanding officers of the regiment on active service together — a record.

March 30th. Coy parades 7-8 a.m.
Bn. parade 10.30 a.m, attack formations. Drafts paraded for musketry in the afternoon.
Inspected route to trenches, to be taken over.

March 31st. Rested in billets.
Divisional baths in SAILLY.
CO. & Coy: cmdrs: inspected the trenches we take over tomorrow.

13th (Kensington) London Regt

Operations 10th – 14th

On the night of the 9/10th the Battalion (13th London R.) after a hot meal at BOUGE CROIX, arrived at the support trenches at 4.30am. The artillery bombardment started at 7.30am and ceased at 8.0am. At 8.30am the Battalion moved to the breastwork just vacated by the Rifle Brigade – German prisoners began to arrive.

Casualties "Everyday" approximately Shashes —

am One Company detailed as working party to unite trenches of 4th Lincolns – Half Company to be permanently attached to O.C. 2nd Field Coy R.E.

At 11am the Batt. moved to the firing trench.

At 12.30pm an Officer was detailed to go out on a reconnaissance to get into touch with the Indians, on no account to cross the line. The report was handed in and given to the G.O.C.

5.30pm Orders were received to prepare to advance

7.30pm Orders cancelled

11pm 50 men detailed to take ported ? to Rifle Brigade and R.I.R.

March 11th 10.15am 50 men the party working for the R.E. was caught by a shell casualties 3 killed 15 wounded

2.15pm Breastwork heavily shelled

3 pm Orders to reinforce Rifle Brigade

2nd Bn. The Rifle Brigade R⁄S 58

Report on Operations at NEUVE CHAPELLE
10th to 13th March 1915

The day of the 10th March 1915.

I. Instructions and orders for the operations were, owing to being strenuously insisted on, issued out. Copies of these marked App 'A' and App 'B' are attached.

II. At 8-26 a.m. the battalion was lying down behind the firing line of the Berks Regt, ready for the 2nd advance.
Formation - Four lines of small columns, each of ½ a Platoon.
At 8-36 a.m. the order was given for the Forward line to advance. Rapidity was insisted on.
At 8-50 a.m. the first line had reached the village itself and the Support Dorsen Trench was being cleared by scouts and bombers. A message to this effect was sent to Bde HdQrs at 8-54 a.m. A few of the enemy were killed and about 50 prisoners taken during

the advance through the village.
Most of these were got out of
cellars by the 1st Brig.
The First Line was ordered not
to stop for prisoners but to get
to the far side of the village
as quickly as possible. Touch
was at once obtained with
the Guards who were level
with us on our right and
with the R.I. Rifles slightly
behind us on our left.

III The Battn. was now on the
line given to it as its objective
and a position to entrench
was at once chosen and work
commenced. This is the position
now held. During the morning
I sent a message to Bde. H. Qrs.
saying that there seemed to be
very few of the enemy in front of
us and asking if a further
advance was to be made. I was
told that our left was held up
and that we could not go on
until they got through.
(N.B.) (I cannot find a copy of these

messages, my Adjutant was killed
and his message book, and
messages are (XY)
We continued to dig all day, but
we lost a good many men from
the fire of their field guns burst
near (17) and (9?) and from a
maxim which moved up and down
the road in front of the wood.
At 6.30 p.m. the Indians on our
right advanced to a position
near the R. Des Layes a good bit
in front of our line. The night
passed quietly. Our casualties on
this day were 4 officers and 112
men killed and wounded.

Day of the 11th March 1915.
1. The enemy began to shell the
village early in the morning.
He also had commenced during
the night a new trench
_____ the edge of the Bois
DE BIEZ which joins his other
trenches about (76). This trench
is about half way between
the wood and the R. DES. LAYES.

and is now their main trench.   61

II. During the morning I received orders to withdraw when relieved by the West Yorks Regt and to *form* up with the rest of the Bde behind the line (21)–(43) in order to become a reserve to the 24th Bde. The West Yorks Regt never took over our trenches and the Battn remained where it was.

About midday I received an message from Bde HQrs saying that if the enemy counter-attacked I was to attack him in turn and follow him up. I replied proposing to attack (97)(98) and asking for support of the rest of the Brigade, & said there was no sign of a counter attack by the enemy. To this I received a reply saying the attack could not be sanctioned at present. Shortly afterwards a staff officer of the DEHRA DUN brigade came to me saying they were about to attack. I showed him the message I had received and told him that we were not moving forward.

Day of the 13th March.

I. About 1.a.m. I received orders to form up ready to attack at 7 a.m.

The objective was the line (97) (98) and I proposed to move my left until it rested on the water ditch

62

bounding the Chateau Garden on its northern side. It was best to advance in this manner parallel to the water ditches and perpendicular to the R. DES LAYES and not at an angle to these obstacles as we afterwards did.

II. About 2-30 a.m. the Indians reported that they were leaving their forward trench and would hold the line of the South Breastwork Trench and nothing to the left of the Brewery Road.

III. The Battn. was getting ready for the above move, when about 4-45 a.m. the enemy made a counter-attack against the whole front. This was easily repulsed. When daylight came the ground in front of us was strewn with their dead and there was a great number close to the enemy's new trench, showing that we had caught the enemy's supports and reserves as they were forming up.

IV. At 7-30 a.m. the time of the attack

63

was altered to 10.30a.m, and at
10.30a.m the General altered it
to 12.30p.m to be preceded by a
bombardment from 12 noon.
I endeavoured to co-operate with
the said [...], but they had orders to
bombard from 12.30p.m to 4p.m and
attack at 4p.m.

[...] you [...] attempted
a second [...] attack, which
was [...] up in the [...]
for [...] the [...].

At 4.30 [...] our leading line advanced
and was immediately met by cross
fire of M guns & Rifles from the
neighbourhood of (75) and (90) and from
the new enemy [...] to the
R. [...] trenches are [...] to
500 yards from her position, the
intervening ground being open though
intersected by dykes [...] a small
percentage of our leading lines
reached the [...] Dereh Trench.

about to (56) the remainder were
all ki[lled] [or] wounded. I ordered
the attack to stop, as it was obviously
impossible to cross this ground under
heavy M. Gun and rifle fire from
front and both flanks.

VII. At 4-05 p.m. I received orders to attack
again at 6-15 p.m. and to rush these
trenches regardless of loss. The guns
were to bombard until 6-15 p.m. This
bombardment did not in any way
lessen the amount of rifle and M. gun
fire from the enemy. The second attack
failed the same as the first with
even more casualties.

VIII. In my opinion the attack failed for
the following reasons:-

(1) Because of the nature of the ground:-
Heavy plough and terribly heavy
going.

(2) The distance was too great for any
possibility of rushing the enemy's trenches.

(3) The enemy had been strongly
reinforced, was well dug in, and
had many machine guns.

65

(4) The Artillery bombardment was ineffective, probably from want of knowledge of the exact position of these new enemy trenches.

(5) Under these conditions it was impossible for Infantry to succeed, however large numbers are thrown into the attack.

Days of the 13th and 14th March 1915.

Work was continued on new line. The enemy's shelling was very heavy.

The total casualties in the Battn. from the 10th to 14th both days inclusive was 12 officers and 365 other ranks killed and wounded.

R. B. Stephen.
Lt-Col
Comdg 2:B: Rifle Brigade

March 18th /15

APP. A

Instructions for Operations on March 10th 1915.

1. <u>Information of Enemy.</u> Maps of N.C. have been issued and will be shown to as many N.C.O's and men as possible. Notes by Intelligence Staff have been issued and will be explained similarly.

2. <u>Information of us.</u> The attack is part of a big show. The Indian Corps on our right and the 7th Division on our left will take part. Our attack will be supported by five hundred guns. The 25th Brigade is the point of the attack and the Battalion will become the most advanced portion of the Brigade.
The 23rd Brigade is on our left and the 24th Brigade in reserve.

3. <u>Intention.</u> The 25th Brigade is to take the village of NEUVE CHAPELLE. The objective of the Brigade is the line of trench ㉛ ㊺ ㉚ and the attack will be pushed on with the utmost determination until we get that line. Rapid movement is of the first importance in order to capture the village before the enemy recovers from the effect of the bombardment.

4. <u>Dispositions:-</u> The 25th Brigade is disposed as follows:-
   <u>1st Line:-</u> Left. Lincoln Regt. Right. Berks Regt.
   <u>2nd Line:-</u> Left. Irish Rifles. Right. Rifle Brigade.
The First Line is to capture the enemy's trenches and to get as far as ㊵ ㊴ ㊳.
The Second Line is then to go through them and capture the village.

5. <u>Formations.</u> The Battalion will be formed as in accompanying diagram in the cover trenches provided. "A" and "C" Coys will be first line under Major Harrison. "B" and "D" Coys. in reserve. As soon as the Berks Regt leave the Fire Trench, the Battalion will move up there and will continue to move on, filling the places of the Berks Regt as they move forward. These moves behind the Berks Regt will be carried out in small columns.
When the front line of the Berks Regt is reached, our first line will lie down behind them, and wait the order to advance.

P.T.O.

6. __Objective.__ The objective of the Battalion is the line of trench ⓖⓖ ㉚
The direction is the road ㉞ to ㊾ CHIMNEY CRESCENT.
"A" Coy will be on the left of this. "C" Coy on the right.
Similarly in 2nd Line "B" Coy will be on the left, and "D" Coy on the right.
Machine Gun Dett will move along the road in the centre with the Machine.

7. __Blocking Parties.__ Only two will be required. One from "C" Coy and one from "B" Coy.
"C's" Blocking Party will block the trench near ㉒
O.C. Machine Gun Dett. will detail one gun to accompany this party.
"B" Coy's Blocking Party will follow "D" Coy and be used as required, under orders of the C.O.
Both parties to have blue flags.

8. __Ammunition.__ The men will carry from billets, one bandolier in addition to their pouch ammunition. Two more bandoliers per man will be served out on the RUE TILLELOY. These two will be put down where ordered, probably when the Berks Firing Line is reached.

9. __Tools.__ The two Reserve Coys will carry 300 shovels which will be put down when ordered.

10. __Rations.__ Each man will carry two days rations i.e:- The Iron Ration and one other days rations. Waterbottles will be full.

11. __Wounded.__ Our own Stretcher Bearers will bring all wounded to the road. ㉔ - ㉞ whence they will be taken back by the Field Ambulance bearers. All men are to be warned that they are not to stop to help wounded, but are to push on with the utmost vigour.
Headquarters will be first at the junction of the RUE TILLELOY with CHIMNEY CRESCENT, afterwards it will move forward in the centre of the Reserve.

P.T.O.

12. **Time.** All watches will be compared and set during the halt for a meal at ROUGE CROIX.

R B Stephen
Lieut Colonel,
Comdg. 2nd Bn. The Rifle Brigade.

App B.   4

Battalion Orders
by
Lieut-Colonel. R. B. Stephens.
Comdg. 2nd Bn. The Rifle Bde.
                    9th March 1915.

1. The Battalion will march at 11.5 p.m tonight. Starting point X Roads at AID POST, 200 yards S.W. of "C" Coy's billets.
Order of march:- B. A. D. C. Coys.
Route:- Road junction M.7.6 - RIEZ BAILLEUL road junction M.19.6 - CROIX BARBÉE - ROUGE CROIX - thence to position of assembly.
The Battalion will halt for a meal at road junction ½ mile north of CROIX BARBÉE

2. The Battalion will carry out the operations described in the instructions issued yesterday.

3. At 7.30 a.m. the guns open.
At 8.5 a.m. the guns will lift and the first infantry (Royal Berks) attack will advance.
At 8.35 a.m. the guns will again lift and the Battalion will advance.
The 1st two Companies of the battalion will be immediately behind the Berks firing line ready to advance at 8.35 a.m.

                                P.T.O

6

4. Silence and concealment are most important at the position of assembly. No smoking or lights after leaving ROUGE CROIX until daylight.

5. The Indian Corps on our right will mark their blocking parties with a pink flag. 8th Division blocking parties are marked with a blue flag.

6. The new bright cap badges will be covered with mud.

Issued at.
6-30 p.m
9/3/15.

R B Stephen
Lieut- Colonel.
Commdg 2nd Bn. The Rifle Bde.

2/A.B.

8th, Division.

25th, Brigade.

2nd, Rifle Brigade.

April, 1915.

121/5254.

25th Brigade 5.

2nd Rifle Brigade

Vol VI 1 - 30.4.15

2nd Battalion The Rifle Brigade.

April 1915

48

April 1st

Took over trenches of number one section VIII Div from 4th Cameron Highlanders, completing relief about 9 p.m. Enemy very quiet. We had frequent patrols out all along the line & sniped pretty freely when not patrolling. Work was done on the parapet & entanglements improved. No casualties.

April 2nd Continued work in the trenches, filling & building up sandbags. Sniped vigorously all day to which the enemy only made a feeble reply. [Sgt Wiley killed in fire trench] Rifle with telescopic sight arrived & we made free use of it — a great success. A great deal of work was undertaken at night & the parapet & wire considerably improved. A working party of the R.I.R. filled in a large portion of the network of Knyvets in front of D Coy. A large German patrol was seen by this Coy & it was heavily

fired upon. Rain fell during night.
GOC Div visited lines during day.
April 3rd
Rain fell at intervals.
Sniped more vigorously than ever
to which the enemy made even
a feebler reply than yesterday.
Six Germans were actually seen
hit & fall, four to the telescopic
sight. Officers of RIR visited
trenches in morning & afternoon
with view to taking over.
GOC V Corps visited lines
during afternoon.
Night work was handicapped
by the weather — a rainy & very
dark night: however a good
deal of work was got through
D Coy filling & laying 400
sandbags & putting out 8 coils
of barbed wire.
D Coy reported at 3.20 a.m.
that a large body of the enemy
could be heard marching along
the road in rear of enemy
lines towards their front
trench. Nothing came of this
— possibly reliefs or ration party.

April 4th. Relieved by R.I.R. — but into Brigade Reserve billets — A Coy clic up to the firing line on Rue Tilleloy.

April 5th. Rested in billets

April 6th. Rested in billets — Telescopic sight on .303 sporting rifle issued from 6th Div.

April 7th. Relieved R.I.R. in Trenches — a quiet night but very wet.

April 8th. Heavy rain. Trench mortar arrived & was fired in afternoon with great success by Lt Watney. Coys got through a good deal of work — but the state of the trench was very wet & muddy. Experimented with French parachute lights which was also a great success. Enemy very quiet.

51

April 9th. A good deal of rain fell & the trenches became very wet Tuesday. A quiet day. One burst ho lar in afternoon — it is very accurate. Work continued on the trenches. B Coy reported a large German working party out in front of their trenches but did not fire on them owing to request of R.E. officer who was in charge of a large party working just behind our line. Tramway lines completed from our H.Q. to B Coy trench. Fired some dozen rounds from trench mortar about 7.30. B Coy reported mysterious noises under their parapet.

April 10th. The weather cleared up & a great deal of work was done cleaning up the trench which soon became very dry with the help of a strong wind. One man shot through the head & killed in A Coy. Our guns registered on enemy's wire in our front.

Relieved by 5th in the evening & marched into Bde reserve billets on Rue du Bouchers.

April 11th. Rested in billets.

April 12th. Brigadier inspected Coys in marching order in billets — highly satisfied with appearance & clothing of Bn. Marched into Div Res N of SAILLY.

April 13th. 7–8 am Coys practised blocking parties. 10.30 am Bn parade route march & attack practise. 2.30 – 3.30 pm Last drafts on musketry & arm drill parade.

April 14th Parades under O.C. Coys. Working party last night of 375.

April 15th. B & C coys went for long route march, dinners out.

April 16th Coy officers inspected the trenches. Divisional

baths all day. Working party 375 at night. One man killed one wounded.

April 17th. C-in-C inspected the Brigade at 2.30 pm.

April 18th. Relieved E. Lancs in No 5 section. [Marched from billets at 3.30 pm, halting for teas at Steenbeck. Relief completed 8.50 pm.] C Coy commenced new trench with help of large working party from D Coy. Two men wounded. Routine orders show Sgt Bollinger & Rfn Knut as being awarded DCM in connection with recent operations at Neuve Chapelle also Cpl Looslourgh if he had lived.

Officers & NCO's W. Riding Division attached for instruction.

April 19th. [One man killed, two wounded in fire trench during course of day.] Very quiet on the whole. Beautiful warm weather. Officers attached yesterday left & new lot arrived. Man wounded last night died this evening.

April 20th
Two men killed two wounded, one died of wounds received yesterday. Fine warm weather. Quiet night work progressed rapidly on new trench.

April 21st Three men killed. Relieved by RIR & marched into billets in Fleurbaix.

April 22nd. Rested in billets

April 23rd Rested in billets

April 24th Relieved RIR in trenches. Finished off C Coys new trench. One Coy of the York & Lancs territorials attached for instruction.

April 25th One man killed. three wounded. Territorial Coy relieved by another. Quiet night.

April 26th. Very misty during early morning — fine all day. Five men wounded. Relieved by 1/4th York & Lancs territorials & moved into Div reserve billets at BAC ST MAUR.

April 27th. Rested in billets. Draft 1 Officer 105 men joined.

April 28th. Took over old trenches in E lines relieving 1/6th West Yorks. Territorials. Two men slightly wounded. No work hardly during night owing to lack of stores. A good deal of firing throughout night. Scots Guards 7th Div. held D lines on our right. RIR taking over F lines.

April 29th. Bright sunny day. Enemy shelled slightly late in afternoon. Work continued on the wire, parapet & parados during the night. The enemy sniped freely to which we replied with heavy machine

gun + rifle fire. German
trench mortar fired some
rounds on the right of B
Coy. One man killed + two
wounded from rifle fire.
Very strong wire entanglements
were noticed in front of
German trenches opposite
left of A Coy. All coys reported
having noticed enfilade fire
coming from the right during
the night.

April 30th. Beautiful warm
day. Relieved by R. Berks
+ moved into Bde Reserve in
Rue Dosquin.

~~May 1st~~

K. 13. W. 13.

8th, Division.

25th, Brigade.

2nd, Rifle Brigade.

May, 1915.

Capt b?

131/553/3

S/L Simson
25th Brigade

2nd Rifle Brigade

Vol VII 1 – 31.5.15

2nd Battalion The Rifle Brigade.

May 1915

57

May 1st. Rested in billets. About 4.30 a.m. the battalion stood to arms for about two hours on account of Germans shelling area behind NEUVE CHAPELLE very heavily. No development.

May 2nd. Rested in billets. About ½ doz shells fell in Laventie killing two women.

May 3rd. Relieved Royal Berks in E Lines. Quiet night — very wet. One man wounded. Little work done owing to weather.

May 4th. Rainy day. Relieved by W. Yorks (Territorial), & marched to billets on RUE BATAILLE, not completing move till 2 AM 5th. Very dark night & Territorials delayed. Enemy fired a good deal during relief, but no casualties.

May 5th Rested in billets. The whole of B Coy worked on wire in front of No.2 Sec: 5 Casualties in the Coy. 1 Killed. A Coy sent working party of 100 to work under Bd. sig. of in No 2 sect. two casualties, 1 died of wounds.

May 6th Rested in billets. C. Coy on working party in No 1 Sect. Coy officers reconnoitred during night position of & approach to assembly trenches. Orders received for operations.

May 7th Rested in billets. ~~Battn paraded 11am to march to assembly trenches in No 1 sect.~~ Operations postponed for 24 hours.

May 8th Rested in billets. Battalion paraded 11am & marched to assembly trenches.

59

May 9th & 10th.

Instructions & orders for assembly & the first advance were issued & were accurately carried out.

When our bombardment opened a good many shells dropped short. Some of our men began to retire from the advanced sap & from the fire trench. The movement was stopped but our first line suffered severe casualties from our own shell fire.

At 5.40 a.m. the first line advanced & the other lines moved into the forward sap & fire trenches.

The first line B & D Coys, took the German trench opposite to them & continued the advance.

The second line, A & C Coy, Machine Gun & Headquarters moved across into the enemy's trench. Both lines suffered severe loss, the machine guns were unable to get across. Headquarters were dispersed, & the organised bombing & blocking parties were broken up & were most difficult to find afterwards.

Our men occupied the line 826 - 827 - 828 in accordance with orders. They had the red & yellow distinguishing flags up. All the first line had gone up & most of the second.

The attacks on our right & left had not succeeded & bombing parties were organised for both ends of the captured trench. It was extremely difficult to find bombs & bombers but about 50 yards to the west of the SAILLY - FROMELLES road was gained & a bit to the east making our front perhaps 250 yards in all.

Meanwhile the Coys at

61

826 etc were subjected to a very heavy machine gun fire from both flanks, chiefly from the 'back' of the German trench on our right & left. Nearly all the Coy officers were killed or wounded on this line & about 8 o'clock the men began to retire & continued to dribble back from these advanced positions all day.

They all reported that they encountered very little opposition or fire from their front, but were being very badly enfiladed & taken in reverse.

The defence of the German fire trench was organised & several attempts to bomb our flanks were repelled. About 12 noon, 2/Lt Gray brought up reinforcements; about 50 started from our Sap but they lost very heavily crossing the open, & only about 20 arrived. 2/Lt Gray got the captured

machine gun working.
The CO also received a
message at this time that
General Cole had been killed
+ he was in command of the
Brigade.
About 7.30 pm the enemy
counter attacked but were
beaten off helped by the
fire of the captured machine
gun. About 8.30 pm all was
quiet. The CO then returned
to our parapet & put up
all our men who could
be collected, about 70, 2
machine guns & two bombing
parties of the Royal Berks
to help hold the trenches.
This was as many men as
the trench could hold.
About 2.30 am the enemy
started another counter attack
bringing a large force against
the front of the trench &
bombing heavily from both
flanks, our flanks were driven
in in spite of the blocks
we had put up.

had than no bombs with which to repel this attack.

Our machine guns were very gallantly fought & are said to have caused the enemy very heavy loss, but eventually about 3 a.m. the remnants of the battalion were driven out of the trench.

About 5 a.m. the battalion, consisting of 3 officers & about 195 men marched back to billets near SAILLY.

May 11th. Rested in billets & reorganised. Capt Nugent arrived from the third battalion & took over command of the battalion. Capt Bligh & Lts Young & Boswell also arrived & a draft of 70 NCO's & men.

May 12th. Rested in billets. Casualties during recent engagement:- 77 killed — 340 wounded — 194 missing, 18 wounded & missing. Officers 9 killed — 8 wounded — 4 missing.

64

May 13th Restd in billets. Parade postponed owing to weather. Acting Brigadier inspected the draft.

May 14th Bn. Route March. Restd in billets.

May 15th Restd in billets. C.O. inspected billets & Coys paraded under OC Coy for arm drill & musketry.

May 16th. Coys paraded under OC Coys during the morning. A Coy found a working party of 25 men for loading stores on Rue Petillon; in addition a working party of 100 paraded for work near Neuve Chapelle.

May 17th. Divisional baths at Sailly. The By. moved into billets in Estaires.

65

May 18th. In billets at Estaires. Bn paraded for route march at 10.30 a.m.

May 19th. In billets at Estaires. Coys paraded under OC Coys. Six subalterns joined last night for duty.

May 20th. In billets at Estaires. Route march. Inspected by Brigadier Stephens en route. Working party of 100 men under Lt. Bailie worked near Neuve Chapelle in the fire trenches. Party conveyed to rendezvous in six GS wagons.

May 21st. Parades under OC Coys.

May 22nd. Bn route march. CO & OC Coys inspected D lines trenches. Draft of 2 officers and 249 men arrived.

66

May 23rd. Voluntary church parades. GOC Bde inspected draft at 10 am. Working party of 50 men at 8.30pm under Lt. Poe in D lines. One man wounded from shell fire.

May 24th. Cleaned up billets & took over D lines from E Lancs regt. A quiet night. Little work done besides a general inspection of wire & parapet. One man killed.

May 25th. Enemy shelled promiscuously throughout the day with light field gun & light field howitzer. One man killed at night by rifle fire. All coys worked on wire & thickening parapet. A quiet night.

May 26th. Enemy continued shelling. Two men killed two wounded by our own field guns. One man killed

and one wounded by rifle
fire during the night &
two wounded by rifle grenade.
Coys worked on the wire &
parapet. 2/Lt Gray appointed
Bde MG officer.

May 27th. Enemy used
rifle grenades against our
trenches killing 4 men &
wounding one. Two men
wounded by rifle fire. A
warm day. Work continued
on our parapet & wire.

May 28th. A warm, quiet
day. Very hot in the trenches.
Work on wire & trench
continued. Enemy were
exceptionally quiet at night &
was at work on his wire &
trench.

May 29th. A quiet day.
Two men were wounded on
patrol at night. Grass in
front of trenches is now very
long. Coys started to cut it
tonight. The communication
trench into C Coy was
improved. Enemy was also

at work all night & very quiet.

May 30th. Enemy shelled our trenches with small howitzers early this morning, with no effect. Shelling continued in the vicinity of trenches intermittently during the day. 2Lt E.P. Smith joined today. Coys continued cutting the long grass & improving the trench. Enemy's transport reported to be moving from S to N about 9 pm.

May 31st Enemy shelled P.P. HQ & Rue Bacquerot about 8 am with "woollybears", one man wounded. They also shelled trenches between 8 am & 9 am & between 10 am & 11 am with trench mortars & 5.9 howitzers. Two men were bruised. Our artillery not being allowed to fire could not retaliate. Two officers,

2 Lt G.T. Sheridan & Lt W.W
Monkith joined today.
Enemy shelled Bn H.Q.
with field guns again during
afternoon. One man killed
in fire trench by rifle bullet.
One Coy relieved by R.I.R.
about 9 pm the remainder
by Middx left about 12
midnight. Bn moved
into Bde Res in Laventie.
About 9 pm enemy's transport
was again reported moving
S to N.

121/5930

8th Division

2nd Rifle Brigade

Vol XIII 1 — 30.6.15

2nd Battalion The Rifle Brigade.

June 1915

June 1. Rested in billets. Draft of 1 officer (Capt. Jenkyns) & 36 other ranks arrived - all these were men previously wounded with the battalion. Brigadier spoke to the battalion at 7 pm & praised them for their gallant conduct on 9th May. A working party of 100 men under Lt. Chapman rendezvoused at HQ D lines at 8.30 pm.

June 2. CO inspected draft at 10.30 am & billets at 11 am. Draft 1 officer 36 men arrived

June 3. Rested in billet. Respirators inspected by MO Relieved R.I.R. & Middx Regiment in trenches taking over D lines (left) as last time. Waterbottles sterilised in the morning.
One man wounded during relief.

June 4. Work continued as usual on the trenches.

A quiet day.

June 5. One man killed at stand to arms. Extremely hot day. Two men told off with shot gun to watch house suspected of containing carrier pigeons for use by spy. A few pigeons shot. Draft of 2 officers + 38 men arrived. Enemy shelled Rue Bacquerot at intervals during day

June 6. A very hot day. One man killed last night on patrol. Enemy shelled Rue Bacquerot towards evening. New telescopic rifle received today (Government issue). Relieved by Royal Irish rifles + marched into Bac billets in avenue.

June 7. Rested in billets. A better day than yesterday. Working party of 100 men under Lt Whateley working in vicinity of Neuve Chappelle on an emergency trench, to be used in case of gas attacks. The bombardment in South Faorain continued for 36 hrs. Another officer of the Oxford and Bucks. L.I. arrived. Divisional total for 1/2 B=C. 9 Kings Lt.

June. 8. Rested in billets. Extremely hot day. Thunderstorm at 2 p.m. Coy parade carried out with bombing, sword exercises, and work with respirators on. A Coy made a pathway from Fauquissart crossroads to Trolley head left D. line. Bombardment in South continues. Enemy dropped 16 shells in front of Laventie. Working party of 50 men under Lt. E. R. Smith working in vicinity of D. night lines on redoubt and communication trench. No casualties. 9 Kings Lt.

June. 9. Rested in billets. Rained heavily in afternoon; Lecture on asphyxiating gas by an expert from G. H. Q. Working party of 50 men under 2/Lt. V. C. Martin in vicinity of D. lines. No casualties. 9 Kings Lt.

June. 10. Rested in billets. Battalion went

73

march at 4.30 p.m. about 6¼ mls. Machine guns carried out practice on range during morning. 2 working parties of 50 men each under Lt. W. Sheridan and 2/Lt. W.W. Young; the latter working at beginning of the "Duck's Bill", the former same as last night. No casualties.
　　　　　　　　　　　　　　　2/Bg.Lt.

June 11. Rested in billets. Divisional bath for remaining half battalion. A draft of 3 officers arrived. 4 machine guns and two detachments sent to trenches to man D.1 and S.H. & 9. Bombing field used. A working party of 30 men under 2/Lt. J.W.K. Boswell working on a new fire trench in front of present parapet. A suspected man sent to Brigade office, chield cutting telephone wires.
　　　　　　　　　　　　　　　2/Bg.Lt.

June 12. Rested in billets. Two men suspected of sending up pigeons sent to Brigade Hdqrs. Took over same trenches from R.I.R. as before at about 10 p.m.

　　　　　　　　　　　　　　　2/Bg.Lt.
June 13. One man killed in early morning. 2. Lt. Sewel returns to duty. Work on trenches carried on, chiefly on

74

support trenches. A new "Periscopic
Rifle Rest" sent for trial proves excellent.
Enemy very quiet.
                                    a/y lt.

June 14. Quiet day. Work in evening very slight,
owing to demonstration bombardment
of E. Lines from 4.p.m. Enemy shelled D.1.
Three casualties.   a/y ft.

June 15. Work continued on our support trenches.
About 8.50 a.m. miner exploded a small mine
below a German gallery; gallery broken &
destroyed. Miners went down again too
soon, several of whom then became gassed
by "after gas". Enemy shelled our cutting
slightly. G.O.C. inspected the trenches.
Demonstration bombardment in evening.

June 16th. A quiet day &
very hot. Our trench
mortar fired about 6 p.m.
Enemy shelled & were
replied to by our heavies.
Work continued on trenches.
A considerable amount of
firing continued throughout
the night.

75

June 18. DF blown in a hostile gallery successfully. A very quiet night, enemy apparently not at work on their trenches. One man wounded at stand to arms. Relieved by RIR in the trenches about 10 pm

June 19. Rested in billets. CO inspected billets. Draft of 1 officer + 108 men joined.

June 20. Church parade. GOC Division distributed DCM ribbons. ½ bn had baths at La Crosne during afternoon.

June 21. Coys paraded under OC Coys. Working party of 50 men at night.

June 22. Bn route march. Blankets withdrawn. C Coy attended bombing school in evening for instruction. Working party of 50 men at night.

76

June 23rd. Coys at disposal of OC Coys. Half Bn went to Divl baths La Gorgue. Working party of 50 men at night.

June 24th. Coys at disposal of OC Coys. Relief of Irish rifles in D lines cancelled. Working party of 50 at night.

June 25th. Coys at disposal of OC Coys. Orders received to move to SAILLY. Marched at 8 pm & billetted in Divisional baths.

June 26th. Officers inspected No 4 Section trenches & Bn relieved 5th West Yorks in same marching at 8 pm. Relief completed about 11·15 pm

June 27th. Practically no work done last night. Wire was inspected & weak places in parapet found. GOC visited Headquarters in the afternoon. Four men wounded, owing to slight hostile shelling.

June 28th. A good deal of work was got through last night — trenches are very weak in parts — much too broad. GOC inspected trenches about 6 a.m. Work continued at night on wire & trench. One man wounded, one killed.

June 29th. A quiet day & night — work continued as usual.

June 30th. GOC inspected trenches. Work at night as usual

8th, Division.

25th, Brigade.

2nd, Rifle Brigade.

July, 1915.

121/6306

25th 8th Division

2nd Rifle Brigade

Vol IX 1 — 31.7.15

2nd Battalion The Rifle Brigade.

July 1915

79

July 1st. Took over No 5 Section from 1 Lincolns & handed over ½ No 4 Section to 7th Middx. "Watling Street" Communication Trench traced out

July 2nd. Two men wounded, rifle fire in fire trench. Relieved by RIR in trenches.

July 3rd. Rested in billets. Working party 150 at night.

July 4th. Parades under OC Coys. Working party 150 at night.

July 5th. Parades under OC Coys. Working party 150 at night. One man wounded.

July 6th. Parades under OC Coys. Working party 150 at night.

July 7th. Parades under OC Coys. Working party 150 at night.

80

July 8th Relieved R.I.R.
in trenches.

July 9th Following intelligence
report sent in :- "Enemy
heard driving in pickets about
opposite S.P. Germans very
quiet till 1.30 am when brisk
fire was kept up till daylight.
Enemy seen at work on his
parapet. About 12 Germans
seen using a path during
daylight about 800 yds in front
of S.P. & behind their own
trench. A patrol which was
out in front of SS from 11 pm to
12.15 am reported gorse patch
clear & enemy driving in
stakes in front of his trench
but he stopped on one
round being fired by our
field guns. About 12 midday
a party of Germans
cutting grass were dispersed
by our snipers."
Work was carried out on
new shelter trench.

81

July 9th 10th. Capt Roe wounded working on wire last night. Work continued on the fire trenches + new support & communication trenches. Strong officers patrol went out from H.P under Lt Byrne Johnson making a useful reconnaisance. A patrol from 54 reported enemy working on their wire & a sap. Another strong patrol under Lt Monteith went out from the left of the line & surprised a party of 10 Germans cutting grass, who ran away & thus avoided capture.

July 11th. Watling Street was worked on again last night & considerable progress made. The usual maintenance worked was carried on in the trenches & the new defence works improved. In the evening our trench mortars fired with success on enemy's parapet. The enemy replied with about 30 small shells slightly damaging our parapet, whereupon our guns fired about 7 rounds at enemy's trench. Trench Mortars then fired a second time & the enemy again replied being answered by our guns. Our Snipers gained complete ascendancy over the German Snipers today & still maintain it.

Patrols reported the enemy very quiet & doing no work on their lines.

July 12. Lt. Bull slightly wounded by shell fire today but remained at duty. One man was wounded by rifle fire. Usual maintenance worked carried out in trenches also work on new trenches & "Working Sheet".

At 4.30 pm, according to a pre arranged plan with the 33rd Bde R.F.A. our trench mortars opened fire on German trench. The enemy replied with 20 small shells doing little or no damage, but our guns, who immediately answered, fired about 15 rounds on German trench with some success. Our trench mortars continued to fire, although one was out of action owing to a jam. The mortars fired 116 rounds in all with considerable accuracy & apparently doing no little damage. One of our batteries silenced the hostile battery, but a German howitzer battery then opened fire & was immediately answered by our howitzers while our field guns & trench mortars continued to fire on the German trench. About 30 yards of the German parapet was blown in. By this time the German guns had ceased altogether. Our snipers continued to fire at

84

the German parapet throughout the action, but not a shot was fired by the enemy's snipers. Our field guns continued to fire intermittently for some time without getting any reply from the German guns. A message of congratulation was sent to the Bn. by the Brig. Genl. Cuddy on the success of this small action of which he was a spectator.

July 13. Two men killed by rifle fire & three wounded by shell fire. Maintenance work continued on trench, also work on "walking street" & new defences. Machine guns were laid on the parapet knocked about by our guns yesterday & great inconvenience was caused to working parties there. Our snipers continue to maintain the ascendancy & two hostile snipers were shot by them, also numerous periscopes were smashed.

85

July 14th. Bn HQ were shelled throughout the morning from 9 am to 12 noon by a 4.2 howitzer battery, 91 shells dropping close round; but no damage was done. In the trenches one man was killed by rifle fire & four wounded by an accidental explosion of a hand grenade.
Usual work continued last night. Our snipers claim two more Germans this morning & 5 periscopes.
Relieved by RIR in trenches tonight & marched to DW Res in Bac St. Maur. A pouring wet night.

July 15th. Coys at disposal of OC Coys. Fitting clothing. Digging party 200 men at night.

July 16th. Coys disposal OC Coys. CO inspected billets. MO inoculated some men. Digging party 200 men at night.

86

July 17th. Parades under OC Coys. Digging party 200 at night.

July 18th. Church parade. GOC Bde presented DCM to Rfn Vondehauk. Digging party 200 at night. About midnight CQMS Houlton captured single-handed a spy signalling from a house in Fleurbaix, who went for him with a drawn sword.

July 19th. Parades under OC Coys. Inspection of smoke helmets by MO & Divisional baths for the Bn. Digging party 200 at night.

July 20th. Relieved R.I.R. in the trenches. A quiet night.

July 21st. A very quiet day. 2/Lt Frisch joined in the evening. Usual work carried out on trenches, but shortage of sandbags is a severe handicap. Enemy used searchlight frequently last night. Usual work again carried on at night. Watling Street is improving rapidly.

July 22. Lt. Norris joined for duty. A quiet day. Work continued as usual.

July 23. We have got the upper hand of enemy's snipers & can easily silence them.

July 24. Conditions quite normal. Nothing worth recording occurred. All telephonic communication readjusted ~~with us~~ in accordance with new scheme for defence.

July 25. At 3.30 pm an ~~aeroplane~~ aeroplane having arrived to observe for our guns,

88

We commenced to bombard the enemy's trenches with our trench mortars & rifle grenades. The Germans made no reply for some time but eventually fired a few whizz-bangs doing us damage. A brigade of our field guns & a battery of howitzers replied to the German fire & our trench mortars & rifle grenades continued to shoot, & 30 trench mortar shells & 30 rifle grenades were finally fired with success into the German trench.
The enemy remained very quiet.

July 26th Relieved by R.I.R. & marched into Bde reserve.

July 27th Parades under O.C. Coys in billets. Digging party 150 at night.

89

July 28th. Parades under OC Coy — Digging party of 150 at night.

July 29th. Parades under OC Coy — Digging party 150 at night.

July 30th. Parades under OC Coy. A draft of 91 joined the battalion. Digging party 150 at night.

July 31st. Parades under OC Coy. Draft of 49 joined. Relieved RIR in trenches & took over subsection 4S in addition from Middlesex.

<u>8th, Division.</u>

<u>25th, Brigade.</u>

<u>2nd, Rifle Brigade.</u>

<u>August, 1915.</u>

25/8

121/6737

8th Division

2nd Rifle Bde
M X
August 15

2nd Battalion The Rifle Brigade.

August 1915

August 1st. Conditions normal. Capt. Wolseley-Jenkins joined for duty & took over command of A Coy. Practise alarm at 3.30pm - Bn H.P. & reserve platoons turned to their allotted positions. One man killed.

August 2nd. A patrol under Lt. Howkith reached the German wire & reported a relief having taken place. A quiet day.

August 3. Weather unsettled - a good deal of rain making trenches very muddy. The gunners destroyed a machine gun emplacement this morning which had been discovered by C Coy. A very quiet night. One man wounded.

August 4th. - More rain early this morning but

fine afterwards. Lincolns
on our left bombarded
enemy with trench mortars
at daylight. Enemy
unusually quiet.
Relieved by S.R. at night
Marched into Bac de
S of Fleurbaix.

August 5. Parades under
OC Coys. A party of 200
digging at night — Lieut W W
Young wounded, not dangerous.
Digging party also in morning.

Aug 6. Parades under OC
Coys. Br. Gen inspected last
draft. Digging parties in
morning & at night. One
man wounded.

Aug 7. Parades under
OC Coys. 200 digging at night.
Two men wounded.

Aug 8. Church parade.
Relieved R.I.R. in trenches.

92

Aug. 9. A very quiet night. Heavy cannonade heard in direction of Ypres at dawn. Registered with trench mortar in the afternoon. Enemy shelled ground in rear of trenches promiscuously & slightly. Our artillery were unusually active. One man wounded.

Aug. 10. A quiet morning & very hot. GOC visited lines. 12th Pn RB attached for instruction went into the trenches in the evening. A very quiet night.

Aug 11. Our Snipers & Patrols were very active & did some good work. GOC Divn & attached Bde visited lines. 12th Bn RB changed the platoons under instruction for others in the evening.

War Diary Cont.

Aug 12th. One man wounded. During attachment of 12th Bn they have had one killed & one wounded. A quiet day. Relieved by R.I.R. in the morning & marched into Bde Res billets.

Aug 13th. Rested in billets. Digging party 350 & 25 in the morning & 200 at night.

Aug 14th. Digging party 100 in morning, 250 at night. Divl Horse Show in afternoon.

Aug 15th Church Parade. Digging party 170 morning 250 at night.

Aug 16th Marched into Divl Reserve N of River Layes about 8 pm.

Aug 17th Rested in billets. Divl band played in billets in afternoon.

Aug 18th. CO inspected billets.

Aug 19th. Gas expert 1st Army gave a demonstration which was attended by 5 officers & 45 other ranks of the battalion.

Aug 20th. Divisional baths for the battalion.

Aug 21st. Held battalion sports & competed for Coy shield which was won by A Coy. GOC Div attended.

Aug 22nd. Church parade in evening. Adjutants parade in morning. Officers inspected pivt defence works. Working party 250 at night.

Aug 23rd. Battalion inspected by Corps Commander who made special mention of smart appearance of the troops. Held a concert in the evening.

Aug 24th Battalion route march. Working party 150 at night, one man wounded.

Aug 25th Working party 100 in the morning & 200 at night

Aug 26th Bn. paraded for route march & tactical exercises. Sgt Maj Kemp received commission in 9th Bn. & Sgt Eastwood in 4th Bn.

Aug 27th. Band played in the evening.

Aug 28th. 200 working party in morning, 300 at night.

Aug 29th. Church parade

Aug 30th. 50 working party in the morning. Battalion route march.

Aug 31st Divisional Baths

8th, Division.

25th, Brigade.

2nd, Rifle Brigade.

September, 1915.

25/8

121./7076

8th Division

2nd Rifle Brigade

Vol II

Sept 15

2nd Battalion The Rifle Brigade.

September 1915

Sept. 1st 100 men at Divisional Baths. Relieved Worcesters & Northamptons in No 5 &c marching at 7 pm. A very quiet night.

Sept. 2nd GOC Bde visited the lines. Rained hard all day — trenches very wet & muddy. One man wounded by rifle fire. Our artillery very active on targets behind German lines opposite us.

Sept 3rd. GOC Bde again visited trenches. Lt Seymour & seven other ranks joined for duty. Two men wounded by rifle fire. Enemy particularly inactive.

Sept 4th. Another wet day. Relieved by FIR & marched into Bde Res.

Sept 5th. Church parades.
Divl. baths.

Sept 6th. Working party in morning — one killed by shell fire.

Sept 7th. Parades under OC Coys. Relieved R.I.R. in trenches.

Sept 8th. Two men wounded by rifle fire in fire trench, & one killed. A quiet day & night.

Sept 9th. One man wounded rifle fire in fire trench. Very misty during morning. Lr Cobbold killed by stray bullet while going round his machine guns in the second line works.

Sept 10th. Two men wounded by rifle fire in fire trench, & one in rear of trenches. Relieved by R.I.R. & marched back to usual billets.

Sept. 11th. Ptes under OC Coys.

Sept. 12th. Ptes under OC Coys. Church parade in Evening.

Sept. 13th. Relieved R.I.R's in trenches.

Sept. 14th. Two men wounded by rifle fire. A quiet night & day.

Sept. 15th. Line readjusted. 2/E Lancs. took over our line except D Coy. Two coys marched to billets. HQ & remainder stayed in trenches after readjustment.

Sept. 16th. Trench Coys relieved by 1/London Regt & marched back to usual billets. A Coy found 100 working party at 6pm.

Sept. 17th. Rested in billets. Working party 100 at night.

Sept 18th. Rested in billets. 100 working party at night.

Sept 19th. Church parade. Relieved 1/London regt in the evening in the trenches.

Sept 20th. One man killed by rifle fire in fire trenches. Relieved by Worcesters & marched back to usual billets.

Sept 21st. Bombardment of enemy's trenches & works commenced.

Sept 22nd. Parades under OC Coys. Bombardment continued. 100 working party at night.

Sept 23rd. Parades under OC Coys. Orders for operations issued to the Battalion.

Sept. 24th Paraded
9.30 a.m. for inspection
by GOC & church parade
but owing to shelling
parade was dismissed.
Machine gun billets burnt,
but only a few articles
of kit were lost.
Bn paraded at 6.15
pm for operations &
after an address by
GOC Brigade, marched
to positions of assembly.

September 25th The Bn was ordered to
assault and capture CORNER FORT
and the German trenches to our left
of it for about 200 yards.

The Bn was in the "position of assembly"
at 10 pm on the 24th September, and in
"the position of assault" at 3-45 am on
the 25th.

At 4-25 am the final artillery bombardment
commenced, and, as far as this Bn was
concerned, was extraordinarily effective
and well aimed.

The actual assault was carried out
by "C" Coy and 80 specially trained

bombers.

They had been ordered to crawl forward during the final bombardment, and this they did so effectively that they assaulted the German front line trench at almost the same moment as our guns lifted.

The left of "C" Coy and the left bombing party were hampered by some uncut wire, but, otherwise, the assault was a complete success.

"C" Coy and the bombers, in accordance with instructions issued beforehand, immediately bombed to right and left, and up to the German 2nd line trench.

Before 1 am the German 2nd line trench was captured.

"A" Coy and the machine guns followed "C" Coy, moving along the "ROSSIGNOL" communication ditch.

Captain H. L. RILEY D.S.O. went with them and took over command of the front two companies on arrival in the German trench.

"A" Coy was seriously impeded by some quite new wire in the ditch between the German sap and their parapet, but, in spite of this, and some very heavy fire from the German ANGLE to our left, reached the German front line trench without any very great losses.

Our guns, at this time, were firing on the German third line trench, and to our right of CORNER FORT.

It was very important that C's & A' coys and the bombers should bomb along and join hands with the Berkshire Regt to our left in the German 1st and 2nd line trenches.

Owing to the fact that the right coy of the Berkshires never reached the German trenches, this was not accomplished.

At about 5-15 am 'B' coy (less 50 men) was ordered to go up to the German captured trench with blocking parties and shovels, along the ROSSIGNOL communication ditch.

'D' coy was kept in reserve.

At about 6-50 am owing to strong German bombing attacks, to the impossibility of joining up with the Berkshires, and to difficulty in getting bombs up for our side, it was found necessary to abandon the German 2nd line trench.

By 10 am, however, a firm position had been established in the German front line trench, blocks being made to our right and left.

Many bombs were sent up to the German trench, supplies for this being used from D' Coy, from the 8th Middlesex and the cordons.

Also 2 trench mortars and one Lewis Lanes machine gun.

In spite of constant bombing attacks by Germans from both flanks and from their 2nd line trench our position in their front line trench was maintained.

At about 3 pm a fairly determined counterattack on our left was easily repulsed, and our artillery bombarded heavily.

At about 3.45 pm information was received that the Lincolns and the Berks had withdrawn from the German captured trenches, and orders were given for our companies to withdraw.

C Coy had already been withdrawn ~~and this coy had been told~~ as our front was so small and this company had been held in reserve with part of "B" and "D".

By about 4-45 pm the whole withdrawal was completed.

Our losses were 6 officers killed, 3 officers wounded, 32 other ranks killed, 173 other ranks wounded, and 29 other ranks missing. Total 243.

They were due to the German rifle fire and to the really hard hand to hand and bombing fighting in the German first and second line trenches, the enemy being on both our flanks, and in their second line trench during practically the whole day.

Many Germans were killed and wounded, and about 15 captured, including 11, who were shot by German machine guns.

At night the Bn was relieved by the Worcester Regt, and reached billets in near FLEURBAIX at about 6 am on the 26th September.

The evacuation of the wounded was extraordinarily well carried out, practically no wounded being left behind.

The majority of the wounds were comparatively slight.

Sept 26th. Rested in billets reorganising & fitting clothes. A shell bursting in one of the billets slightly wounded 2/Lt Whatley who remained at duty. One man was also wounded.

Sept 27th. The G.O.C. Div inspected the Bn at 2 pm & addressed the troops. He expressed his high appreciation of & admiration for the gallant & good work done by the battalion. The Bn moved into billets N of the R. Layes in the evening. 2/Lt Daniels V.C. joined for duty.

Sept 28th. Rested in billets.

Sept 29th. General Pulteney cmdg III Corps inspected the Brigade in the morning. He addressed the Bn & spoke some words of high praise for their gallant work.

Sept. 30th. Draft of 96 other ranks joined for duty: quality very good.

8th, Division.

25th, Brigade.

2nd, Rifle Brigade.

October, 1915.

Gen Kirwin

2nd Bde.

24 Oct
2. RB to 70 L3 Bde

Dec 15

Vol XII

H/7435

2nd Battalion The Rifle Brigade.

October 1915

October 1st. Draft inspected by GOC Bde. Divisional tailor for portion of Battalion.

October 2nd. Baths for remainder of Bn. Divisional band played in billets during the afternoon. Relieved 2/E Lancs regt in trenches (No 5 Sec), taking over new trench line dug after recent operations. Enemy trench mortar very persistent all night. Two Sergeants of B Coy were wounded by it. New trench not nearly complete, affords no protection from the weather.

October 3rd. A fine day. Enemy's trench mortar very active during the night despite the answer of our field guns & howitzers. Three men wounded by trench mortar. Large working party digging on new trench last night.

October 4th. The trenches are now very wet & muddy owing to the heavy rains. Enemy remarkably inactive & very quiet. Work continues on the new trench.

October 5th. Still raining. Enemy's trench mortar very active at night one shell killing 2 men & wounding 2. One man wounded by rifle fire. Large working party on new trench. Our guns replied with effect to enemy's trench mortar. A trench mortar of our own is badly required to answer with, but is at present unobtainable. 2/Lt A.E. Burnell joined for duty.

Oct. 6th. 2Lts Kennedy, Kennard, Cramer, Dawson, Trice joined for duty. Enemy shelled our trenches during the day & his trench mortar was active at night.

Oct 7th. Relieved by R.I.R in trenches. Draft 38 other ranks joined for duty.

Oct. 8th. Rested in billets. 150 working party at night.

Oct 9th. Rested in billets. Working party 150 at night.

Oct 10th. Church parade. Draft 81 other ranks joined the Bn. Relieved R.I.R in the trenches. A quiet night.

Oct 11th. Enemy shelled fairly vigorously behind our lines & on our flanks during the morning. One of our aeroplanes brought down an enemy aeroplane from directly above the lines. Draft which arrived yesterday after inspection by G.O.C. joined their coys in the trenches in the evening. A few trench mortars were fired in the early part of the evening doing no damage. Our guns replied. Some rain at night. Enemy's machine guns very active at stand to arms. One man wounded in fire trench.

Oct 12. 2/Lt Payer joined for duty. Enemy's snipers active all day. Only two trench mortar shells were fired during the night but enemy machine guns were very active. One man wounded by rifle fire.

Oct 13. Enemy opened a heavy rifle fire during early part of the evening & shelled our trenches with trench mortars & guns — our guns & machine guns replied — Enemy's operations were in the nature of a demonstration, the whole thing lasting about an hour. One man killed & 3 wounded by trench mortar.

Oct 14th. Relieved by RIR & marched into billets about 7.30 pm.

Oct 15th. Rested in billets — Parades under Co Comd. — 150 working party at night

Oct 16th. Rested in billets — Parades under Co Comd. — 150 working party at night.

Oct 17th Church Parade — 150 working party at night

Oct 18th Relieved RIR in trenches. One man wounded.

Oct 19th 2/Lt Begg joined for duty. Very quiet day & night — no shelling & practically no rifle fire at night. One man wounded by rifle fire.

Oct 20th Very quiet day. Work on new breastworks carried on.

Oct. 21. 2 Lt Kemp killed and two other
ranks wounded. Trist rain for
same days.

Oct. 22. One man wounded. Relieved
in trenches by R.I. Rifles.

Oct. 23. Parades under O.C. Coys. 150 men
for digging at night. Capt Austin
joined for duty.

Oct. 24. Relieved by 6 K.O.Y.L.I. in 21st
Bde went to Paissy St duty. Bde
in place of 11th Hameard toe enters church
parade in morning.

Oct. 25. Working-party of 50 men under
2Lt Yarris in morning. Rain all day.
Parades under O.C. Coys.

Oct. 26. Parades under O.C. Coys.

Oct. 27. Parades under O.C. Coys. 25 men
under Lt. Cremer for working party.
Relieved 8. York and Lanc. in trenches
N 52 - N 54. La Boutillerie. Very quiet.

Oct. 28. Very wet day. One man wounded.
Inspection of trenches by G.O.C. 70. Bde.
arrest

Work on wire and parapet commenced.
2Lt. Buxton joined for duty. Enemy
very quiet. One man killed during night.

Oct 29. 2 other ranks joined for duty.
Enemy shelled to right of Bodavaters.
Very wet day. Enemy otherwise very quiet.

Oct 30. G.O.C. division inspected Bn. line.
Enemy very quiet.

Oct 31 G.O.C. Bde inspected Bn. line and
expressed himself so pleased with
the work done in last few days, that
working parties ordered tomorrow would
be cancelled. Relieved in trenches by
8. Yorks and Lancs. Regt.

8th Division

2/A.I.S.

Nov / Vol XIII

12/7671

Ph Prov: rejoined 26 L.B.Bde

2nd Battalion The Rifle Brigade.

November 1915

Nov. 1st. Rested in billets. Working party of 25 for RE in morning.

Nov 2nd. Coys sent up working parties to trenches during morning but very heavy rain prevented work. Divisional band played during afternoon.

Nov. 3rd. Divisional baths.

Nov 4th. GOC 70 Bde inspected billets — Relieved B Y & L in trenches.

Nov. 5th. Trenches in a very bad state having fallen in in many places owing to last 4 days rain. Enemy quiet & patrols had nothing to report

Nov 6th. Last night was fine & a lot of work was got through. Enemy fired a few shells & trench mortars on our left but were otherwise very inactive.

Nov. 7. A draft of 72 joined the Bn & was posted to Coys in the trenches during evening.

Nov. 8. Relieved by 8 Yr L in the trenches.

Nov. 9. Rejoined 25th Bde. Relieved by 11 Sherwood Foresters in billets, & relieved 8 Y L I in billets.

Nov. 10. CO inspected draft.

Nov. 11. Divisional baths. GOC Bde inspected both last drafts.

Nov. 12. Relieved R.I.R in the trenches. A quiet night but very wet & windy. Trenches in an awful state.

Nov. 13. Wet morning. GOC inspected trenches. Party from RIR came up to coy. Two men slightly wounded at night by rifle fire. A clear fine night. Enemy very quiet.

Nov 14. GOC Div inspected trenches. A fine frosty day. Nothing unusual occurred. Much work was done on lines.

Nov. 15. One man killed & one wounded by rifle fire in trenches. Enemy very quiet & inactive. Work continued as usual.

Nov. 16. Relieved by RIR in trenches & marched to Div Res billets. GOC Bde visited lines.

Nov. 17. Rested in billets. Usual working parties in the morning, one man killed. Working party of 50 per coy at night. 2/Lt Dashwood left Bn to take up ADC duties.

Nov. 18. Usual working parties in morning. Marched to Div Res billets North of River Lys in afternoon.

Nov. 19. Rested in billets.

Nov. 20. Working parties by day (355).

Nov. 21. Rested in billets. Coys at disposal of OC Coys.

Nov. 22. Marched to billets in Bleu, arriving 6.20pm.

Nov. 23rd Marched to billets at Les Ciseaux into GHQ Reserve 13½ miles — Troops marched well. Established in billets 5.30pm.

Nov. 24th Rested in billets & prepared for coming training. CO inspected billets.

Nov. 25th. Training commenced. Three officers + 450 OR joined for duty. Coys at disposal of OC Coys for drill. NCO's under Sgt Major in early morning. Guard mounting + rifle calls commenced. NCO's under SM in morning.

Nov. 26th. Bn parade for drill. Parade for inspection by C in C cancelled owing to weather.

Nov. 27th. Fine sunny day. NCO's under SM in morning. Coys at disposal of OC Coy's for digging trenches for bombing practice.

Nov. 28th. Church parade.

Nov. 29th. Training continued

Nov. 30th. Training continued

8th, Division.

25th, Brigade.

2nd, Rifle Brigade.

December, 1915.

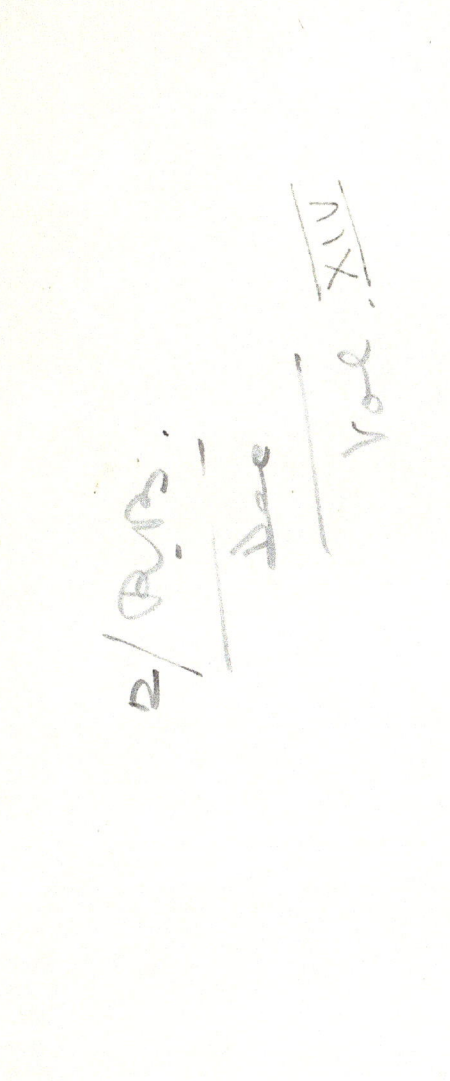

Army Form C. 2118

WAR DIARY
or
INTELLIGENCE SUMMARY

(Erase heading not required.)

Instructions regarding War Diaries and Intelligence Summaries are contained in F. S. Regs., Part II. and the Staff Manual respectively. Title Pages will be prepared in manuscript.

Place	Date	Hour	Summary of Events and Information	Remarks and references to Appendices
	1915 Dec. 1st		Battalion Route March in morning.	
	" 2nd		Usual Training	
	" 3rd		Training Continued. Adjutants Parade in afternoon. "A" Coy played "C" Coy for Bn. Football Shield — Result C3 – A2.	
	" 4th		Commanding Officers Parade. Draft of 62 other ranks joined for duty.	
	" 5th		Church Parade. 30x range completed. "B" Coy played "D" Coy football, Bn. Shield Competition — B4 – D1.	
	" 6th		Training Continued. G.O.C. Brigade inspected draft.	
	" 7th		Training Continued. "A" Coy played "D" Coy football, Bn. Shield Competition A.4 – D.3.	
	" 8th		Battalion Route March. "B" Coy played "C" Coy – B.0. C.0	
	" 9th		C.O's Parade. Training Continued	
	" 10th		Training Continued. "B" Coy beat "A" Coy 4 – 1, thereby winning the Shield. Divisional Band played in afternoon.	
	" 11th		C.O's Parade for tactical exercises. Lts. Pennefather, Inisch, Buxton and Knowles joined for duty.	

Army Form C. 2118

WAR DIARY
or
INTELLIGENCE SUMMARY
(Erase heading not required.)

Instructions regarding War Diaries and Intelligence Summaries are contained in F. S. Regs., Part II. and the Staff Manual respectively. Title Pages will be prepared in manuscript.

Place	Date	Hour	Summary of Events and Information	Remarks and references to Appendices
	Dec '15 (cont'd)			
	12th		Church Parade.	
	13th		Training Continued.	
	14th		Bn. Route March.	
	15th		C.O's Parade for tactical exercises.	
	16th		Training continued	
	17th		Brigade Route March.	
	18th		Training continued. 2nd Lt. Mackamant joined for duty.	
	19th		Training continued. Bn lined the road for departure of F.M. Sir J. French.	
	20th		Divisional manoeuvres commenced.	
	21st		Divisional manoeuvres.	
	22nd		Divisional manoeuvres.	
	23rd		Returned to Baillet.	
	24th		Rested in Billets.	
	25th		Xmas Day.	

1875 Wt. W593/826 1,000,000 4/15 J.B.C. & A. A.D.S.S./Forms/C. 2118.

WAR DIARY
or
INTELLIGENCE SUMMARY
(Erase heading not required.)

Army Form C. 2118

Place	Date	Hour	Summary of Events and Information	Remarks and references to Appendices
	Dec (cont.) 26th		Machine Gun Detachment won the Six-a-side football competition.	
	27th		C.O's Parade – "B" Coy played "A" Coy 1/London Regt in B.E. football competition. Result. B3. London 1.	
	28th		Coys at disposal of O.C. Coys.	
	29th		"B" Coy beat "C" Coy Royal Irish Rifles in final of Brigade football tournament. Result 6–4. Pou. night operations in evening. 2/Lts. Morris & Buxton + 29 other ranks	
	30th		Training recommenced. Transferred to Brigade Machine Gun Coy.	
	31st		Training continues.	

B.E.7.
1st January 1916

F. R. Chichester-Buxlake
Captain & Adjutant
for Lieut Colonel
Commdg 2nd Bn. The Rifle Brigade

<u>8th, Division.</u>

<u>25th, Brigade.</u>

<u>2nd, Rifle Brigade.</u>

<u>January, 1916.</u>

2 Rifle Bore
Jan
Vol XV

Army Form C. 2118

WAR DIARY
or
INTELLIGENCE SUMMARY
(Erase heading not required.)

Instructions regarding War Diaries and Intelligence Summaries are contained in F. S. Regs., Part II. and the Staff Manual respectively. Title Pages will be prepared in manuscript.

Place	Date	Hour	Summary of Events and Information	Remarks and references to Appendices
Rest Billets BOESEGHEM.	JAN '16 1.		Battalion Route March.	
	2nd		Church Parade.	
	3rd		Battalion paraded for demonstration with smoke & flares in the attack. Corps & Army Commanders present. Divisional Band played in afternoon.	
	4th		Coys at disposal of O.C. Coys. Lieut. Colonel Nugent proceeded on leave.	
	5th		Battalion Route March.	
	6th		Coys at disposal of O.C. Coys. In afternoon football match between Battalion team & 21st R. Berks Regt - Stopped owing to rain.	
	7th		All surplus baggage handed into store preparatory to move back to front line.	
	8th		Rested in Billets.	
Line of March	9th		Battalion marched to Billets N. & close to Estaires. Draft of 50 other ranks arrived	

1875 Wt. W593/826 1,000,000 4/15 J.B.C. & A. A.D.S.S./Forms/C. 2118.

WAR DIARY
or
INTELLIGENCE SUMMARY

Army Form C. 2118

(Erase heading not required.)

Place	Date	Hour	Summary of Events and Information	Remarks and references to Appendices
Sing of March	Jan 10		Battalion marched to billets in Brigade Reserve to front line. Enemy shelled battery just S of Fleurbaix with 4.2 Howitzers during afternoon.	
Fleurbaix	11th		Rested in billets. Germans continued to shell same battery intermittently throughout morning & afternoon & evening.	
	12th		G.O.C. inspected lines. One platoon per Company worked on front line trenches at night. One man killed on road in rear of fire trenches.	
	13th		Rested in billets - Same working parties as last night. Relieved 12 men per Company worked on front line during morning.	
	14th		R.I.R's in trenches. 2nd Lieut. C.B. Soga + 3 men wounded and 1 man killed by rifle fire at night.	
	15th		2nd Lieut. Trisch wounded and 1 man killed. Rifle fire from trenches very active. Many parts of trenches dangerous owing to parapet having been allowed to fall down. Trenches taken over very bad state of repair by previous Division. One man killed on patrol by rifle fire in evening. Co's worked on repairing trench + barricades were erected to prevent enfilade fire.	

WAR DIARY
or
INTELLIGENCE SUMMARY

(Erase heading not required.)

Army Form C. 2118

Instructions regarding War Diaries and Intelligence Summaries are contained in F.S. Regs., Part II. and the Staff Manual respectively. Title Pages will be prepared in manuscript.

Place	Date	Hour	Summary of Events and Information	Remarks and references to Appendices
Trenches	Jan 16th		Our snipers have now gained ascendancy over hostile snipers, whose fire has been considerably reduced. Our artillery active - enemy made no reply except a few rounds on our battery about 2.30pm. Our patrols encountered several enemy patrols, shots being exchanged and one of our men was wounded. Much work was done on the trenches. One man was killed by rifle fire in trench. Last night our patrols went out to verify maps of the ground between the trenches and brought back much valuable information. An organised artillery operation commenced at 1pm and effected much damage; our aeroplanes co-operated flying very low and firing their machine guns at the German front line & enfilading their retaliation was considerable on various portions of our defences. No damage however was done and only one man killed in the fire trench by shell fire.	
	18th		Our artillery were very active. The enemy again retaliated very strongly on one of our posts and communication trenches, no damage. Relieved by 2/Middlesex in the trenches & marched to Divisional Reserve billets in BAC. ST. MAUR.	

WAR DIARY
or
INTELLIGENCE SUMMARY

Army Form C. 2118

(Erase heading not required.)

Place	Date	Hour	Summary of Events and Information	Remarks and references to Appendices
Bac St Maur	Jan'y 19.		Rested in billets. Br. General. R.B. Stephens presented Cup to "B" Coy as winners of Brigade Football Competition.	
	20th		16 Officers & 385 men on working parties during the day. C.O. inspected billets. Divisional Band played at Headquarters during the afternoon. Battn. football team beat Royal Berks in Divisional football competition.	
	21st		Rested in billets.	
	22nd		Working parties during day & evening	
	23rd		Church Parade. G.O.C. Division presented Sgt. Sidonick "Croix de Guerre" for gallantry on 25-9-15.	
	24th		C.O. & Coy. Commdrs visited works in Laventie area. Working parties of 4 Officers & 350 men during day. Bn. practised manning posts from Divisional Reserve in the evening. Four other ranks joined for duty.	

WAR DIARY
or
INTELLIGENCE SUMMARY

(Erase heading not required.)

Army Form C. 2118

Instructions regarding War Diaries and Intelligence Summaries are contained in F.S. Regs., Part II. and the Staff Manual respectively. Title Pages will be prepared in manuscript.

Place	Date	Hour	Summary of Events and Information	Remarks and references to Appendices
Bac St. Maur	Nov 16 25th		C.O. & Cy Commrs visited works in Bois Grenier area. Working party of 3 Officers & 100 men during day. Bn allotted Divisional Baths at Sailly.	
	26th		Working parties of 3 Officers and 146 men during day. At dusk Bn moved up into Right Brigade Reserve Billets relieving 8th KRRL. H.Q. Weathercock House, had been severely shelled about mid-day with effect.	
	27th		Coys at disposal of O.C. Coys. In the evening working parties of 1 platoon per Company to R.I.R.	
	28th		Rested in Billets. C.O. visited new trenches in right Brigade area. Usual working parties of 12 men in morning and 1 platoon in evening for Company.	
	29th		Coys at disposal of O.C. Coys. Usual working parties. 1 Rk killed.	

1875 Wt. W593/826 1,000,000 4/15 J.B.C. & A. A.D.S.S./Forms/C. 2118.

WAR DIARY
or
INTELLIGENCE SUMMARY

(Erase heading not required.)

Army Form C. 2118

Place	Date	Hour	Summary of Events and Information	Remarks and references to Appendices
	Jan '16 30		Usual working parties in aboumony. In the evening Battalion relieved R.I.R's in trenches, with one Company of Tyneside Scottish (34 Division) for instruction instead of 'A' Coy which remained in billets; all quiet in the trenches.	
	31st		Fog during day. Tyneside Scottish Coy relieved by another, Leeds Coy of 8/12 of L.I. came in between B + C Coys to take over a small piece of line prior to making a raid – They her 1N.C.O. killed a 1 wounded whilst patrolling the ground. Body brought back by us. One of our patrols brought back sample of strong German wire.	

(B2.)
2 February 1916

W.B. Mm——
Captain & Adjt.
2n/6 for the Rifle Brigade

8th, Division.

25th, Brigade.

2nd, Rifle Brigade.

February, 1916.

Army Form C. 2118

WAR DIARY
or
INTELLIGENCE SUMMARY
(Erase heading not required.)

Instructions regarding War Diaries and Intelligence Summaries are contained in F.S. Regs., Part II. and the Staff Manual respectively. Title Pages will be prepared in manuscript.

Place	Date	Hour	Summary of Events and Information	Remarks and references to Appendices
	1916 FEBRUARY 1st		Quiet day - no shelling: "A" Coy relieved 2/Tyneside Scottish Coy on the trenches. Colonel Rankin 3/9th Kings Liverpool Regt. attached to us for instruction. 8th KOYLI patrol reported Germans Coy active in front of their lines - during the morning G.O.C. the Division inspected the trenches.	
	2nd		Enemy put 5 shells into V.C. corner - 2 hostile aeroplanes over our lines in the morning. Lieut General Sir W Pulteney Comdg. 3rd Corps visited the trenches about 10.30 AM. 8th Bn. K.O.Y.L.I abandoned idea of raid and left the trenches.	
	3rd		In early morning about 2.45 A.M. Lieut Daniels V.C. went out on patrol to investigate report of 8th K.O.Y.L.I. - no signs of the enemy were found in front, though they were working at a saphead on their own wire. G.O.C. Brigade inspected trenches. Enemy shelled along Rue-du-Bois morning & afternoon. Battalion relieved by R.I.Rs in evening and marched back to Brigade Reserve Billets with Bn. Headquarters at Rouge-de-Bout. 2 R/Rs wounded.	
	4th		Rested in billets - Lieut Colonel L.H. Knoc?, D.S.O. appointed to command 164th Infantry Brigade with temporary rank of Brigadier General - he left in the evening - Captain the Hon. R.C. Grosvenor took over command. Usual working parties for R.I.Rs	

WAR DIARY
or
INTELLIGENCE SUMMARY

Army Form C. 2118

(Erase heading not required.)

Place	Date	Hour	Summary of Events and Information	Remarks and references to Appendices
	1916 FEBY 5th		Coys at disposal of O.C. Coys. Battalion Hqrs. opened at Battalion Headquarters. Usual working parties for R.I.R's and party of 1 Officer + 50 men for R.E.	
	6th		Coys at disposal of O.C. Coys. Usual working parties for R.I.R - two parties by R.E. 1 Officer + 50 men + 1/6 Officer + 60 men. 2 Rs wounded.	
	7th		R.E. party 1 Officer + 50 men, usual working party in afternoon for R.I.R - Battalion relieved R.I.R's in trenches (with 1 Coy of 20 Tyneside Scottish for instruction) "B" Coy remained in billets.	
	8th		A great deal of shelling took place on the part of the line trenches were not shelter but V.C Corner, Two Tree Farm, etc., came in for a lot of attention. Lieut. J.P. Kennedy wounded while on patrol, attempting to capture some of the enemy - enemy expected a raid owing to activity of our patrols and became very vigilant. 20 Tyneside Scottish relieved by own "B" Coy in morning	
	9th		Heavy shelling by both sides - we fired a number of phono. mortars with good effect. Two men killed by shell in afternoon. A quiet night. Officers & N.C.O's of 26 Northumberland Fusiliers attached for instruction.	

Army Form C. 2118

Instructions regarding War Diaries and Intelligence Summaries are contained in F.S. Regs., Part II. and the Staff Manual respectively. Title Pages will be prepared in manuscript.

WAR DIARY
or
INTELLIGENCE SUMMARY
(Erase heading not required.)

Place	Date	Hour	Summary of Events and Information	Remarks and references to Appendices
	1916 FEBY. 16th		We carried out an organised Bombardment of the enemy's lines about mid-day. Our Trench Mortars co-operated. The enemy retaliated strongly on our trenches & posts & on the roads & Billets in rear. No casualties resulted on our side. An enemy Trench Mortar was discovered opposite "D" Coy & believed to be destroyed by gun-fire. An unsuccessful attempt was made by two Officers' patrols with Lewis Guns & with the help of a searchlight to capture a prisoner on surprise an enemy working party, but the enemy did not come in front of their trenches. Our snipers maintain their superiority. Artillery activity on both sides was considerable all day.	
	11th		Artillery activity on both sides continues. Relieved by R.I.R's in trenches & marched to Brigade Reserve Billets.	
	12th		Rested in Billets. Usual working parties for R.I.R's & three parties for R.E's.	
	13th		Church Parade. Enemy shelled vicinity of Bn. H.Q. intermittently from Noon onwards with light field guns. Four working parties for R.E.	
	14th		Practise Gas Alarm 7 A.M - Very satisfactory. R.E. working party of 50 in morning. Relieved in Billets by 5th Northumberland Fusiliers & marched to Div Reserve Billets in BAC-ST-MAUR. 19 other ranks joined for duty.	

1875 Wt. W593/826 1,000,000 4/15 J.B.C. & A. A.D.S.S./Forms/C. 2118.

Army Form C. 2118

WAR DIARY
or
INTELLIGENCE SUMMARY
(Erase heading not required.)

Instructions regarding War Diaries and Intelligence Summaries are contained in F. S. Regs., Part II. and the Staff Manual respectively. Title Pages will be prepared in manuscript.

Place	Date	Hour	Summary of Events and Information	Remarks and references to Appendices
	1916 Feby 15th		5 Officers & 300 men on R.E. working parties.	
	16th		R.E. working party. 1 Officer & 50 men. Divisional Baths for Battalion.	
	17th		5 Officers & 330 men on R.E. working parties.	
	18th		Bn Football Team beat R.A.M.C. 4 - 2 in Div: Football Cup	
	19th		R.E. working parties of 5 Officers & 240 men.	
	20th		Church Parade.	
	21st		Relieved 20th Northumberland Fusiliers in the trenches. A quiet night.	
	22nd		C.O. inspected the trenches. Two men wounded. Snow fell & a frost set in.	
	23rd		More Snow. Orders came that 152nd Brigade would relieve the Battalion, but were later cancelled. Hard frost. Quiet night.	

Army Form C. 2118

WAR DIARY
or
INTELLIGENCE SUMMARY
(Erase heading not required.)

Instructions regarding War Diaries and Intelligence Summaries are contained in F. S. Regs., Part II. and the Staff Manual respectively. Title Pages will be prepared in manuscript.

Place	Date	Hour	Summary of Events and Information	Remarks and references to Appendices
	1916. Feb. 24th		A little more artillery activity than during the past three days. Enemy have been very inactive. Warning of Gas received at 12 midnight coming from 3rd Divn: — cancelled ½ hour later.	
	25th		Relieved by R.I.R's in the trenches — more snow. Slightly heavier.	
	26th		1 Officer 65 men working party in the morning. Thaw set in.	
	27th		Church Parade. Working parties 116. Capt. W. S. Alston went as Staff Captain to 25th Inf. Brigade.	
	28th		The C.O. inspected billets. Working parties 110.	
	29th		Relieved R.I.R's in trenches. Draft. Lieut. Kennard and 19 other ranks arrived. A very quiet day night.	

F.C. Chichester–Constable Captain O.C.
2nd Bn. The Rifle Brigade.

8th, Division.

25th, Brigade.

2nd, Rifle Brigade.

March, 1916.

WAR DIARY or INTELLIGENCE SUMMARY

(Erase heading not required.)

Army Form C. 2118

Instructions regarding War Diaries and Intelligence Summaries are contained in F.S. Regs., Part II. and the Staff Manual respectively. Title Pages will be prepared in manuscript.

Place	Date	Hour	Summary of Events and Information	Remarks and references to Appendices
	March 1916 1st		Our Snipers very active. Hostile shelling with 4.2 Howitzers about midday, no damage or casualties, our Howitzers replied. One man wounded on patrol and one man in fire trench by rifle fire.	
	2nd		One of our working parties was caught in the open and shelled, no casualties. Our trench mortars & rifle grenades were active at night. One Corporal killed by rifle fire while working on the parapet.	
	3rd		A good deal of rain fell. Enemy's artillery very quiet. G.O.C. Division inspected trenches. Heavy rain & snow at night.	
	4th		G.O.C. Brigade inspected line. Relieved by R.I.R. in trenches & marched to billets in Brigade Reserve. Draft of 38 other ranks arrived, very wet day.	
	5th		Rested in billets. Church Parade. R.E. working parties during morning. Battalion Football team beaten by Divisional Mounted Troops in Semi Final of Divisional Football Cup. Score 4-1.	
	6th		R.E. working parties during morning.	
	7th		R.E. working parties morning & night. G.O.C. inspected drafts and presented Sgt. Bennett with D.C.M. ribbon.	

Army Form C. 2118

WAR DIARY
or
INTELLIGENCE SUMMARY
(Erase heading not required.)

Instructions regarding War Diaries and Intelligence Summaries are contained in F. S. Regs., Part II. and the Staff Manual respectively. Title Pages will be prepared in manuscript.

Place	Date	Hour	Summary of Events and Information	Remarks and references to Appendices
	Mar 1916 cont'd 8th		Divisional Baths for Battalion. Relieved R.I.R's in trenches at night. Very active mining operations during night. Our Miners broke into German galleries.	
	9th		Our Howitzers shelled hostile mine shafts and enemy retaliated with field guns and H. E. Rosg; no damage.	
	10th		Enemy exploded a camouflet and fired a mine close to our parapet doing no damage. The crater was wired and examined by our patrols.	
	11th		The enemy exploded another mine doing no damage. Artillery on both sides active. Night was quiet. Our patrols attempted to bomb an enemy covering party, but the Germans would not leave their wire.	
	12th		Relieved by R.I.R's at night and marched to Billets in Brigade Reserve.	
	13th		Rested in Billets. Draft of 2 Officers + 13 other ranks arrived. Usual working parties.	
	14th		Working parties in the morning and evening.	
	15th		Working parties. 2nd Lieut. Marchetti killed while superintending a working party.	
	16th		Relieved R.I.R's in trenches. A Coy 13/R. Sussex Regt came into trenches under instruction. "C" Coy remained in billets.	

1875 Wt. W593/826 1,000,000 4/15 J.B.C. & A. A.D.S.S./Forms/C. 2118.

WAR DIARY
or
INTELLIGENCE SUMMARY
(Erase heading not required.)

Army Form C. 2118

Place	Date	Hour	Summary of Events and Information	Remarks and references to Appendices
	Mar 16 Contd 17th		One Sergeant accidentally wounded by a Sniperscope. One man accidentally killed by a Sniperscope. A quiet day. Enemy machine guns & snipers very active at night. One man wounded by rifle fire. We exploded a mine at 11.30 p.m. with the object of destroying a hostile gallery and its occupants.	
	18th		Our Snipers were very active and met with some success. Artillery of both sides were active. There was a good deal of sniping & machine gun fire at night. Captain A.C. Bunnell was killed while bringing in the dead body of an a/Cpl killed on a wiring party - one stretcher bearer was wounded at the same time both by rifle fire. Two other men wounded by rifle fire in fire trench. A bright moonlight night - weather very hot & summit for time of year. "B" Coy 13/R. Sussex Regt. relieved "A" Coy 13/R Sussex Regt.	
	19th		A quiet day but artillery of both sides active. Warm weather continues. "C" Coy joined B.H.Q in Bie Trench in evening. 13/R. Sussex Regt marching back to billets. Two Coys 16th Bn. Rifle Brigade attached for instruction. Weather still fine and warm. One man wounded by rifle fire in rear of trenches.	
	20th		Relieved by R.I.R.s in Trenches & marched to Brigade Reserve.	

WAR DIARY
or
INTELLIGENCE SUMMARY

(Erase heading not required.)

Army Form C. 2118

Instructions regarding War Diaries and Intelligence Summaries are contained in F. S. Regs., Part II. and the Staff Manual respectively. Title Pages will be prepared in manuscript.

Place	Date	Hour	Summary of Events and Information	Remarks and references to Appendices
	Mar 16 Cont'd 21st		Rested in billets. Usual R.E. working parties.	
	22nd		R.E. Working parties.	
	23rd		Divisional Baths for Battalion. R.E. Working parties. Heavy snow, weather turned much colder.	
	24th		Relieved P.I.R's in the trenches. Two Coys of 16th Bn. Rifle Brigade in trenches under instructions. One man killed rifle fire for trench. Anyway Quiet night.	
	25th		Weather improved. General Stephens visited lines to say good bye to the Battalion on taking over command of a Division. Officers of 17th Royal Scots (35th Division) visited lines preparatory to taking over. Pte-du-Bois was slightly shelled with field guns about 3-15pm. Quiet quiet night.	
	26th		Attached Coys of 16th Bn. Rifle Brigade withdrew from the trenches, one man wounded rifle fire, fire trench. Patrols of 14 Royal Scots came into the line in the evening.	
	27th		Advanced parties of 17th Royal Scots arrived early in the morning. Relieved by Royal Scots in evening & marched back to billets in Sailly.	

WAR DIARY
or
INTELLIGENCE SUMMARY

(Erase heading not required.)

Army Form C. 2118

Place	Date	Hour	Summary of Events and Information	Remarks and references to Appendices
	MAR 16 contd 28th		Marched to Lestrem, where Battalion entrained - 27 Officers 911 other ranks.	
	29th	4.30 A.M.	Arrived Longueau. Detrained and marched through Amiens to Flesselles.	
	30th		Rested in billets.	
	31st		Coys at disposal of O.C. Coys for drill and physical exercise. Divisional Band played in afternoon.	

F.C. Chichester-Constable
Captain + Adjutant
2nd Bon. The Rifle Brigade

B.2.2.
1st April 1915

8th, Division.

25th, Brigade,

2nd, Rifle Brigade.

April, 1916.

WAR DIARY
or
INTELLIGENCE SUMMARY

Army Form C. 2118

(Erase heading not required.)

Place	Date	Hour	Summary of Events and Information	Remarks and references to Appendices
	April 1916			
	1st		Coys at disposal of O.C. Coys. Divisional Band played in afternoon.	
	2nd		Church Parade. Divisional Band played in afternoon.	
	3rd		Battalion Route March – very hot day	
	4th		Coys at disposal of O.C. Coys. Medical Officer inspected the Battalion.	
	5th		Marched to Billets in St Gratien	
	6th		Marched to Huts in Henencourt Wood, in Divisional Reserve.	
	7th		Coys at disposal of O.C. Coys. Various working parties & details sent away to R.E. Bomb School etc.	
	8th		Coys at disposal of O.C. Coys. Divisional Band played in afternoon. C.O. Brigade inspected the lines.	
	9th		Marched to Billets in Domancourt with "A" & "B" Coys in Posts in Becourt Wood – Brigade Reserve.	
	10th		C.O. inspected Billets. Officers and 50 men working party for R.E. had baths at Albert. About 4 pm the enemy commenced an intense bombardment on the R.1.R.2 trenches. 40 Bavs went up in support but after waiting some time, were ordered back to billets which they reached about midnight. The Germans effected a raid on the trenches & captured some prisoners. We had one killed & eight wounded.	
	11th			Shell fire on Becourt Wood

WAR DIARY
or
INTELLIGENCE SUMMARY
(Erase heading not required.)

Army Form C. 2118

Instructions regarding War Diaries and Intelligence Summaries are contained in F.S. Regs., Part II. and the Staff Manual respectively. Title Pages will be prepared in manuscript.

Place	Date	Hour	Summary of Events and Information	Remarks and references to Appendices
	April 16 12th 13th		Officers inspected trenches. 4 Officers & 100 working party at night. Relieved R.I.R. in the trenches, with the exception of Trench Mortar Battery a very quiet night. The trenches are very bad.	
	14th		Hostile Trench Mortars were active during the afternoon & all night, also hostile machine guns. Our Mortars, Artillery & machine guns replied. G.O.C. Brigade visited the line by night.	
	15th		Usual trench mortar activity during the afternoon which increased considerably at night. Our mortars & Artillery replied vigorously. Much work is being done on the trenches which are gradually improving.	
	16th		A very quiet day with slight hostile rifle grenade activity towards evening. Our Heavy & field artillery were active all day. Our Trench mortars and rifle grenades firing two bombs to the enemy's one completely silenced him at night. Three officers joined for duty - 2nd Lt. Pascoe, Jones & Peckham. 3 men wounded by rifle grenades. Enemy's mortars & rifle grenades again silenced the enemy at night. Gen. Witaloly with one man made a close inspection of the German wire. Work on the trenches is making great progress.	
	17th			
	18th		1 killed, 1 wounded rifle grenade. Trench mortars were again active on both sides.	

WAR DIARY
or
INTELLIGENCE SUMMARY

Army Form C. 2118

(Erase heading not required.)

Place	Date	Hour	Summary of Events and Information	Remarks and references to Appendices
	April '16 19th		French Headquarters moved from Chateau to Chapes Spur. 1 man killed rifle grenade, 1 man wounded shell fire. Enemy's French mortars and grenades were much less active, in spite of renewed activity on our part. Officers 70th Brigade visited trenches	
	20th		2 men wounded by rifle grenades. Enemy now only fires his French mortars & rifle grenades in retaliation to ours. Our Artillery & French mortars carried out a demonstration in the afternoon. "A" & "B" Coys were very active with rifle grenades.	
	21st		1 man wounded, rifle grenade. Relieved by R.I.R's and marched back to billets in Doullencourt which we did not reach till 1.30 A.M. "C" & "D" Coys remained in Beaumont Hamel Redoubt.	
	22nd 23rd		Rested in billets Usual working parties for R.I.R's & two parties for R.E. at night. C Rural Parade in the morning. Divisional Baths all day.	
	24th		Coys at disposal of O.C. Coys	
	25th		Bn relieved by 11th Sherwood Foresters. "C" & "D" Coys + 2 platoons of "A" Coy marched to Hennencourt Wood in Divisional Reserve. The rest of the Bn. remained at Doullencourt to work under 11th Railway Coy R.E.	

WAR DIARY
or
INTELLIGENCE SUMMARY

Army Form C. 2118

Place	Date	Hour	Summary of Events and Information	Remarks and references to Appendices
	April 16 26th		Coys under O.C. Coys. Respec.	
	27th		Coys under O.C. Coys for training purposes	
	28th		Training Continued. Working party of 50 under R.E. on road making	
	29th		Training Continued. " " " " " " " " " "	
	30th		Church Parade	

F. Gwil Lieut & Adjt.
2nd Batn The Rifle Brigade

8th, Division.

25th, Brigade.

2nd, Rifle Brigade.

May, 1916.

WAR DIARY
or
INTELLIGENCE SUMMARY

Army Form C. 2118

(Erase heading not required.)

2 Rifle Bde Vol 19

Place	Date	Hour	Summary of Events and Information	Remarks and references to Appendices
HEMENCOURT WOOD	May 1916 1st		Coys at disposal of O.C. Coys. Working parties of 1 Officer, 50 men & 1 Sgt & 20 men to work on the roads, under the R.E's. 1 Officer per Coy visited the trenches ALBERT.	
	2nd		Coys at disposal of O.C. Coys. O.C Coys & Coy Sgt Majors visited trenches. Two more Lewis Guns received making a total of eight for the Battalion.	
ALBERT - TRENCHES Left Sub-section	3rd		Relieved 2nd Bn Scottish Rifles in the trenches by daylight. Two Coys in the front line, one Coy in the Second line, "D" Coy in ALBERT. Very quiet night. 2 Officers & 94 men came up from "D" Coy to work in the trenches. The trenches are quite good and there is a considerable amount of wire out.	
	4th		Very quiet day. G.O.C. Brigade went round the trenches. 2 Officers & 80 men came up from "D" Coy to work in the trenches.	
	5th		G.O.C. Division and Brigade Commdr. visited lines. A raid was carried out by the Division on our left. Our Artillery co-operated on our front. The enemy replied strongly — no casualties.	
	6th		A quiet day. Two Platoons "D" Coy were moved up into the trenches owing to the Battalion line being extended to the right. Enemy snipers rather more active at night.	
	7th		Artillery of both sides active during the day. Weather much cooler, some rain fell. Enemy used lachrymatous shells on our second line during the afternoon. About 11 p.m a systematic bombardment of our front & support lines commenced which increased in intensity till about 12.30 A.M. when slackened and finally ceased at 1 A.M. Our guns & machine guns replied vigorously throughout. M Rhodes Major Commdg 2nd Bn the Rifle Brigade	

Army Form C. 2118

WAR DIARY
or
INTELLIGENCE SUMMARY
(Erase heading not required.)

Instructions regarding War Diaries and Intelligence Summaries are contained in F.S. Regs., Part II. and the Staff Manual respectively. Title Pages will be prepared in manuscript.

Place	Date	Hour	Summary of Events and Information	Remarks and references to Appendices
ALBERT-TRENCHES Sy Sub-section	MAY 1916 7th (Continued)		The enemy made no attempt to leave his trenches. Casualties one killed four wounded by shell fire.	
	8th		A cloudy day, gusty & some rain. Enemy quiet – nothing to report. One man wounded by rifle fire.	
	9th		A dull rainy day and quiet. No activity during daylight. A few small shells only were fired by enemy. A quiet night. Two men wounded by shell fire.	
	10th		Our artillery was very active during the day; the enemy however made scarcely any reply. A raid was carried out by a Battalion on our immediate right about 2 A.M. The enemy replied vigorously to our bombardment with light & heavy guns & also trench mortars. Our casualties were 2 killed – 15 wounded.	
	11th		A quiet day. Relieved by 2nd/W. Yorks in the evening & marched to Divisional Reserve in Millencourt.	
MILLENCOURT	12th		Rested in Billets. 88 men working party in morning	
	13th		Coys at disposal of O.C. Coys. Working parties of 26 Officers & 88 on roads and 2 Officers & 180 men on trenches. A coy of 8 D.R. arrived.	
	14th		Coys at disposal of O.C. Coys. Working parties of 2 Officers & 88 men on roads & 1 Officer & 40 men Royal Flying Corps, Sheets. S.O.S. sent from NAB at 11 P.M. – no action.	

A. Maude Major
Commdg 2nd Bn the Rifle Brigade.

Army Form C. 2118

WAR DIARY
or
INTELLIGENCE SUMMARY

(Erase heading not required.)

Instructions regarding War Diaries and Intelligence Summaries are contained in F. S. Regs., Part II. and the Staff Manual respectively. Title Pages will be prepared in manuscript.

Place	Date	Hour	Summary of Events and Information	Remarks and references to Appendices
MILLENCOURT	MAY 1916 15th		Working Parties 3 Officers & 150 men on trenches at night - 2 Officers & 88 men on roads by day. Draft of 32 other ranks joined.	
	16th		Draft of 20 other ranks joined. Working party & 1 Officer & 40 men in trenches.	
	17th		Working parties 2 Officers & 88 men on roads, 1 Officer & 40 men on trenches.	
	18th		Working parties 2 Officers & 48 men on trenches. Commanding Officer inspected draft.	
	19th		Relieved by 8th York & Lancs and marched to Billets in ALBERT relieving 2/W Yorks. Working party of 30 men in morning on roads. G.O.C. Brigade inspected Draft.	
	20th		Rested in Billets. Working parties 2 Officers & 100 men on front line. One Billet slightly shelled - no damage. 2/Lieut. N.R. Harvey joined for duty.	
ALBERT	21st		Church Parade. Baths at ALBERT for 'A' 'C' & 'D' Coys. 2 Officers & 160 men working party under R.E.	
	22nd		Coys under O.C. Coys. Working parties 1 Officer & 60 men in morning 2 Officers & 126 men at night.	
	23rd		Coys under O.C. Coys. Working parties 3 Officers & 180 men in morning, 1 Officer & 40 men at night under R.E. Baths for 'B' Coy, all detachments & casuals. 60 other ranks joined for duty.	

N. Braud Major
Commdg 2nd Bn the Rifle Brigade

WAR DIARY
or
INTELLIGENCE SUMMARY
(Erase heading not required.)

Army Form C. 2118

Instructions regarding War Diaries and Intelligence Summaries are contained in F.S. Regs., Part II. and the Staff Manual respectively. Title Pages will be prepared in manuscript.

Place	Date	Hour	Summary of Events and Information	Remarks and references to Appendices
MILLENCOURT	24th		Rain till. Coys under O.C. Coys. Commanding Officer inspected draft. Working parties of 2 Officers & 120 men in morning, and 1 Officer & 20 men in evening under R.E.	
ALBERT TRENCHES LEFT SUB-SECTOR	25th		Wet weather continues. The Battalion relieved the 2nd Royal Berks Regt in the trenches during daylight, in the left sub-section. One man slightly wounded.	
	26th		Wet weather continues. The enemy were very active with trench Mortars day & night.	
	27th		At 2.30 A.M. the enemy opened a heavy bombardment on our front line & support trenches. Our guns replied. Casualties. Four killed. 6 wounded. Two of whom died from the effects of wounds same day. The Battalion was relieved in the trenches by the 8th Bn. York & Lancs Regt. during the afternoon, and marched to Camp in Henencourt Wood. Divisional Reserve.	
	28th		Rested in Camp. Church Parade. Draft of 15 other ranks joined. Dau Sims	
	29th		Coys under O.C. Coys. 1st training during the morning. "Battalion parade" in afternoon. 1st extended order drill.	
HENENCOURT	30.		Coys under O.C. Coys. Baths at Henencourt for "A" & "B" Coys. 20 Officers went to Bresnvillers to see Practise attacking ground. Rain during morning cleaning up in the afternoon.	
	31		Coys under O.C. Coys. 1st training during the morning. Franvillers 1st rehearsal on practise attacking ground. All officers went to Exhibition with the Bangalore Torpedoe was given by R.E. Officer near Camp	

R. Bund, Major
Commdg. 2nd Bn. the Rifle Brigade

8th, Division.

25th, Brigade.

2nd, Rifle Brigade.

June, 1916.

Army Form C. 2118.

2 Rifle Bde
Vol 20

WAR DIARY
or
INTELLIGENCE SUMMARY
(Erase heading not required.)

Instructions regarding War Diaries and Intelligence Summaries are contained in F. S. Regs., Part II. and the Staff Manual respectively. Title Pages will be prepared in manuscript.

Place	Date	Hour	Summary of Events and Information	Remarks and references to Appendices
Hencourt Wood	June 1916 1st	1.40AM	Battalion paraded & proceeded to Tranvoillers & took part in attack on flagged position with the Corps. Working party 150 men under C.R.E.	
"	2nd		Battalion paraded in B training & General. Trench Mortar Demonstration by a Battery of Stokes. Working Parties 3 Officers 130 men	
"	3rd		Coys at disposal of O.C. Coys. miniature Range allotted to Battalion. 2/Lieut. Cremen went to Trench Mortar Demonstration at 4th Army School at Valhuineux. D.C.M's awarded to Riflemen Welshen & Benton by G.O.C. 8th Division.	
"	4th		Church Parade in morning. Battalion marched to Albert-Bouzincourt Defences in afternoon, relieving 2nd Bn W. Yorks. Major the Hon. R. Brand to be companion of the Distinguished Service Order. Distinguished Conduct Medal awarded to Sgt. Riddett. Military Medal to Riflmn Burgess & Fido.	
Albert	5th		Coys at disposal of O.C. Coys. Working Parties 126 in morning 200 at night	
"	6th		Coys at disposal of O.C. Coys. Working Parties 150 in morning	
"	7th		Coys at disposal of O.C. Coys. Working Parties 150 in morning 200 at night.	
"	8th		Baths at Millencourt for C & D Coys & Machine Gun Detachment. Working Parties 150 morning 200 at night.	
"	9th		Coys at disposal of O.C. Coys. 2O.C. Division presented Medal Ribbon to Sgt. Riddett, Riflmn Burgess & Fido. Working Parties 150 in morning & 200 at night.	

Army Form C. 2118.

WAR DIARY
or
INTELLIGENCE SUMMARY

(Erase heading not required.)

Instructions regarding War Diaries and Intelligence Summaries are contained in F. S. Regs., Part II. and the Staff Manual respectively. Title Pages will be prepared in manuscript.

Place	Date	Hour	Summary of Events and Information	Remarks and references to Appendices
Albert	June 1916 10th		Coys at disposal of O.C. Coys. Working parties 190 in morning & 170 at night.	
"	11th		Church Parade. Working parties 200 in morning & 150 at night.	
Louvencourt	12th		Battalion relieved 2nd Bn. Scottish Rifles in left Sub-section of the Trenches. Quiet night.	
"	13th		Heavy rain for 36 hours. G.O.C Brigade visited trenches. Quiet day.	
"	14th		Rain of first five hours. Captain C.L. Sommerfelt killed, 2/Lt. H. Daniels wounded by Germans Bomb whilst reconnoitring No Man's Land. 3 other ranks wounded by Shell fire.	
"	15th		Officers of Coldstream + Irish Guards inspected trenches. Blind H.E gas shell fell in "C" Coys area, no damage. 35 other ranks joined for duty.	
"	16th		Weather improved. Relieved at night by 8th Bn. York + Lancs. Regt. Marched to Ribemont in Long Valley, arriving at 5 A.M. 17th night.	
Long Valley	17th		Rested in Bivouac. Working parties 250 day & 150 at night.	
"	18th		Moved from Bivouac Long Valley to Billets in Millencourt. Working Parties	
"	19th		Capt. S.A. Harland rejoined from Base Duties. 24 other ranks joined for duty. Working Parties 200 in morning, 100 at night. Battalion rested in Billets.	
"	20th		Rested in Billets. Working parties 250 in morning, 150 at night. other ranks as nominated	

Army Form C. 2118.

WAR DIARY
or
INTELLIGENCE SUMMARY
(Erase heading not required.)

Instructions regarding War Diaries and Intelligence Summaries are contained in F. S. Regs., Part II. and the Staff Manual respectively. Title Pages will be prepared in manuscript.

Place	Date	Hour	Summary of Events and Information	Remarks and references to Appendices
Millencourt	Jan 16 21st		Rested in billets. 150 working party by day. skin raids + one wounded. Demonstration by Raiding Party at night. Two 'Bangalore Torpedoes' blown up, good results. Sect. C.D. Caswell joined for duty.	
	22nd		Very fine day. Rested in billets. Working Party 150 in morning.	
	23rd		Relieved R.J.R's in Centre Sub-Section. Tenerife Storm raged from 4.30 p.m. to 5 p.m. Relief carried out. Eny Emergency Rocket very slow. Stokes mortar joined for duty.	
Trenches	24th		Bombardment commences at 4 A.M. Fine casualties during day. Gas put off on account of too slight a wind. Not much reply by enemy. Raid also put off. Fine day.	
"	25th		Fine day. Bombardment continues. Enemy replied on Albert + Avenluy. The latter at 5 A.M. 2 p.m. intense at 11 p.m. MAB heavily shelled 2 p.m. + 11 p.m. 3 enemy observation balloons destroyed, one enemy aeroplane brought down by our aircraft guns + landed in Begnies. Gas put off owing to wind changing round. The Battalion carried out a very successful raid on the enemy trenches opposite Avenluy at midnight. The raiding party consisted of 2/Lt Murray, 2 lcpl + 25/R Anderson + 50 men. At 11.20 p.m 2/Lt Anderson laid out tapes from three spouts in our wire to a position 100 yds from enemy wire, then laid a tape across showing where the party would die, + from the centre of that position he laid a tape up to enemy wire. At 11.55 p.m the whole party, led by 2/Lt Murray filed out lay down along the grass tape 100 yds from German wire. They carried 3 Bangalore Torpedoes 30' long in 3 sections to this position. At 12 midnight the artillery opened	

2449 Wt. W14957/M90 750,000 1/16 J.B.C. & A. Forms/C.2118/12.

WAR DIARY
or
INTELLIGENCE SUMMARY

Army Form C. 2118.

Place	Date	Hour	Summary of Events and Information	Remarks and references to Appendices
	June 10th 25th Continued.		on the German trenches. 12 bars at 4.55 on the front line & Heavies - Howitzers on the approaches. The parties in charge of the Bangalore torpedoes joined the Bombers at 12.16 am. The Artillery gradually lifting. The raiding party moved forward to within 50 yards of enemy wire. The Bangalore torpedoes parties moving up to the wire laid their torpedoes & fired them. The right centre torpedo exploded and cut clear lanes through the German wire. The left failed. The Raiding Party pushed in through the 2 gaps. The left party having no gap filed through the one on the right and proceeded along German parapet bombing the Gnomes till they reached their proper point forty both outside parties worked forward's centre party using revolvers, dagger, club & bombing the dug-outs. All parties met with great success in the hand to hand fighting in the trench, killing all the men in the trench or driving them into the dug-out or over the parados. The dug-outs were bombed & investigation by torches showed them to be crowded with dead & wounded. One prisoner of the 126th Wurtembergers was brought back by our party. The enemy put up a stout resistance & there were many bombs from behind the Parados. At 12.40 AM as previously arranged the Raiding Party withdrew from the enemy trench, bringing back all their casualties 1 killed & 10 wounded. at 12.45 AM the Artillery ceased fire. The Raid was carried out with great dash and proved wholly successful. The enemy casualties were estimated to be at least 50.	

Army Form C. 2118

WAR DIARY
or
INTELLIGENCE SUMMARY

(Erase heading not required.)

Instructions regarding War Diaries and Intelligence Summaries are contained in F.S. Regs., Part II. and the Staff Manual respectively. Title Pages will be prepared in manuscript.

Place	Date	Hour	Summary of Events and Information	Remarks and references to Appendices
Trenches.	June 26th		Artillery Programme carried out, bombardment increases. Smoke liberated along our front 10.10 A.M. causing enemy to shell our front line until 5 p.m. Our casualties 14 O.R. wounded all slight. Gas liberated 7.15 p.m. Enemy opened fire with Machine Guns & Rifles but only slight. Relieved by R.I.R's at night.	
Long Valley.	27th		Arrived in Long Valley. Reveille at 5 A.M. Bn rested. G.O.C. 3rd Corps inspected raiding party at 11.30 A.M. Officers conference 9 p.m. 2/Lt Sheridge joined for duty.	
	28th		Bn rested in Camp. Relief in trenches cancelled. Very wet day.	
	29th		Paraded under O.C Coys. Relieved R.I.R's in left centre sub section "B" area. Weather slightly improved. Six officers joined for duty.	
Trenches	30th		Bombardment continues. Enemy retaliation slight, chiefly on unused support lines. At 12.30 p.m. Bn took over final assembly positions from R.I.R's at Donnet Post. Quiet night. Special Patrol sent out, unable to enter enemy trenches owing to lack of time. 2nd Lt Huddart killed, other ranks 4 killed 6 wounded.	

J. V. Byrne afsham
Captain & Adjutant
for O.C.
2nd Bon. The Rifle Brigade

D.A.G.
G.H.Q.
3rd Echelon.

Herewith War Diary of
this Battalion for month
of June.

B B Pascoe Lt & Lt Col
Comdg: 2nd Rifle Brigade

BM C/319

O.C.
  2nd/7th Rifle Batt.

Ref your Preliminary operation orders,
attached :—
The Brigade commander does not
quite approve of the last para as
if all Units in front of you have
been unable to cope with the "cleaning
up", you being the last Unit will
have to assist otherwise there will
be no one coming behind to do
it.
Will you amend it accordingly
please. & return.

                    Ashford Capper
                    Batt. Major
                    25th Batt.

29/6/16

"A" Form
Army Form C. 2121.

MESSAGES AND SIGNALS.

No. of Message_____

Prefix_____ Code_____ m. | Words | Charge | This message is on a/c of: | Recd. at_____ m.
Office of Origin and Service Instructions. | | | | Date_____
| Sent | | _____Service. | From_____
_____ | At_____ m. | | |
_____ | To_____ | | (Signature of "Franking Officer.") | By_____
_____ | By_____ | | |

TO LE

Sender's Number.	Day of Month	In reply to Number	**A A A**
* 12B416	23.6		

Reference operation order issued
this days aaa Please make
following amendments aaa
Page 3 line 2   for 22 word 27000a
Page 3 line 3   for 22 word 27000a
The mistake is much regretted.

From C.M.
Place
Time 7.10 p.m.

"2nd Bn. The Rifle Brigade"

Amendment to Operation Orders Page 3.

Cancel last para: Clearing up.

This should read:-

The rear two Coys ("C" & "A") will detach parties of as small a number as possible to cope with any 'clearing up' that may be required.

Bombers will always be sent as part of the personnel of such parties.

BEF.
24-6-16

R. Brand. Major.
Commdg. 2nd Bn. The Rifle Brigade.

To: Headquarters
25th Infantry Brigade

Herewith Amendment as requested.

J. N. Bryne Johnson. Capt & Adjt.
for
2nd Bn. The Rifle Brigade

24.6.16

SECRET

2nd. Bn. The Rifle Brigade.

Preliminary Operations Orders.

Position previous to assault.

B. & A. Companies.   Mellin and Donnet Streets.

D. & C. Companies. Ribble Street between WENNING and John O'Gaunt.

Bn. Hq. and Lewis guns in Donnet Posts.

The Coys will be situated in such a way that B. followed by A. can file up John O'Gaunt, and D. followed by C. up Wenning and Pendle Hill.   On Orders received from Bn.Hq. D. Coy followed by C. Coy will file up Wenning, Coniston, Pendle Hill, D.Coy branching into front line in ½ Coys by Pendle Hill and Cartmel, and in the front line stretching from Pendle Hill to Rivington Tunnel.

C. Coy will follow D. Coy branching off and occupying Yewdale.

B.Coy at the same time will file up John O'Gaunt, Barrow, Furness, Broughton into the front line occupying it from Rivington Tunnel to Sap 6.

A.Coy following will lead straight on past Broughton occupying Ulverstone and Furness between Rivington and Broughton.

Bn.Hq.and Lewis Guns(4) will be situated at Junction of Cartmel and Yewdale.

Orders to Advance.

On orders being given to advance by Brigade Hq.through Bn.Hq. two platoons of D. and two platoons of B. D.on the left, B.on the right will advance in artillery formation, by half platoons at 25 paces interval, followed by their two remaining platoons, in the same order at 50 paces distant. The right of B.being the centre and marching on sap at X.8.a.7.4.

As the two rear ½ Coys of D.and B.Coys leave their trench in the front line, the leading two platoons of C. and A.Coys will leave Yewdale and Ulverstone, Furness, respectively, in artillery formati formation)

and will follow the two rear half coys. of the leading coys at 100 paces distant, being in their turn followed by the two remaining half coys of C and A coys. at 50 paces distant and in the same order,

The two rear coys will move all the way over the open from Yewdale and Ulverstone.

Battalion Hq. and four Lewis guns will move up in the centre of the rear line of platoons.

The battalion will then advance in this order, their centre marching on the following points (46),(88),(10),44),(79), thence tram track to (65),(89),(22), and at this point prepare to assault the 3rd. objective, in conjunction with two platoons of the Bde. grenade coy, who will be attached as the battalion passes the 2nd. objective, the other being and two sections of the Bde. M.G. coy, one of which will be attached as the battalion passes the 2nd. objective, the other being brought with the battalion from position of assembly in our own lines.

The assault.

As the battalion comes up to the 2nd. objective, the two leading coys will not enter the trench, but the does will advance and take up a position along road (48),(27),(44),(51), and the two rear coys will halt 50 paces behind the 2nd. objective and lie down there.

Battalion Hq. will enter the trench and establish itself as near as possible to pt. (22).

D and B coys in front will send out officers patrols in force to reconnoitre and see if there is a good line of defence, which can be taken up running from (48),(80), and if on the decision of the senior officer in the front two coys. there is such a position about this line D and B coys will move forward and take up a position there.

D coy will be on the left, B coy will be on the right.

The two platoons of the Bde. grenade coy will be held responsible for the communication trench running through (22), towards (44),(09).

The following points will receive the names as attached.

(48)   Young.   (44)   Baby.

.3.

names contd).

(22)   June.   (51)   Gull.

(48),(22),will be garrisoned and held by D coy

(44),(51),   "   "   "   "   "   " B coy.

The reserve Lewis guns will be sent up to whichever point that may require their support.

The greatest care will be taken to consolidate the strong points as soon as possible.

Lewis guns.

Eight Lewis guns will accompany the battalion into action One will be attached to each coy. and will be under coy arrangements. The remaining four will be in reserve, and will be under the orders of the battalion commander, and in charge of the M.G1O.

Lewis guns can be used for consolidating strong points in the final objective, but are on no account to be used for this purpose before.

Bombers.

The bombing sections of each platoon will be on the outside flank of each platoon. These will be used mainly for keeping connection with the regiments on our flanks, namely the 70th. Bde on our left, and the 1st. Bn. Royal Irish Rifles on our right.

Stretcher bearers.

All stretcher bearers will be under the orders of the M.O. during the action. They will be accomated in Donnet Post prior to the advance from the assembly positions, and not with their coys.

Cleaning Up.

It must be clearly understood that on no account must men be detached for the purpose of cleaning up portions of trenches that cause a slight obstruction, as these are being accounted for by other units, and it is necessary to maintain the largest number of men possible until the final objective.

23.6.16   R W Maud. Major
Comdg 2nd Bn R.H.R.

Report on Raid carried out by
2nd Bn Rifle Brigade on 25th June
against trenches x7b96 - x7b94.

At 11.20pm One officer and a few men of raiding party
went out from 3 lanes in our wire and
laid white tape in 3 lines one on road
the 2 others 15 yards on either side till they
reached the position 100 yards from German
wire they then laid a tape across showing
the party where they would lay up then.
He also ran a tape up road nearly to German wire

At 11.55 Party left our trench & lay up on this
tape.

From 12 mid. Bombardment excellent, one casualty in
till 12.16 raiding party

12.16 - Raiding party went forward to close to
12.21 German wire. The three torpedoes parties
went forward & laid their torpedoes under
the wire. The right & centre torpedoes
exploded and blew 2 excellent gateways
through the wire. The left torpedoes did
not explode in spite of 2 attempts to do
so. The raiding party came up through
the gaps, the Left Party getting through
the centre gap as previously arranged &
filing under the parapet to their objective.

12.21 Centre Party got in at junction of road &
12.40. trench, no opposition met with while getting
through wire but as soon as party landed
in trench they met the enemy who shouted
"Whois der" "Whois dat", our scottvre man
immediately killed 3 of these men. Lt
Murray then found a dug out under the

parapet he throws 6 bombs in the dug out sentry having already been killed. Lt Murray then went down into the dug out which had 6 or 7 steps and flashed his torch in it, he says at least 20 men were killed & wounded in this dug out. The party met a few more Germans round this part of the trench who fought them & were killed. The Germans some of whom had climbed over the parados then started bombing the party in the trench from behind the parados. Lt Murray then time being up, sent his party out of the trench.

The Right Party got into the trench with no difficulty led by 2Lt Anderson though it appears that they entered the trench between B & C instead of at C. They found no dug outs & joined up with centre party at B. The officer then led them towards C and he killed a sentry in the trench with a bomb. The party had some fighting with bombs with Germans behind the parados. It is not known how the enemy got behind the parados in this part of the line but it is suspected that they either got there by underground ways from dug outs or were already in position there or came from 2nd line. Lt Anderson got his party out at 12.40 and sent them back down the tape to our own trench. He & a corporal remaining behind and carrying the one man killed back to our lines.

The Left Party their torpedoe having failed made for centre gap got through & worked along under parapet to A. Sgt Marsh who was leading shooting a sentry who was shooting at him, with his revolver. The party after a bit of bomb throwing captured 3 men in Sap F who were taken off & kept under parapet. The party entered trench at A

and started to block the French line with their
blockers. the party then led by the swordsmen
went down the trench towards B. our swordsmen
killed 3 Germans. I they will have been given
about 6 bombs each the Sgt and other men
testify to ~~very amount~~ each dug being full of
dead. This party towards the end of the time in
the trench had some fighting with enemy over the
barricades. when they were leaving the trench they
were fired on & bombed at by a large party
of Germans who had got astride the trench by
Sap T. this party had some further fighting in
the trench and they killed Germans in every bay.
Of the 3 Germans captured 2 were killed owing to
disinclination to accompany our conductor back.
The left party had some difficulty in getting into
enemy trench a great number of bombs having
to be thrown in as the trench was full of Germans.

All parties carried out programme as laid down
and worked by time. The tapes were very useful
and in the assembly position the tapes had
been laid thus

the torpedoe parties
lay at the T pieces of the tape the
enabled the officers to find them the
moment they wanted them. The torpedoe parties
had no difficulty in joining the 3 sections of
their torpedoes together. these junctions had been
well oiled previously and the torpedoes were
brought up to the front line in daylight so
as to prevent them being damaged

The explosion of the two torpedoes was excellent &
cut clean lanes right through the wire.
The wire was good in all places except
where the torpedoes cut it.

The trench was in good condition 8'x8'
sloping sides not damaged, well boarded
dug outs under the parapet, possibly connected
by tunnel to behind the parados.

The prisoner wounded in the face was 180th
Bartenkyer. More prisoners would have been
brought back but the enemy made a stout
fight in the trench which was crowded
with men either in dug outs in the fire trench
or behind it. This made it almost
impossible to attend to them as it was never
arranged to bring back more than 2 or 3.

The party all reached our trench the Germans
firing rifle fire from the flanks of the trench
and a machine gun from 23d line.
It was found that the idea of coming up
the road through dead ground & going back
that way was good as the enemy when our
party retired naturally opened heavy rifle &
machine gun fire on the Russell bend of
our trench & 76. The enemy also sent away
number of different coloured flares up as our
party retired, green & red

R. Strand Major
26.6.18
O in C S. & R. R/L Brigade

German letter attached.

Headquarters,

   3rd Corps.

   ****

I forward report by O.C. 2nd Rifle Brigade on the raid carried out by his battalion last night.

I consider it would have been a well-planned enterprise which was most gallantly carried out with successful results.

                                                                            sd. H. Hudson.

8th Division,   Major-General,

26th June, 1916.   Commanding 8th Division.

25th Inf.Bde.
8th Div.

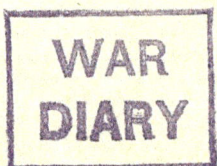

2nd BATTN. THE RIFLE BRIGADE.

J U L Y

1 9 1 6

Army Form C. 2118

2 Rifle Bde

WAR DIARY
or
INTELLIGENCE SUMMARY

(Erase heading not required.)

Instructions regarding War Diaries and Intelligence Summaries are contained in F. S. Regs., Part II. and the Staff Manual respectively. Title Pages will be prepared in manuscript.

Place	Date	Hour	Summary of Events and Information	Remarks and references to Appendices
OVILLERS — LA BOISELLE	July 1916 1st		At 6.25 a.m. a very intense bombardment was opened on the German trenches at Ovillers-La Boiselle lasting till 7.30 a.m. at which hour the 2nd Berks & 2nd Lincolns attached with the R.B's coming up in support. The Battalion being in Reserve left the assembly trenches at 7.30 a.m. and proceeded up the communication trenches to the front line. The leading troops and about half the supporting troops were met with heavy machine gun rifle and shrapnel fire and only succeeded in reaching the enemy trenches at a few points whence they were soon driven back, the Battalion being checked in the trenches. Came under intense shell fire from guns of all calibres. As it was decided to attempt no further infantry attack, A.B. & C. Coys were withdrawn to the support line, while D. Coy with details of the rest of the Brigade held the front line. Shortly before dark details of other Battalions were withdrawn and relieved by "A" Coy in the front line. The Battalion was relieved by the Queens of West Kents of the 37th Brigade shortly after midnight and returned to Bivouac on the Long Valley. Casualties nearly all shell fire, consisted of 5 officers Wounded, Capt. A.M. Curtis, Capt. W.R. Boswell, 2nd Lieut. H. Daniels V.C. 2nd Lieut. C. Rowbridge, 2nd Lieut. C.B. Sayer and 128 other ranks killed and wounded. 2nd Lieut. C.S.P. Shera found for duty.	
Long Valley. (Ainval)	2nd		Arrived Long Valley about 4 a.m. Entrained at midnight at Dernancourt	
	3rd		Arrived at AILLY-SUR-SOMME and detrained. Marched to billets at St Saviour. Very good billets.	
	4th		Rested in billets. Parades under O.B. Coys. Marched to billets in Howdiney in evening	

Army Form C. 2118.

WAR DIARY
or
INTELLIGENCE SUMMARY
(Erase heading not required.)

Instructions regarding War Diaries and Intelligence Summaries are contained in F.S. Regs., Part II. and the Staff Manual respectively. Title Pages will be prepared in manuscript.

Place	Date	Hour	Summary of Events and Information	Remarks and references to Appendices
	July 1916 5th		Inspections and parades under O.C. Coys. C.O. inspected Battalion Billets, and afternoon inspected draft at 12 noon.	
	6th		Marched to LONGEAU, 15 kilometres, to entrain for Bethune area - leaving billets at 4 P.M. Detrained at PERNES 6.30 P.M. and marched to billets at MARLES-SUR-MINES, about 6 kilometres, good billets.	
	7th		Rested in billets until 5 P.M. Orders to move in an hour received. Marched to ALLOUAGNE about 3 kilometres to billets.	
ALLOUAGNE	8th		Rested in billets. C.O. inspected billets.	
	9th		Rested in billets. Church Parade 10.30 A.M.	
	10th		Parades under O.C. Coys. G.O.C. Division inspected the Battalion in the afternoon to present medals awarded for raid on June 25th.	
	11th		Parades under O.C. Coys. Inspected as a Brigade by G.O.C. 1st Army at 3 P.M. at Aerodrome Enguinhem. Draft of 1 Officer + 50 other ranks 5.O.B. reported for duty. Posted to "C" + "D" Coys.	
	12th		Parades under O.C. Coys. "A" + "B" Coys proceeded to SAILLY-LA-BOURSE, to 15th Division on a fatigue party. Working party of 150 men + 1 Officer 1 P.M. for work on range. C.O. visited forward area of 15th Divn. Capt. R.C. Crichester - Constable M.C. appointed S.O. 3 - 8th Division.	

2449 Wt. W14957/M90 750,000 1/16 J.B.C. & A. Forms/C.2118/12.

Army Form C. 2118.

WAR DIARY
or
INTELLIGENCE SUMMARY

(Erase heading not required.)

Instructions regarding War Diaries and Intelligence Summaries are contained in F. S. Regs., Part II. and the Staff Manual respectively. Title Pages will be prepared in manuscript.

Place	Date	Hour	Summary of Events and Information	Remarks and references to Appendices
	13th		Captain W.P.C. Gundry posted as Assistant A.P.M., 8th Divn. Captain S.A. Harland sent as reinforcement Officer to Lapugnoy. Following casualties caused by our Shell near Vermelles Church to our two Coys. working under 18th Division. 2nd Lt. R.A. Davison and 4 other ranks killed, 8 died of wounds & 23 wounded. Parades under O.C. Coys. Eng. inspected last draft 10.30 A.M. Working party 180 men x rays.	
	14th		Parades under O.E. Coys. C.O. Adjt. & O.C. Coys visited Cambrian area during morning. The Battalion marched and billets at Annequin, S. about 14 Kilometres, and one Brigade Reserve to 23rd Infy. Brigade in Cambrian Sector to La Bassée Canal, taking over from 12th R. Sussex Regt. at 2 A.M.	
	15th		Parades under O.E. Coys. Rested in billets. Capt. S.A. Harland rejoined for duty.	
	16th		Church Parade. Rested in billets. Roads E of Killer shelled at 11 A.M. and 7 p.m. No damage. Lewis Gun Sniping Instruction Classes carried on.	
	17th		Parades under O.C. Coys. Slight shelling of roads & batteries E. of Annequin. No damage.	
	18th		Working party 1 N.C.O. & 20 men on front line trenches and 2 Working Parties. Baths for "C" & D Coys. Bombardment from 12 – 5 p.m. by our artillery. Retaliation by enemy E of Annequin. Being in Army Reserve, ordered to be at 2 hours notice to move. R.S.M. Turvey awarded the Military Cross by - C. in - C.	
	19th		Parades under O.E. Coys. Working party of 1 N.C.O. & 12 men carrying away gas cylinders from Cambrian Sector. Baths for B. Coy. H.Q. & M. Gun Sect. (Standing by) on 2 hours notice to move. G.O.C. Division visited the Battalion.	

Army Form C. 2118.

WAR DIARY
or
INTELLIGENCE SUMMARY
(Erase heading not required.)

Instructions regarding War Diaries and Intelligence Summaries are contained in F. S. Regs., Part II. and the Staff Manual respectively. Title Pages will be prepared in manuscript.

Place	Date	Hour	Summary of Events and Information	Remarks and references to Appendices
Annequin	July 20th		C.O. inspected form supporting posts allotted to the Bn. in Cambrin Sector. Baths for 'C' + 'D' Coys.	
	21st		Parades under O.C. Coys. C.O. + O.C. Coys inspected Hohenzollern Sector during the morning. Baths for 'A' 'B' Coys + Machine Gun Sect.	
	22nd		Relieved the 9th Seaforths in Hohenzollern Sector, marching off from Annequin at 7.30 p.m. Very good relief, enemy being fairly quiet. Hostile rifle, dart and rifle grenades active between 10 p.m. + midnight. 2 men killed 2 wounded.	
	23rd		Very quiet day. 3 wounded. 3 Minenwerfers on our right + one at Border Redoubt. Very quiet night. Very few grenades or bombs by either side. G.O.C. Division inspected our trenches.	
	24th		Quiet day. Enemy shelled Reserve Line and Quarry at 6 p.m. at 9 p.m. We appear to be silencing his darts + T.M's by our Stokes Guns + Rifle Grenades. One killed 4 wounded. G.O.C. Corps inspected our trenches, also the Bde., 25th Brigade. Enemy threw bombs in front of his parapet all night.	
Hohenzollern	25th		Far more active day. Our Reserve Line + Quarry heavily shelled. Our Trench Mortars, Rifle Grenades, Mills throwers and Artillery kept up a retaliation on enemy all day. Enemy sniping our loop-hole plates with a sort of a pom. pom. A good deal of work had to be done to damaged trenches on our left. Lieut. Bond, from 1 Coy, attacked for instruction. Casualties 3 killed 2 wounded. Our Stokes appear to greatly annoy the enemy	

Army Form C. 2118.

WAR DIARY
or
INTELLIGENCE SUMMARY

(Erase heading not required.)

Instructions regarding War Diaries and Intelligence Summaries are contained in F. S. Regs., Part II. and the Staff Manual respectively. Title Pages will be prepared in manuscript.

Place	Date	Hour	Summary of Events and Information	Remarks and references to Appendices
Itancourt	26th		Same places as yesterday shelled. Not much damage. Our Stokes are doing very good work and annoy the enemy very much. Aerial darts fired by enemy from 5 p.m. One German shot. Enemy bombed his craters at night. Casualties 1 killed 5 wounded.	
	27th		Usual bombing activity, also Stokes Mortars. Enemy apparently registering our lines about M.10. trench. Casualties 10 wounded.	
	28th		Captain J.C. Maclean rejoined for duty. Bombardment in evening of enemy mortars, fairly successful. Usual bombing activity. Casualties 1 killed 1 wounded.	
	29th		Usual activity, rather quieter. Enemy appeared to be registering our lines as before. Enemy raided our lines about Bayou 116 at 9 p.m. At 8.40 p.m. enemy commenced a very large barrage forming two barrages, one inside the other. The wires are including about 40 yards of our lines at head of 116 which were nearly untouched and which were raided. Owing to not having a line from the left Coy, but only a Central Station, it took over an hour to hear from the left Coy, i.e. he raided one. But a good deal of use was made by using the Station in Cannon St, and artillery fire was accordingly directed from here or first. Great difficulty was experienced however owing to the enormous amount of dust raised. At 9 p.m. SUPPORT G.4.4 - G.4.3 was sent. At 9.51 p.m. the enemy bombardment was going on as hard as ever, our guns replying. So an S.O.S. was sent. The O.C. Devons previously had been asked to try and fire one of his Lewis Guns on to our left flank. The right Coy Comdr, now came to our Central Station & gave us news that his Coy ie "C" & the centre "B" were never raided, but "B" was knocked about a good deal & all bombing parties were ready.	

2449 Wt. W14957/M90 750,000 1/16 J.B.C. & A. Forms/C.2118/12.

WAR DIARY or INTELLIGENCE SUMMARY

Army Form C. 2118

Place	Date	Hour	Summary of Events and Information	Remarks and references to Appendices
Loos - Hohenzollern	29th (continued)		"A" Coy in support also reported his parties were all correct. The raiding party appears the extent about 116, probably about 9.20 p.m. Being very closely hanged by his own T.M. fire, these timely worked were exceptionally large. It is practically certain that prisoners were taken and another 3 men are missing. Some of these may be buried in a mine shaft explosion the large size which resulted. It is estimated that the enemy were only in our trenches 5 to 10 minutes. Our bombing parties worked up but found no enemy. Several forage bags, bombs and one mine-portable were found abandoned by the enemy. The damage by bombardment was intense and entirely flattened out the trench in most places and also up two bays to front line entirely. A good deal was cleared by daylight, but none could be made fit for prolonged defence.	
	30th		Relieved at 10 A.M. by 2nd Royal Sussex, moved back into Brigade Reserve vacated by them. Working parties of 170 during day. Casualties for last 24 hours 5 killed 15 wounded 17 missing. G.O.C. inspected damage to lines at 6 P.M. Baths A Coy. Rested in billets. Working parties of 310 men. Baths in Vermelles for B & C coys.	
	31st			

J.Wynyard(?)

Captain & Adjt.
2nd Batn. The Rifle Brigade.

G.S.F.
3rd August 1916

8th, Division.

25th, Brigade.

2nd, Rifle Brigade.

August, 1916.

D.A.G.
3rd Echelon
Base.

Herewith War Diary for
month of August 1916.
Please acknowledge.

B. Pascoe 2nd Lieut
          A/Adjutant.
          for O.C.
2nd Bn. The Rifle Brigade.

B.E.F.

Army Form C. 2118

2 Rifle Bde

WAR DIARY
or
INTELLIGENCE SUMMARY
(Erase heading not required.)

Instructions regarding War Diaries and Intelligence Summaries are contained in F.S. Regs., Part II. and the Staff Manual respectively. Title Pages will be prepared in manuscript.

Place	Date	Hour	Summary of Events and Information	Remarks and references to Appendices
Reserve Trenches	Aug 1st		Rested in Billets. Working Party of 310 men. Baths in Vermelles for "C" & "D" Coys. Captain E.C. McGrigor joined for duty.	
"	2nd		Working Party of 340 men. Baths for Headquarters Party & Lewis Gun Detachment. O.C. Coys inspected the line to be taken over.	
Trenches	3rd		Relieved 2d Lincoln Regt in Centre, Hohenzollern Section. A Great deal of work to be done on mines.	
	4th		Large amount of work done on mines. Aerial darts fairly active. Mines blown on our left by us at 8 p.m. Casualties one wounded. Captain J.H.G. Kenward attached to 33rd Battery R.F.A. for 24 hours instruction.	
	5th		2/Lieut G.H.G. Anderson wounded by mine concussion. Other casualties 2 killed 9 wounded Mine blown by us at 2 A.M. Enemy bombarded our lines 1·30 – 2·30 A.M. Test Gas Alarm 4·30 A.M. Fairly quiet day. G.O.C. inspected Trenches.	
	6th		Quiet day. Casualties Nil	
	7th		Relieved by 2/K.O.Yorks in trenches & marched to billets at Fouquières. Coy & part of "D" Coy, 138 men in all, left behind as "Spade Party". Billets very good. Return shelled by enemy. Heavy civilian casualties. Working party of 20 to Div School to dig trenches.	

1875 Wt. W593/826 1,000,000 4/15 J.B.C. & A. A.D.S.S./Forms/C. 2118.

Army Form C. 2118

WAR DIARY
or
INTELLIGENCE SUMMARY
(Erase heading not required.)

Place	Date	Hour	Summary of Events and Information	Remarks and references to Appendices
Fouquires	AUG '16 8th		Rested in Billets. Working Party by day. 35 O.R.	
"	9th		Rested in Billets. Fitting Clothing. Lecture by Major Campbell on Sword fighting.	
"	10th		Rested in Billets. Parades under O.C. Coys. Working party 20 by day.	
"	11th		Parades under O.C. Coys. Draft of 39 other ranks joined for duty.	
"	12th		Guard of Honour - 100 men under the Adjutant for Pres. Poincarie. The President failed to turn up.	
"	13th		Church Parade. G.O.C. Division presented medal ribbon to R.S.M. Tuey (Military Cross). Ref: Sweeting Hutching (Military Medal.)	
"	14th		Capt. A. Hadland to Instructor, Reinforcements, Etaples. Parades under O.C. Coys.	
Brigade Reserve (trenches)	15th		Draft of 40 O.R. joined for duty. Marched to night Quarry Section of the trenches in Brigade Reserve, relieving 1st Bn. Worcester Regt at 5 p.m. Intended Gas scheme put off. Working Party at night 4 Officers, 40 O.R.	
"	16th		Working Party 1 Officer & 150 men under R.E. in front line. "C" of relieved off Spoils Party and came to trenches at 11.30 A.M.	

Army Form C. 2118

WAR DIARY
or
INTELLIGENCE SUMMARY
(Erase heading not required.)

Instructions regarding War Diaries and Intelligence Summaries are contained in F.S. Regs., Part II. and the Staff Manual respectively. Title Pages will be prepared in manuscript.

Place	Date	Hour	Summary of Events and Information	Remarks and references to Appendices
Brigade Res Trenches	Aug 16 17th		Working Party of 1 Officer & 150 men for R.E's. Quiet day	
	18th		Working Party of 1 Officer & 125 for R.E's. Conference held at Bn Headqrs re raid on August 25th. 2n. Lieut B.C. Pascoe rejoined from Trench Mortar Battery.	
	19th		Baths for Lewis Gun Detachment, Headquarter Staff & A Coy	
	20th		Church Parade for Companies in Support. Working Party of 1 Officer & 145 men for R.E's. T.M Battery. Gas was liberated on our front - No retaliation	
	21st		Working Party 1 Officer & 140 for R.E's	
Front Line	22nd		Relieved 2n Bn Lincoln Regt in O.R.1. Support Section. Capt & Adjt J.W. Byrne-Johnson killed - G.S. Head, when visiting the front line trenches	
	23rd		2 Lieut B.C. Pascoe took over the duties of Act Adjutant. Casualties - 5 O.R. wounded. Capt R.C. Chichester-Constable D.S.O. attached for offensive operations. Enemy shelled front line with Trench Mortars	

1875 Wt. W593/826 1,000,000 4/15 J.B.C. & A. A.D.S.S./Forms/C.2118.

WAR DIARY
or
INTELLIGENCE SUMMARY
(Erase heading not required.)

Army Form C. 2118

Place	Date	Hour	Summary of Events and Information	Remarks and references to Appendices
Front Line	Aug 1/16 2/16		Capt. W.W. Young, Commdg. "D" Coy went out on patrol with 2nd Lieut. S. Murray D.S.O. The patrol split up and Capt. Young went off with one man, both he and the man failed to return and have been reported missing. Part of front line G.12.a.17. was blown in during the night by minenwerfers. 2nd Lieut. J. Moore & Lieut. R. Hobbs reported from leave. On 24th/25th the Battalion made a raid, about which the following report was written. "Wire was cut on the front G.12.5 – 9.12.1. From 10 A.M. until dark by 18 bars, assisted by 2nd Lieut. J. Montais on the evening 24-8-16. Though the wire was not cleared entirely in front of German front line, there appeared to be several gaps made through it, more especially on the South side of the Hulluch Road. At 8 p.m. a large explosion was observed to take place in the German lines opposite G.18.5, which had the appearance of a small mine; it could not be definitely located. At 11 p.m. the 3 Companies detailed to raid this portion of the German line were in position in our front line, between Boyau 49 and 44. The 4th Company had 2 platoons in the support line between Boyau 49 & 44, 3 one platoon near Methyr Sap in front line. Lewis Guns were as detailed on the scheme - two each, on the Saps & two with "C" Coy. At 11.25 p.m. the two leading Companies commenced to get out in front of our wire followed by the 3rd Company and the Lewis Guns. At 11.31 p.m. all troops were in position outside our wire & the 2 platoons from the support line were filing into the front line. The enemy sent up one red flare from his second line on third line opposite our front at 11.35 p.m.; no action followed, but the Companies lying out had one or two casualties from machine gun fire which was intermittent.	

1875 Wt. W593/826 1,000,000 4/15 J.B.C. & A. A.D.S.S./Forms/C. 2118.

WAR DIARY
or
INTELLIGENCE SUMMARY

(Erase heading not required.)

Army Form C. 2118

Place	Date	Hour	Summary of Events and Information	Remarks and references to Appendices
	Aug 26 Continued		At 12 midnight the bombardment started and the two lines commenced to crawl forward under the barrage following it closely. The leading line reached the enemy wire at 12.54 A.M. and came under a heavy enemy barrage directed on to the enemy front line and wire and they failed to get through the barrage and the wire. At 12.30 P.M. it was reported that the right leading Coy were on the Germans line but subsequently this report was found to be erroneous though a few men succeeding in getting so far as the German parapet. The burst of fire arranged to take place 1½ hours after "all quiet" was cancelled owing to the necessity of recovering "wounded" from "No Man's Land". It appears that the enemy after the wire cutting, evacuated this portion of his line & arranged a heavy barrage of Artillery, Machine Guns, & Rifle Grenades on his front line and support trench. Our Artillery ceased at 1.15 A.M. fire when our Artillery ceased at 1.15 A.M. Our casualties were:— 1 Officer killed :— 2nd Lieut. Wilson. 4 ,, Wounded :— Lieut. Heaton, Ellis, & Lieuts. Fraser, Lomas, Evans, Drew. 2 ,, "at duty" & Lieut. Murray, D.S.O., & Lieut. Leetham. 3 ,, Missing :— Lieut. Whatley, & Lieuts. Fraser & Oliver. 13 other Ranks killed 20 ,, ,, Missing 66 ,, ,, Wounded	

Army Form C. 2118.

WAR DIARY
or
INTELLIGENCE SUMMARY
(Erase heading not required.)

Place	Date	Hour	Summary of Events and Information	Remarks and references to Appendices
Trenches	Aug. '16. 25th		The enemy have been very quiet throughout the night and this morning. G.O.C. Division came round the trenches this morning and said that he was perfectly satisfied that the Battalion had done its duty during the raid. 2nd Lieut. Hobbs reported sick & evacuated to Field Ambulance.	
"	27th		Yesterday morning a Rifleman came in from 'No Mans Land' having remained outside from the night of the raid 24/25th/8/16. and stated that after the raid made by the Battalion he lost his way & was uncertain as to which trenches were ours. He remained in a Shell Hole in 'No Mans Land' throughout the day 25/8/16, the enemy night fearing that a sentry might mistake him he still remained in the shell hole. He returned to our lines next morning at 'stand to'. He had nothing to report except that he had seen or heard no working parties on the German wire or in their trench & that the enemy was very quiet during the time he was out. Last night a patrol of ours went out from 'A'Coy in front of Q.18.5. and observed an enemy patrol of 5 or 6 men crossing the Nullah Road; Our patrol at once returned & rifle & Lewis Gun fire was at once opened on the German patrol which at once scattered and it was thought that one or more of them were hit.	
"	28.		Battalion received a telegram from General Sir Francis Howard K.C.B. C.M.G. Colonel Commandant of the Bn. "on the Regimental Birthday 25th August" "My best wishes are with you to-day". The enemy have been quiet the last 24 hours. At 11 a.m. this morning our T.M. opened fire into the emplacements of the Kaluch-Cross road. Our snipers fired at 2 men in a house at H.13.a.5.8½ and later the snipers of the Battalion on our right reported they observed 2 men carried out at back of the house.	

WAR DIARY or INTELLIGENCE SUMMARY

Army Form C. 2118.

Place	Date	Hour	Summary of Events and Information	Remarks and references to Appendices
Aug '16 Continued	28.		A patrol which went out from G.18.5. reported that the enemy were working on their wire & were unable to disperse them with our Lewis Gun fire & rifle fire. Two Germans were thought to have been wounded. A lot of wire was put out during the night.	
	29.		Lieut. Caswell rejoined for duty from Army School & was posted to B.Coy. Lieutenant A patrol reported that there were two German Listening Posts. These listening posts are joined by a supposed advanced German Sap. These listening posts are joined by a flying sentry. A phenomenal thunderstorm occurred today & rain fell heavily.	
	30.		On the night of 29/30 we placed a notice board half way across "No man's land" South of Juttish Road informing the enemy of Roumania's dicission. A bombing party of 1 N.C.O and 6 men went out between G 12.3 and G.12.4. to bomb an old sap used as a listening post. They started at 11-30 P.M. and three men attached a sentry group on the right. & three - a group on the left. The parties crawled to within 30 yards of the German post and threw 12 bombs into the interior post. A given signal. The enemy retaliated with hand grenades immediately thereafter enemy suffered at least 4 casualties. The party withdrew covered by the M.G. & 1 man who threw bombs from some little land the enemy became quiet again	
	31.		Quiet day. Casualties 2 other ranks wounded - weather very unsettled rain at times.	

Serial No:	From / To	No: of letter	date	Purport
1	To 25th Bde CRA	G H 19	17/8/16	Instructions for raid by a Bn.
2	From Bt Corps	854/123 GA	19/8/16	Allotment of Ammunition & calling for Scheme
3	To 25th Bde CRA	G H 19	19/8/16	Allotment of ammunition calling for programme
4	From 25th Bde			Scheme for raid
5	From CDA	8th Div R A 1/82	16/8/16	Points for Saints in 16th & 32nd Div area
6	To 8o Bde	8th Div G 182	20/8/16	Scheme for raid & for Corps for approval
7	To DvoRA RA Inf Bdes &	8th Div G 182/1	22/8/16	Instructions concerning raid by RB on wk/pit
8	DvoRA RA Inf Bdes &	G 182/2	23/8/16	Time to fire for raid
9	25th Bde C/o 116			For raid
10	To same people that 8 went to	G 1182/2 8th Div	24/8/16	Zero hours
11	From 16th Div	R 2045	22/8/16	Programme for feint.

Raid by
2nd:
Rifle Brigade

Secret

① G H 19

H Q's 25th Bde
C.R.A (for information)

1. In confirmation of the verbal instructions given by the G.O.C at your H.Q's this morning the G.O.C wishes you to arrange for a raid to be carried out within the next 8 days anywhere on the present front of your Bde.

2. For the reasons given this morning it is suggested that the raid should be made on the German front line somewhere between H 13 a 2.6 and A 7 C 0.5.

3. The raid is to be made by 1 or 2 battalions and is to include the occupation of the German 2nd line and possibly his 3rd line. The Bn. or battalions doing it will stay in the German lines 1 to 2 hours and will do as much damage as possible before withdrawing.

2.

4. I am to point out that there is no question of consolidating and remaining in that part of the line captured.

5. The 1st Corps have promised a liberal supply of the following kinds of ammunition:-
9.2"
6 inch
60 Pounder
4.5 How
18 Pounder.

6. All arrangements are to be made by you in conjunction with the C.R.A.

7. Feints will be arranged by Div. H.Qs on other parts of the Divisional front and on the fronts of our flank Divisions.

8. The G.O.C. wishes to have your proposals as soon as possible

3.

These are to include the date you propose to carry out the operation and the amount of ammunition you require.

9. Should you wish to overlap 100x or 150x into the 16th Divisional area for a starting off point early information of this should be given to Div. H.Qs so that the necessary arrangements with the 16th Division may be made.

H Hudson
General Staff
8th Division

Aug 17/16

Secret.

8th Division
~~H.A 1st Corps (for information)~~

No 854/123 ga

19/8/16

The following amounts of ammunition are allotted for the operations discussed with you by the Corps Commander —

    18 Pdr   24000 (Suggested distribution 19000 A / 5000 AX)

    4.5" How 1700

In addition the following Heavy Artillery Ammunition is allotted for the same purpose

    60 Pdr   1200 { 800 D / 400 DX
    6" How   500
    9.2" How 100

The following Heavy Artillery is available for the operation —

    8 — 10   60 Pdrs
    6   6" Hows
    2   9.2" Hows

They will act under H.A 1st Corps in accordance with arrangements to be made between you and the GOC RA 1st Corps, and their action will be included in your programme, which should be forwarded to this H.Q as early as possible

W Dunkinyngham Lt Col
Brig General
for General Staff
1st Corps

Secret — DIV RA ③ G 19
25th Bde

The 10th Corps intimate that the following amounts of ammunition are allotted for the operation being carried out by the 2nd Rifle Bde:—

18 Pr: 24000 (Suggested distribution 19000 Shrapnel 5000 H.E.)

4.5": 1700

In addition the following H. Art: Am: is allotted

60 Pr: 1200 { 800 Shrapnel 400 H.E.

6" How 500
9.2" How 100

The following H.A. is available for the operation:—
8 – 10   60 Prs.
   6   6" Hows
   2   9.2" Hows

The H.A. will act under H.A. 10 Corps instructions in accordance with arrangements to be made by these H.Qrs with G.O.C. R.A. 10 Corps.

Please submit your programme as soon as possible

A. S. C— [illegible]
G. S. 8th Divn.

19/9/16

Secret   25th I.B. 211/G./22

H.Q.
   8th Division.

1. Herewith two copies of the scheme by OC of Right Brigade for a raid of the Battalion under his command on the night of August 24-25. Maps (traced from air photograph) are attached.

2. The Brigade Stokes Mortars, M.G. Coy, and other Battalions in the line will co-operate by fire.

3. I shall be glad if 10th Div. Artillery will also assist, as also the Stokes Mortars & M.G. Coy 48th Inf Brigade, or whichever Brigade is then on the left of the 10th Div. I propose to consult G.O.C. 48th Inf Brigade as to this tomorrow morning.

4. The R.E. who will accompany the OC of Right Brigade will finally settle about I.S., every detail as yet quite decided.

5. Kindly acknowledge receipt.

Done
G.O.C.
           19.8.16
                                        Comm McDonald [?]
                                        Colonel 25th Inf Brigade

                                        Lauders

SECRET.

Reference Map attached.

Scheme for RAID to be carried out by 2nd Battalion The Rifle Brigade on the night of 24th/25th August 1916, against hostile front and second line on front H.7.c.1.2¼.(point E) - H.13.a.2.8.(point F.)

-:-

Time.

11.45 p.m. (1) B and D Coys. will get out of our trenches by means of ladders, and will file out through gaps previously cut in our wire, and lie down about 20 yards in front of our wire, B Coy. on the right with its left on the HULLUCH ROAD, D Coy. on the left with its right on the HULLUCH ROAD, both extended to one pace and protected by a covering party.
C Coy.(with two Lewis Guns) will immediately follow these two Companies, and will lie down just in rear of B and D Coys.; they will cover the same frontage as the two leading Companies i.e. just over 200 yards, (extended to two paces), the Lewis Guns on the flanks.
The 2nd in Command of the Battalion will be with this Company and will be accompanied by 6 signallers with telephones.
A party of Royal Engineers will also accompany C Coy. for demolition purposes.
A Coy. will be in our front line between BOYAUX 77 and 79.
Battalion Headquarters with Artillery Officer attached will be in our front line near BOYAU 78. Definite position will be given later.
6 Lewis Guns of the Battalion will be kept in our front trench.

ZERO (i.e. 12. mid-night). (2) Intense bombardment commences on the front G.12.d.5.8. (pt. Z) - Sap, running out to Crater H.13.a.3.2.(pt. Y), especially on front and second lines on the front H.7.c.1.2¼ (pt. E) - H.13.a.2.8. (pt. F).
B and D Companies crawl as close up to the bombardment as possible, C Company following at 50 yards distance.
The flank platoons of B and D Company's and the Centre platoon of C Company will lay out tapes to point of entry in German front line.

12.5 a.m. (3) Guns lift from H.7.c.1.2¼. (pt. E) - H.13.a.2.8. (pt. F) and barrage the box H.7.c.0.5. (pt. G) - H.7.c.1½.5. (pt. H) - along dotted line up to read H.13.a.5.8.(pt. J) - H.13.a.3.6. (pt. K).
The bombardment however remains intense on the flanks.

~~12.15 a.m.~~ ~~(4)~~ B and D Coys. rush over the front line and get into the 2nd line on front H.13.a.3.8. (pt. L) - H.7.c.2.2¼. (pt. M) without going into communication trenches between front and 2nd lines.
C Coy. gets into front line H.7.c.1.2¼ (pt. E) - H.13.a.2.8. (pt. F).

12-15 am. (4). A Coy. sends one platoon out through MERTHYR SAP and holds the nearest of the old trench running from this sap to enemy line at G.12.d.9¾.4¼ (pt. N). 2 Lewis Guns will go with this platoon. A Company will also send one platoon accompanied with two Lewis Guns to hold the near half of an old trench which runs from our sap about G.18.b.8.6½.(pt. O) to the German Sap H.13.a.1½.6½. (pt. P).

(5) D Company on reaching the 2nd line will bomb down to their left and block the junction of 2nd line and communication trench at H.7.c.1½.3½. (pt. Q) - this Company will also be responsible for the blocking of the communication trench at H.7.c.2½.1½. (pt. R) and keeping touch with B Coy. where the HULLUCH ROAD cuts the 2nd line.
B Coy. on reaching the 2nd line will block the communication trench at H.13.a.3¼.7½. (pt. S)
C Company on reaching the enemy front line will extend to its

Right and Left blocking the trench at at H.13.a.2.6½. (pt. T) on the right and G.12.d.9¾.4. (pt. U) on the Left.
C Company will clear all 6 BOYAUX leading from front line to 2nd line and get in touch with B and D Companies, sending its two Lewis Guns to either flanks of 2nd Line to deal with counter attacks.
They will also form a Bomb Depot where the HULLUCH ROAD cuts the front line.

12.15 a.m. to 12.50 a.m.
(6) The bombardment will continue on the Barrage lines but will moderate.
B and D Companies, whilst being ready to repel bombing attacks from the flanks or communication trenches in front will also guard against any attack made over the open from the Third line. They will clear all dug-outs and pass all prisoners and machine guns captured back to C Company, through the BOYAUX.
C Company whilst guarding against attack from the flanks, will clear all dug-outs in front line and BOYAUX and arrange for the removal of prisoners and captured material, over "No man's land" by the HULLUCH ROAD, and hand over to the platoon of A Company in our front line.
During this time as much damage will be done as possible to all the German line occupied, and all papers and other articles of interest will be collected and brought back. Searchers will be told off, and carry sandbags for papers etc.

(7) All wounded will be sent out and cross "No man's land" by the old trenches held on the North and South flanks by two platoons of A Company (see para. 4).

(8) The Engineers who accompany C Company will carry explosive charges and destroy any machine gun emplacements and mine galleries there.are.

(9) Battalion Headquarters will be in telephonic communication with the 2nd in command in the German Trenches, and also with the Artillery, and it is hoped to be able to switch artillery fire on to any special point that is giving trouble.

From 12.50 a.m. to 1.15 a.m.
(10) From 12.50 a.m. to 1.15 a.m. the artillery will increase their fire making it specially heavy on the flanks and paying special attention to the saps and QUARRY near H.13.a.2.5. (pt. V) and also to the salient G.12.d.5.8. (pt. Z)
At 12.50 a.m. the BOYAUX between 1st and 2nd line will be clear and B and D Coys will withdraw gradually and quietly by the 5 BOYAUX which run into the front line between H.7.c.1.2¼. (pt. E) and H.13.a.2.8. (pt. F.) passing through C-Company and regaining our line. The Officer Commanding these two Companies will see to it that all dead and wounded are brought out with him.
C Company will as soon as B and D have passed through them draw in their flanks to H.7.c.1.2¼ (pt. E) and H.13 a 2.8. (pt. F) and then will proceed to withdraw to our line, all dead and wounded being brought out.
At 1.10 a.m. a Claxton Horn will be sounded by the Officer in charge in the German Trench (the 2nd in Command) which will be the signal for anyone who is still in the German trench to withdraw.

1.15 a.m.
(11) The artillery bombardment will moderate and then gradually die down. The two platoons of A Company and 4 Lewis Guns will withdraw from the old trenches in "no man's land to our front line.

(12) Each Company after withdrawal to our lines will

resume its normal position as soon as possible provided the front line and saps are sufficiently held to repulse a possible counter-attack. There will be in any case the two platoons of A Company and 2 Lewis Guns in our front line which have not been used.

(13) Stokes Trench Mortars will co-operate. Infantry on the remaining front (QUARRIES Section) will co-operate with rifles and Lewis Gun fire. M.G.Coy. will co-operate with indirect fire on communications.
The Brigade of the 16th Division on our Right will be asked to co-operate also.

(14) At 2.45 a.m. every gun will fire for one minute on the area bombarded during the raid.

(15) List of stores required is attached.

                                                (Sgd) R.ERAND Major,
19th August 1916.   Commanding 2nd Battn. The Rifle Brigade.

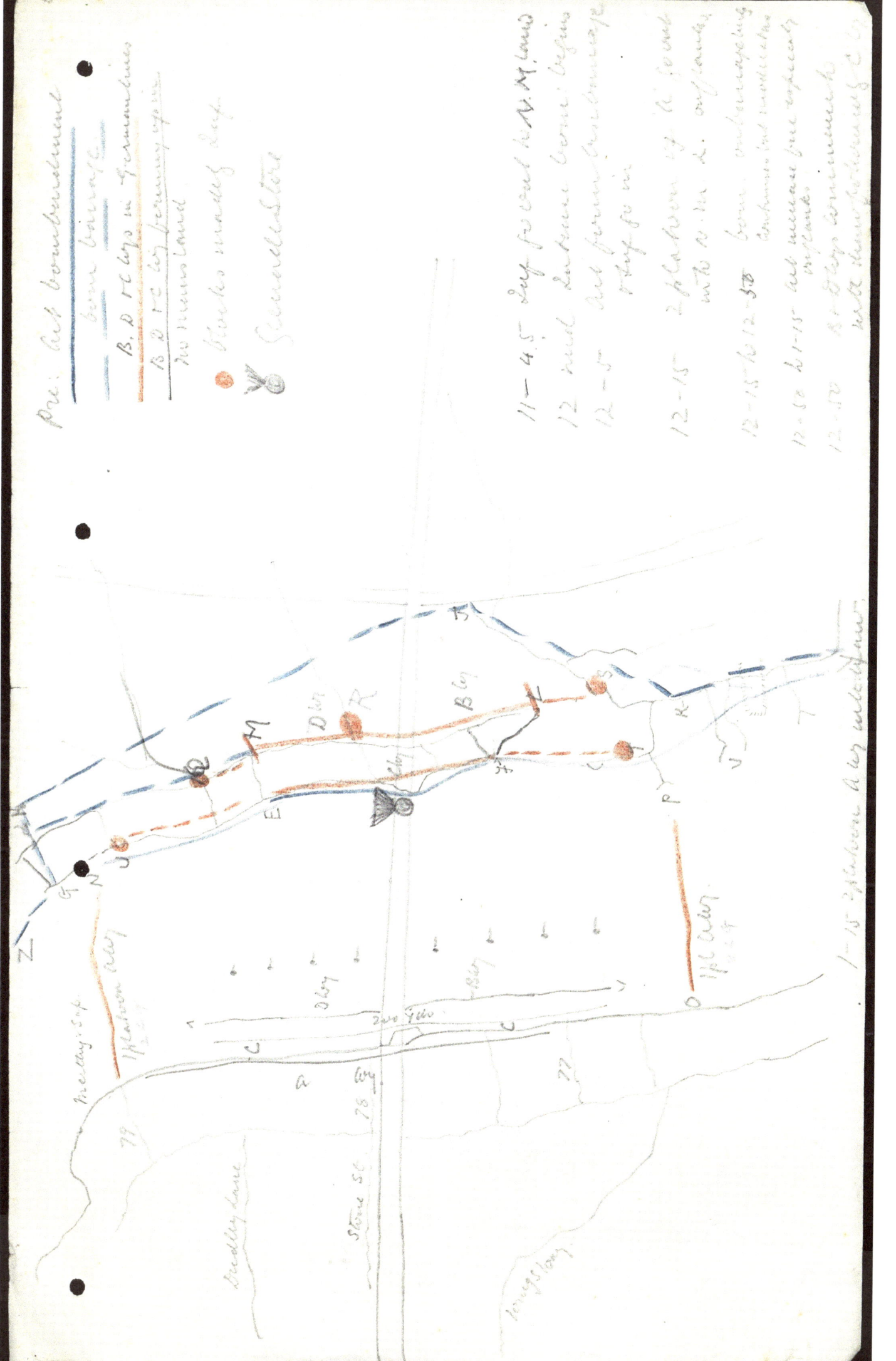

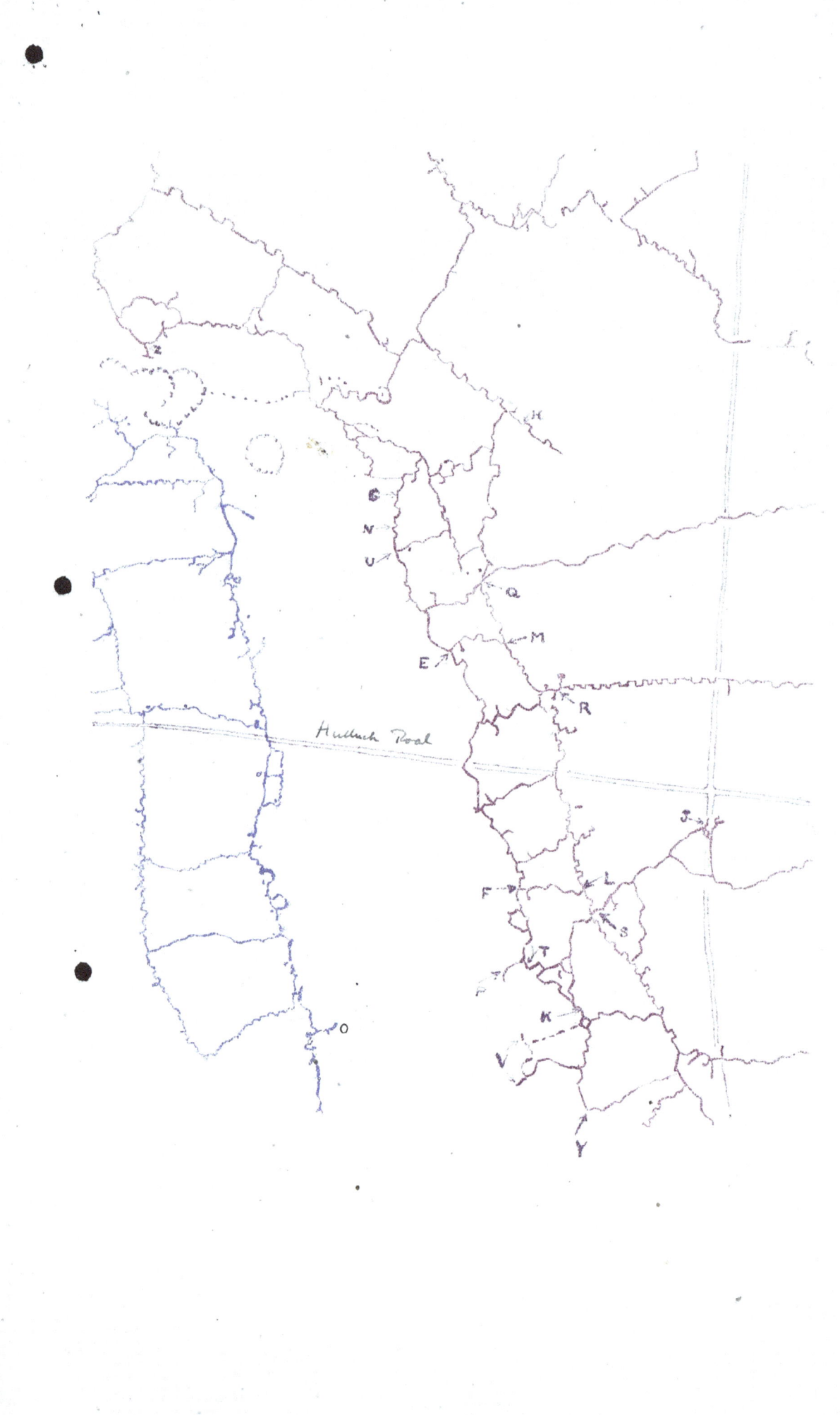

SECRET   8th D.A.   O/82/4

1. Herewith the Artillery Time Table for a Raid to be carried out by the 2nd Battalion, The Rifle Brigade, on the Night of 24th/25th August, 1916.

2. Flank Divisions will co-operate by demonstrating at selected places.

3. One and a half hours after "All Quiet" has been reported, a burst of fire from all natures will be opened on the raided portion of the hostile trenches.

   The exact time will be notified on conclusion of the operations.

                                           Major R.A.
                                    Brigade Major 8th Divn Artillery.

21-8-16.

Copies to :- Right Group
             Left   "
             D.T.M.O.
             5th Bde. RHA
             23rd Inf. Bde.
             24th   do.
             25th   do.
             8th Division (2)
             1st Corps H.A.
             1st Corps R.A.
             War Diary
             Spare (2).

SECRET   O/82/4

ARTILLERY TIME TABLE

FEINT. G 5 c

TIME	UNIT	NATURE	OBJECTIVE	AMMUNITION H.E. S.	REMARKS
3 p.m.	1st Corps H.A.	1 9.2" How.	Jaegar Trench (G 5 c 5.9½ to G 5 c 3.9)	15 rds.	T.M. Emplacements.
4.30 p.m.	H.T.M.	1 9.45	G 5 c 6½.8	6 ,,	do.
	1st Corps H.A.	1-5" How.	G 5 c 9½.½ to G 5 c 3.½	20 ,,	
	do.	1-6" How	G 5 c 5½.2 to G 5 c 3.2	20 ,,	
5. p.m.	do.	1-60 prd.	G 5 c 9.4 to G 5 c 5.4	10	
	do.	1-60 pdr.	G 5 c 9.7½ to G 5 c 4.8	10	
11.30 a.m.	Left Group	1. 4.5" Bty	G 5 d 1.1 to G 5 c 9½.½	50	
12-15 p.m.	do	do	G 5 c 0½.½ to G 5 c 7¼.1½	50	
1 p.m.	do	do	G 5 c 5½.2 to G 5 c 3.2	50	
2 to 4 p.m.	do	5-18 pdr. Bties.	Front line G 5 c 3½. to G 5 c 2.3		180 rounds per Battery 25% H.E. Group Commander will allot portions for Batteries. Half hour Bombardments. One Battery to start at 2 p.m. 1 Battery to start at 3 p.m. 1 Battery to start at 4 p.m. Bombardments to similate wire cutting.
During Day.	T.M's	2-2" T.M's	Front line G 5 c 9½.½ to G 5 c 2.3		As available.

SECRET

ARTILLERY TIME TABLE
FEINT G 5.c

2nd. Sheet.

TIME	UNIT	NATURE	OBJECTIVE	AMMUNITION H.E.	S.	REMARKS
-0.20 to -0.05	1st. Corps H.A.	1 9.2" How.	JAEGAR TRENCH G 5 c 5.9½ toG 5 c 3.9	5 rounds.		After firing 5 rounds switch to new objective.
	do.	1-6" How. 1-6" do 1-60 pdr. 1-60 "	G 5 c 5.5.½ to G 5 c 6½.1½ G 5 c 5.2 to G 5 c 3½.2½ G 5 c 9.4 to G 5 c 5.4 G 5 c 9.7½ to G 5 c 4.8	15 rds. 15 " 5 5	15. 15	
	Left Group	3-18 pdr. Bties.	Front Line G 5 c 9½.1 to G 5 c 2.3	135	405	2 rds. per gun per min.
	T.M's.	2-2" T.M.	do. do.	As available.		
-0.05 to 0.15.	1st. Corps H.A.	1-6" How. do 2-60 pdrs.	As above. G.5.c.8½.8½ do. G.5.c.3½.5. As above As above	3 rds. 3 rds.		
	Left Gp.	3-18 pdr. Bties.	G 5 c 9½.4 toG 5 c 3½.5½	10 180	10 540	Total. Group Cdrs. will allot portions for Bties. (2 rds. per gun per min.)
	T.M's	1-2" T.M. 1-2" "	G 5 c 9½.½ G 5 c 2.3	As available. "		
0.15 to 1.00	1st. Corps H.A.	2-6" Hows. 2-60 pdrs.	As for -0.05 to 0.15. As above	17 rds. " "	Total. 50 Total.	
	Left Group T.M's.	3-18 pdr. Bties. 2-2" T.M8s	Is for -0.05 to 0.15 do	10 200 As available.	610	1 rd. per gun per min.
-0.20 to 1.00	F.T.M.	1-9.45	G 5 c 6½.8	As available.		

SECRET.   3rd. Sheet.

ARTILLERY TIME TABLE.

TIME	UNIT	NATURE	OBJECTIVE	AMMUNITION H.E. S.	REMARKS
0.00 to 0.05.	1st. Corps H.A.	1-6" How.	H 13 a 4.1,1.3 to H 13 a 4.2	Up to 10 rds.	
		1-6" ,,	H 13 a 5½.9½t	do.	
		1-6" ,,	G 12 d 8.7	do.	
		1-6" ,,	G 12 d 5.8	do.	
		1-60 pdr.	H 13 a 7.8 to H 13 a 0½.8½	10	2 rds. per gun per min.
		do.	H 7 c 4⅝.1½ to H 7 d 0.1	10	do.
		do.	H 7 c 3½.4½ to H 7 c 9½.5	10	do. 60 pdrs to rake backwards and forwards.
	Right Group.	1-4.5" Bty.	Three Saps. H 13 a 3.3½ to H 13 a 3.5	)	
		2-4.5" Hows.	G 12 d 9½.6	)	
		do.	G 12 d 8.7¼	) 120	Two rds. per How per min.
		do.	G 12 d 5.8	)	
			H 7 c 2.10 H 7 c 0.8	)	
	do.	4-18pdr. Btsi	H 13 a 2.6½ toG 12 d 9½.4	600	5 rds. per gun per min. On front and 2nd. line Trenches.
	T.M's	2-2" T.M.	3 Saps½ H 13 a 3.3½ to H 13 a 3.5	As available.	
		do.	G 12 d 9½.6	do.	

SECRET   4th. Sheet.

ARTILLERY TIME TABLE.

TIME	UNIT	NATURE	OBJECTIVE	AMMUNITION H.E.	S.	REMARKS.
0.05 to 0.15.	1st. Corps H.A.	4-9.2" How.	H 15 b 6½.7½ to H 15 b 5½.8½	20 rds.		) Total Ammunition for
		do.	G 12 b 9½.7½ to G 12 b 7½.6	"		) whole period 0.05 to 1.15.
		4-6" Hows.	As for 0.00 to 0.05	40 rds.		1 rd per How per min.
		3-60 pdrs.	Objective do.		60	2 do.
	Right Group.	3-4.5" Btys.	Objective do.	120		1 rd. per How. per min
		4.18 pdr. Btys.	Lift and Barrage	300	900	5 rds. do
			H 13 a 5½.8 -H 7 c 5½.7½-			
			H 7 c 4.4½ -H 7 c 2.6.			
	T.M's.	4-2" T.M's.	do.	As available.		
0.15 to 0.50	1st Corps H.A.	2-9.2" Hows.	As for 0.05 to 0.15	140 rds.	150	i.e 35 rds. per How.
		4-6" Hows.	do.			do. gn.
		3-60pdrs.	do.			i.e 50 do. gn.
	Right Group	3-4.5" Btys.	do.	420 rds.		i.e 1 rd. per How per min.
		4-18pdr.	do.	420	1260	i.e 2 do.
	T.M's	4-2" T.M's.	do.	As available.		
0.50 to 1.15	1st Corps H.A.	2-9.2 Hows.	As for 0.05 to 0.15.	80 rds.		i.e 20 rds per How.
		4-6" Hows.	do.		60	i.e 20 do. gun.
		3-60 Pdrs.	do.			i.e 1 rd. per How per min.
	Right Gp.	3-4.5 Btys.	do.	300 rds.	1350	3 rds. do.
		4.18 pdr Btys.	do.	450		
	T.M's	4-2" T.M's.	do.	As available.		

SECRET.   8th D.A. 0/82/4/1.

Reference 8th D.A. 0/84/4. dated 21-8-16.

           Amendment

1. 2nd. Sheet.   Time   -0.05 to 0.15.

    For   1 - 6"   How   -   As above
    "   do   "   do
    "   2 - 60 Pdrs   -   do

    Read   1 - 6"   How   -   G 5. c $8\tfrac{1}{2}.3\tfrac{1}{2}$
             1 - 6"   How   -   G 5. c $3\tfrac{3}{2}.5$
             2 - 60 Pdrs   -   As above.

----

2.   Time   0.15 to 1.00.

    For   2 - 6"   How   -   As above

    Read   2 - 6"   How   -   As for -0.05 to 0.15.

                                                             Major R.A.

22-8-16.   Brigade Major 8th Divl Arty.

Copies to.   Right group.
----------   Left   "
             D.T.M?O.
             5th Bde R.H.A.
             23rd Inf Bde.
             24th   "   "
             25th   "   "
             8th Division.
             1st Corps H.A.
             1st CORPS R.A.

Time Table corrected

JF
22/8

Secret   (5)   8" D.A. 0/82

8' Division.

Reference your G.H.19 dated 17 Aug.
para 7.

The following points would be
suitable for us and are submitted
for approval.

16" Division H.19.d

32" Division ..... RAILWAY POINT
                     and RAILWAY TRENCH
                     (A 28. c + a)

             L.R. Cooper Major
                   for
18 Aug 1916.   L.R.A. 8' Div.

Copy Secret (6) G.1182

Headquarters,
    I Corps.

I forward, for the approval of the Corps Commander, the Scheme for the raid to be carried out by the 2nd Rifle Brigade on night 24th/25th.

Feints will be made by the 16th Division Artillery about H.19.d, and by the 32nd Division Artillery about RAILWAY POINT A.28.c.2.8 at -20.

The Artillery bombardment will be kept up on these two points after zero.

In addition to the above the Trench Mortars and Machine Guns of the 48th Brigade are co-operating.

The OC 2nd Rif: Bde. has been told that, if there is a heavy barrage on "no man's land" at the time arranged for the withdrawal from the German trenches, that the Bn: should remain on the enemy's lines until the barrage dies down.

                                        H. Hudson
8th Division,   Major-General,
21st August, 1916.   Commanding 8th Division.

"A" Form.
Army Form C. 2121.

MESSAGES AND SIGNALS.

Prefix	Code	m.	Words	Charge	This message is on a/c of:	Recd. at	m.
Office of Origin and Service Instructions.			Sent At	m.	Y Service.	Date	
			To By		(Signature of "Franking Officer.")	From By	

TO	CRA	24th Bde
	CRE	25th Bde
	23rd Bde	Q

Sender's Number.	Day of Month	In reply to Number	AAA
* G.442	23		

Ref my G.1182/1 of 22.8.16 para 7 for 23rd line 1 read 24th.

From 8th Divn
Place
Time 9.20 a.m.

Copy

SECRET.   G. 1122/1.
                                                           22 AUG 1916
                                                           8th DIVISION

Div. R.A.
Div. R.E.
23rd Inf. Bde.
24th Inf. Bde.
25th Inf. Bde.
    Q.

1. A raid will be carried out by the 2nd Bn. Rifle Brigade
    on the night 24th/25th August against the hostile front and
    second lines on the front N.7.c.1.6½. - N.13.a.2.2.

2. The Battalion will stop in the German Trenches from one
    to two hours and will do as much damage as possible, secure an
    identity and kill as many Germans as possible.

3. The following Heavy Artillery has been placed at the
    disposal of the G.O.C. 8th Division for the operation:-

                    8 - 10   60 Pounders.
                        6   6" Howitzers.
                        2   9.2" Howitzers.

4. A liberal supply of all types of ammunition has been
    allotted for the operation.

5. Feints will be carried out the same night by the 16th
    and 32nd Divisions on specially selected points on their
    fronts.

6. Our Artillery and Heavy Artillery are carrying out a
    feint on HILL'S BLUFF.

7. The Trench Mortars and Machine Guns of 24th and 49th
    Infantry Brigades are cooperating under arrangements made
    direct between G.O.C. 25th Infantry Brigade and Brigadiers
    concerned.

8. Zero hour will be communicated to all concerned
    separately.

                                            H. Hill
                                            Lieut. Colonel,
                                            General Staff 8th Division.

SECRET.

G.1182/2.

Copy

16th Division
40th Division

Div. R.A.,
Div. R.E.,
24th Inf. Bde.,
25th Inf. Bde.,
97th Inf. Bde.,
32nd Division,
170th T. Coy. R.E.,
180th T. Coy. R.E.,
253rd T. Coy. R.E..

****

  The following is the Time Table for the operation being carried out by 25th Infantry Brigade tonight :-

- 0 - 20 Artillery bombardment begins.

 0 - 0 Zero hour.

 0 - 5 Infantry assault German trenches on the front
    H.7.c.1.2¼. to H.13.a.2.8.

 0 - 50 Infantry begin to withdraw.

 1 - 15 Artillery bombardment will moderate and gradually
    die down.

  Watches will be synchronised over the telephone with 8th Division at 6 p.m..

8th Division,
24th August, 1918.

Lieut.-Colonel,
General Staff.

S E C R E T.   Copy No. 22

25th INFANTRY BRIGADE.

OPERATION ORDER No. 116.

1. A raid will be carried out by 2nd Batt. The Rifle Brigade on the night of 24th/25th August against the hostile front and second lines on the front G.12.d.97.40 - H.13.a.20.75.
A detailed Scheme for the raid has been issued to all concerned.
Zero hour is 12 midnight.

   11.25 p.m   Infantry commence getting into position in "No Man's Land".
   12 midnight. Infantry crawl close up to the bombardment.
   12.5 a.m.   Assault.
   12.5 a.m)
        to   ) Infantry in occupation of German Trenches doing
   12.50 a.m) all damage possible.
   12.50 a.m)
        to   ) Infantry evacuating German lines.
   1.15 a.m)

   1.15 a.m. Infantry resuming normal positions in our Trenches.

2. The Artillery programme has been issued to all concerned.

   11.40 p.m The Artillery will bombard G.5.c. (A Feint)
   12 midnight. Intense Bombardment on the objective.
   12.5 a.m.) Artillery lift and barrage the box to be raided.
        to   ) Intense fire on the flanks.
   12.15 a.m.)

   12.15 a.m) Bombardment will continue on the Barrage lines but
        to   ) will moderate.
   12.50 a.m.)

   12.50 a.m)
        to   ) Artillery fire increases being specially heavy on
   1.15 a.m.) the flanks.

   1.15 a.m. Bombardment moderates and gradually dies down.

   One and a half hours after "All quiet" has been reported a burst of fire from all natures will be opened on the portion raided.

3. Co-operation by the Divisions on our Right and Left will take place.
   Each Division will carry out a feint on specially selected points.
   The Division on our right will also Co-operate with Medium T.M's and Stokes Mortars and Machine Guns on selected localities.

4. The 25th Trench Mortar Battery will concentrate its guns in BOYAU 80 and the vicinity, and will act according to the following Time Table:-
   12 midnight)
        to   ) Rapid fire by all guns on the hostile front line
   12.2 a.m   ) and Northern flank of the objective.

   12.2 a.m   ) Intense fire by all guns on the Northern flank
        to   ) of the objective.   No point South of G.12.d.95.55
   12.5 a.m.) is to be bombarded.

   12.5 a.m   )
        to   ) Moderate fire continued as above.
   12.50 a.m.)

   12.50 a.m)
        to   ) Fire increased on same objective.
   1.15 a.m.)

1.15 a.m. Fire will gradually decrease and eventually cease.

One minute rapid fire over the whole area raided.

Four Stokes Mortars complete with personnel from 23rd Infantry Brigade have been placed at the disposal of 25th Brigade to relieve 4 guns in the line on the left of the Brigade front. O.C. 25 Trench Mortar Battery will arrange guides to meet this party at VERMELLES Church at 4 p.m on 24th and conduct them to their emplacements.

5. The O.C. 25th Machine Gun Company will keep up an intermittent fire on the enemys communication trenches during the whole operation. The Special trenches to be dealt with to be arranged with the O.C. 2nd Batt. The Rifle Brigade.

6. One Company of the 2nd Lincolnshire Regt will relieve the 2nd Batt. Rifle Brigade in the line between BOYAU 84 and BOYAU 79 on 24.8.16. Relief to be completed by 2 p.m.
The 2nd Lincolnshire Regt. will also move up one Company from CURLY CRESCENT putting two platoons in the Reserve Trench between DEVON LANE and WINGS WAY and 2 platoons in O.B.1 & 2 by 11 p.m. All details of this relief to be arranged between Commanding Officers concerned. The normal dispositions will be resumed on completion of the operation.

7. Watches will be synchronised over the telephone with Brigade Headquarters at 6.15 p.m.

Issued at 10 a.m.

24th August 1916.

Captain,
Brigade Major,
25th Infantry Brigade.

Copy No.1 G.O.C.
"   2 Brigade Major.
"   3 Staff Captain.
"   4 2/Lincs. R.
"   5 2/R.Berks. R.
"   6 1/R.Irish Rif.
"   7 2/Rif. Bde.
"   8 25 M.G.Coy.
"   9 25 T.M.Batty.
"   10 25 Sig. Sec.
"   11 23rd Brigade.
"   12 24th Brigade.
"   13 97th Brigade.
"   14 2nd Field Co. R.E.
"   15 15th Field Co. R.E.
"   16 170th Tunnelling Co.
"   17 180th   "   "
"   18 253rd   "   "
"   19 Right Group R.A.
"   20 8th Div. R.A.
"   21 C.R.E.
"   22 8th Division.
"   23 War Diary.
"   24   "   "
"   25 Office.

Copy

SECRET. 16th Div   G.1182/2.

Div. R.A.,
Div. R.E.,
24th Inf. Bde.,
25th Inf. Bde.,
97th Inf. Bde.,
32nd Division,
40th Division,
170th T. Coy. R.E.,
180th T. Coy. R.E.,
253rd T. Coy. R.E..

Reference No. G.1182/2 dated 24th August, forwarding Time Table for Operation by 25th Infantry Brigade tonight, Zero Hour will be 12 midnight.

8th Division,   Lieut.-Colonel,
24th August, 1918.   General Staff.

SECRET

Left Group, 16th D.A.
Centre Group, 16th D.A.
----

1. Herewith Programme of bombardment on night of 24th/25th August, as a feint in assistance of 8th Division.

2. Zero time will be notified later.

3. Wire cutting will take place beforehand under arrangements of O.C., Left Group.

4. Acknowledge.

                                      Major, R.A.,

22/8/16.   Brigade Major, 16th Divl. Artillery.

Copies to:-
  48th Inf. Bde.
  8th Divl. Arty.
  H.A., I Corps.
  16th Division.
  49th Inf. Bde.
  R.A., I Corps.
  Spare 3.

SECRET

TIME TABLE

PHASE A.

Bombardment night of 24th/25th Aug.

Guns	From	To	Objective	Remarks	Ammunition
A/180	-0.20.	0.05	Front trench, 25 yards each side of Communication trench H.19.c.91.77.		7x6x20 = 840 AX
C/77	"	"	Front Trench, 25 yards each side of LOOS-HULLUCH Road H.19.c.95.55.	-0.20 to 0.00 Section Fire 20"	
B/180	"	"	Front trench, on a front of 50 yards midway between trench junctions H.19.d.03.50 and H.19.d.10.35.		
A/77	"	"	Front Trench, H.19.d.11.32 to H.19.d.15.25.	0.00 to 0.05. Section fire 10"	7x12x5 = 420 A.
B/177	"	"	Front Trench from Sap H.19.d.23.19, 50 yards to South east.		
A/177	"	"	Front Trench, 25 yards each side of Trench junction H.25.b.40.95.		
C/180	"	"	Front Trench, 25 yards each side of Sap H.25.b.43.84.		
D/77 (1 How. (do. (do.	" " "	" " "	(Trench junction H.19.d.11.86. (" H.19.d.11.59. (" H.19.d.36.88.	))) One round per) gun every) 3 minutes.))	See phase B.
D/177(1 How. (do. (do. (do.	" " " "	" " " "	Junction of Sap and Front Trench H.19.d.10.35. Trench junction H.19.d.37.20. " H.19.d.48.27. " H.25.b.46.73.		

SECRET   60-pdrs.   PHASES A and B

Guns	From	To	Objective	Remarks	Ammunition
1 - 60-pdr.	-0.20	1.00	C.T., H.19.d.70.80. Search N.E.		⎫
1 - 60-pdr.	-0.20	1.00	C.T., H.19.d.60.30. Search N.E.		⎬ 150 D.
1 - 60-pdr.	-0.20	1.00	C.T., H.25.b.57.40. Search N.E.		⎭ 50 DX.

PHASE B

Guns	From	To	Objectives	Remarks	Ammunition
A/180	0.05	1.00	Front Trench H.19.c.90.77 to H.19.c.95.56.	Section fire 20"	7x6x55 = 2310
C/77	0.05	1.00	C.T. H.19.c.97.57. to H.19.d.12.59 and Support trench H.19.d.12.59 to H.19.d.20.52		
B/180	0.05	0.10	Support Trench H.19.d.20.52 to H.19.d.35.35.	Section fire 20"	A AX
	0.15	1.00		From 0.10 to 0.15	1900 410
A/77	0.05	0.10	Support Trench H.19.d.35.35.to H.19.d.48.17.	drop back on to	Total 18-pr. Ammunition
	0.15	1.00		Front Trench as	
B/177	0.05	0.10	Support Trench H.19.d.48.17 to H.25.b.53.97.	in Phase "A"	A AX
	0.15	1.00		At 0.15 lift again	Phase "A" 420 840
A/177	0.05	0.10	Support Trench H.25.b.53.97 to H.25.b.63.81.	to support trenches	Phase "B" 1900 410
	0.15	1.00			2320. 1250
C/180	0.05	1.00	Support Trench H.25.b.63.81 to H.25.b.68.75. C.T., H.25.b.68.75. to H.25.b.46.71.	Section fire 20"	3570
D/77 (1 How.	0.05	1.00	Trench junction H.19.c.96.57.	1 round per gun every 3 minutes	190 B.X.
(do.	"	"	" H.19.d.11.86.		
(do.	"	"	" H.19.d.36.88.		
D/177(1 How.	"	"	Trench junction H.19.d.48.27.		
(do.	"	"	" H.25.b.68.75.		
(do.	"	"	" H.25.b.80.47.		
(do.	"	"	" H.25.b.56.42.		
9.2 How.	0.05	0.25	Trench junction H.25.d.94.98.	1 rnd. every two minutes	10 rounds

Phase "A"

Scale 1/10,000

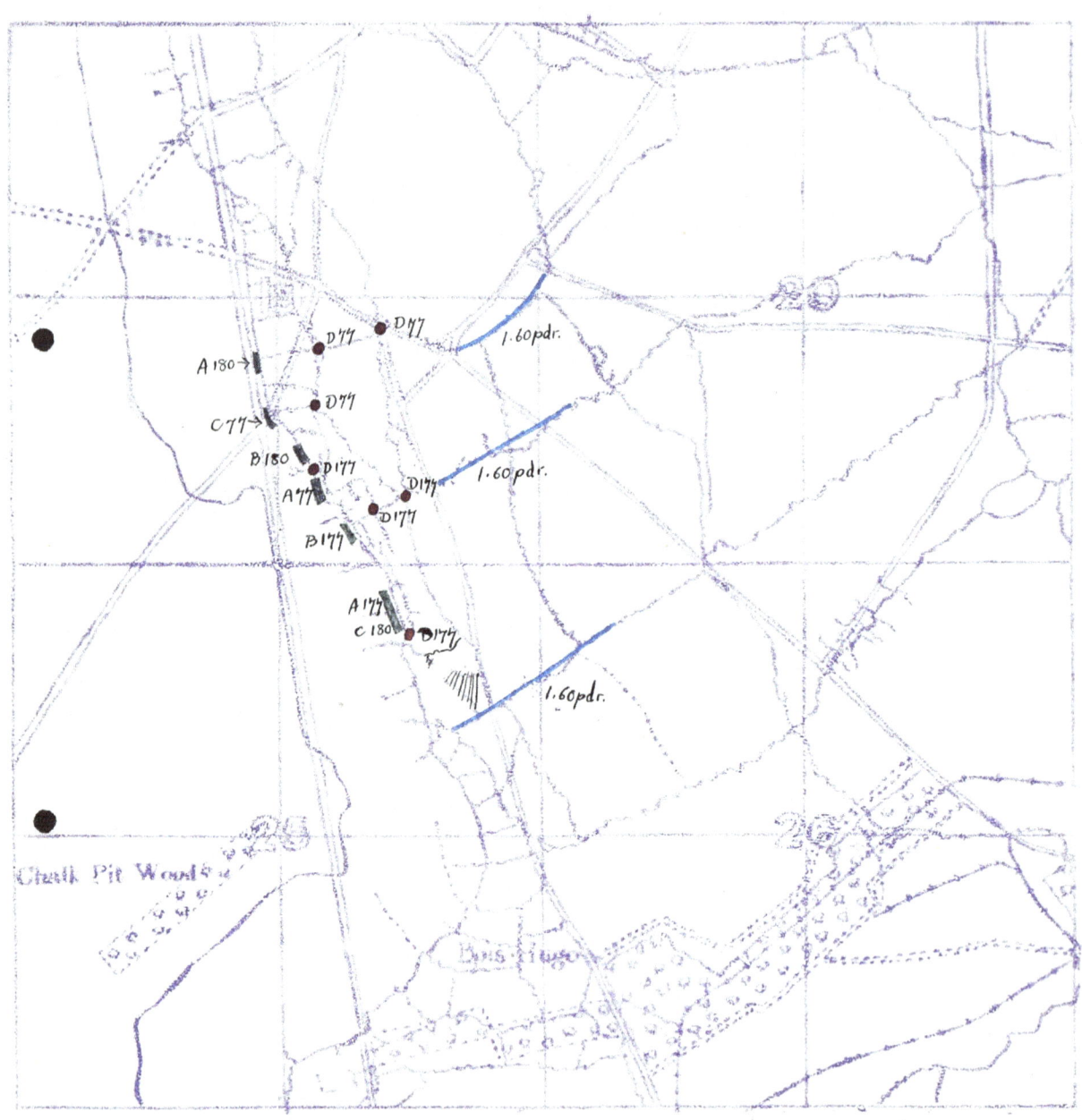

Phase "B"

Scale 1/10,000

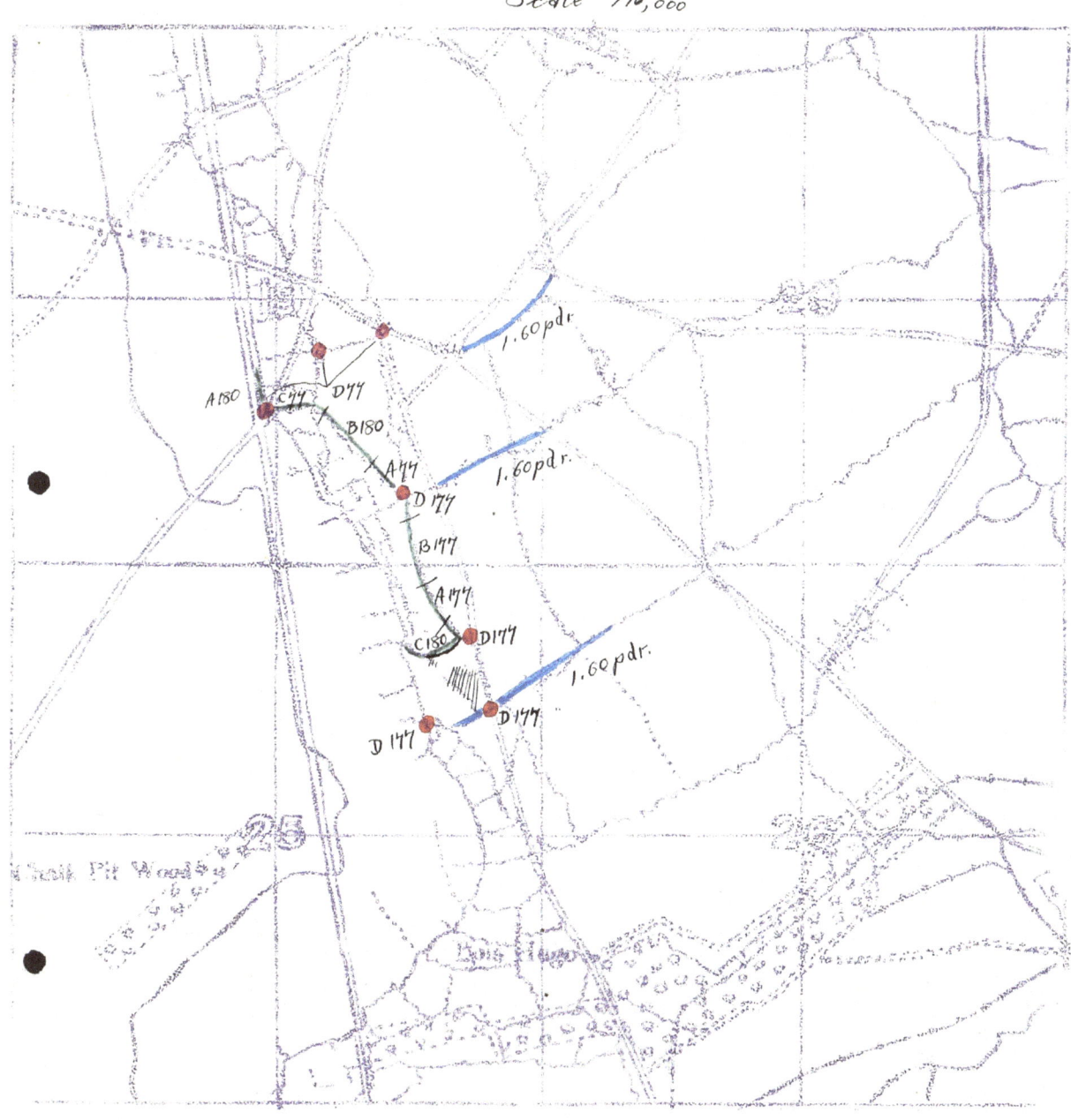

Army Form A. 2007.

CENTRAL REGISTRY.

Central Registry No. and Date. 8. DIV Attached Files.

502/75(G) 25

SUBJECT, AND OFFICE OF ORIGIN. 1st Corps

Minor Operations.
Carried out by 2nd Batt. Rifle Brigade
against enemy positions between H.18.b.½.4
and G.12.b.4.5.

Referred to	Date	Referred to	Date	Referred to	Date
OHe G.26.8.6					
I 28/8/16 mjl					
CE 30/8/16					
J.M. RA 31.8.16					
G 1/9/16					

P. A.	Date
HM	3/9/16

Schedule of Correspondence.

SECRET.

First Army.

No. 854/129(Ga).   25th August, 1916.

    The attached preliminary report on attempted raid by 2nd Battn. Rifle Brigade north and south of HULLUCH road on night of 24/25th August, 1916, is forwarded for your information.

Lieut. General.
Commanding I Corps.

Preliminary report on attempted raid by 2nd Battn.
Rifle Brigade north and south of HULLUCH road
between H.18.b.7½.7. and G.12.b.7.5. on night
of 24/25th August, 1916.

The battalion assembled outside our lines unmolested. One red rocket was sent up by enemy from his front line almost immediately, and some machine guns opened fire. The battalion moved close up to our barrage. It appeared to them that our barrage came back on them; this, however, was the German barrage which was put on very quickly. Enemy barraged his own front line with artillery and rifle grenades. Several hostile machine guns were firing from their front.

A sergeant went along the enemy's parapet for 50 yards but saw no Germans in their front trench. An officer and a sergeant went over the enemy's front line trench and on towards second line. These are now missing.

Enemy's barrage was exceedingly heavy and the battalion unable to get through.

Casualties approximately :-

  Officers - 1 killed.
        7 wounded (2 at duty).
        3 missing.

  Other ranks - 14 killed.
         67 wounded.
         22 missing.

S E C R E T.

First Army.

No. 854/129(Ga). 25th August, 1916.

The attached preliminary report on attempted raid by 2nd Battn. Rifle Brigade north and south of HULLUCH road on night of 24/25th August, 1916, is forwarded for your information.

for Lieut. General.
Commanding I Corps.

Preliminary report on attempted raid by 2nd Battn.
Rifle Brigade north and south of HULLUCH road
between H.18.b.7½.7. and G.12.b.7.5. on night
of 24/25th August, 1916.

The battalion assembled outside our lines unmolested. One red rocket was sent up by enemy from his front line almost immediately, and some machine guns opened fire. The battalion moved close up to our barrage. It appeared to them that our barrage came back on them; this, however, was the German barrage which was put on very quickly. Enemy barraged his own front line with artillery and rifle grenades. Several hostile machine guns were firing from their front.

A sergeant went along the enemy's parapet for 50 yards but saw no Germans in their front trench. An officer and a sergeant went over the enemy's front line trench and on towards second line. These are now missing.

Enemy's barrage was exceedingly heavy and the battalion unable to get through.

Casualties approximately :-

    Officers -   1 killed.
                      7 wounded (2 at duty).
                      3 missing.

    Other ranks -   14 killed.
                        67 wounded.
                        22 missing.

-:-:-:-:-:-:-:-:-

Inter-Office Minutes.

NOTE.—Inside sheets to be attached to this page.

NOT TO BE WRITTEN ON.

8th, Division.

25th, Brigade.

2 nd, Rifle Brigade.

September, 1916.

To. The D.A.G.,
   3rd Echelon
      Base.

———

Herewith War Diary for
month of September 1916.

Please acknowledge.

B Carrol 2nd Lieut. & /Adjt.
                    for O.C.
           2nd Bn. The Rifle Brigade.
B.E.F.
———

WAR DIARY
INTELLIGENCE SUMMARY
(Erase heading not required.)

Army Form C. 2118.

2 Rifle Bde / N 23

Place	Date	Hour	Summary of Events and Information	Remarks and references to Appendices
La Bourse	1916 September 1st		We were relieved by the 2. West Yorkshire Regt at 3 p.m. punctually, in the Hohenzollern Sector, Right sub Section, and marched to billets in Labourse.	
"	2nd		Brig. General Pollard Comdg. 25th Inf. Brigade inspected the drafts the Battalion had received during the last two months. Battalion rested in billets.	
"	3rd		The G.O.C. the Division presented the Military Medal Ribbon to Sgt. Rugley W. Carlile and spoke to Officers & N.C.O's about the raid the Battalion made on night 24/25 August. Sgt. Rugley Carlile won his Medal for work as a Stretcher Bearer on July 1st 1916.	
"	4th		In addition to permanent working party of one officer & 30 men were found for carrying French Mortar Bombs to front line. Parades under O.C. Coys.	
"	5th		Working Parties of 1 Officer & 50 men by day & 3 Officers & 110 men by night.	
"	6th		Two Working Parties cancelled. Parades under O.C. Coys.	
"	7th		Company Football Matches were played morning & afternoon & at 5 p.m. a Boxing Competition was held. There was also a concert at night to celebrate the Regimental Birthday.	
"	8th		Final of Company Football - B. Coy - 4 - A. Coy. Nil. Semi Finals of Boxing. Sgt. Bingham beat Gunner Lambbottom R.F.A. on points & Lieut Oliver & Lieut Pollak joined for duty & were posted to "D" & "A" Coys. round competition	

Army Form C. 2118.

WAR DIARY
or
INTELLIGENCE SUMMARY

(Erase heading not required.)

Instructions regarding War Diaries and Intelligence Summaries are contained in F.S. Regs., Part II. and the Staff Manual respectively. Title Pages will be prepared in manuscript.

Place	Date	Hour	Summary of Events and Information	Remarks and references to Appendices
	Sept 1916 9th		The Battalion relieved the 2nd Bn. East Lancs Regt in the Left sub-section of the Hohenzollern Sector.	
	10th		2nd Lieut S. Knowles rejoined for duty. 2 other ranks killed 8 wounded	
	11th		One man wounded. The enemy were quiet throughout the day. Part of Northampton Trench was knocked in by enemy's shell fire.	
	12th		One man wounded. Enemy have again been very quiet.	
	13th		The Battalion was relieved by the 2nd Bn. Royal Berks Regt. and moved back to Brigade Support Trenches. Working parties of 2 officers & 125 men were found.	
	14th		Daily working parties found. Coys at disposal of O.C. Coys.	
	15th		Working parties as usual. Coys at disposal of O.C. Coys.	
	16th		Working parties as usual. C.O. held Company Commanders conference.	
	17th		The Battalion relieved the Royal Irish Rifles in the Left Sub-section, Hohenzollern Sector. 2nd Lieut. Graham & 8 other ranks joined for duty.	
	18th		Enemy have been very quiet throughout the day.	
	19th		The Enemy were quiet again to-day.	

Army Form C. 2118.

WAR DIARY
or
INTELLIGENCE SUMMARY

(Erase heading not required.)

Instructions regarding War Diaries and Intelligence Summaries are contained in F. S. Regs., Part II. and the Staff Manual respectively. Title Pages will be prepared in manuscript.

Place	Date	Hour	Summary of Events and Information	Remarks and references to Appendices
	20th		Enemy still quiet. An Officers Patrol of 2/Royal Berks Regt. went out from our lines. The enemy fired a red rocket but no action followed.	
	21st		The Battalion was relieved by 2/Royal Berks Regt. and moved into Brigade Reserve trenches, taking over from 1/Royal Irish Rifles.	
	22nd		Working Parties of 160 men. Coy Commanders Conference. Coys as disposed of N.C.Os.	
	23rd		Daily Working Parties found. Remainder of the Battalion employed making dug-outs. Brigade Commander visited the trenches.	
	24th		Daily Working Parties found. G.O. Coys visited trenches to be taken over from 2/R.Berks.	
	25th		The Battalion relieved the 2/Royal Berks in right sub-sector, Rest C, the Battalion before. The trenches were much knocked about by shell fire & heavy minenwerfer.	
	26th		Between 7.30A.M. & 11A.M. the enemy bombarded our lines with artillery and trench mortars. 5 other ranks were buried in a dug-out which was blown in by minenwerfer and could not be dug out.	
	27th		Enemy were quieter. Our artillery bombarded the enemy's trenches opposite C.4.2.7 C.4.3.	

Army Form. C. 2118.

WAR DIARY
or
INTELLIGENCE SUMMARY

(Erase heading not required.)

Instructions regarding War Diaries and Intelligence Summaries are contained in F. S. Regs., Part II. and the Staff Manual respectively. Title Pages will be prepared in manuscript.

Place	Date	Hour	Summary of Events and Information	Remarks and references to Appendices
	Sept 28th		Enemy still fairly quiet. The 14th Brigade carried out a raid on our left at night.	
	29th		The Battalion was relieved by 2/ R. Berks and moved back into Brigade Support taking over support trenches from 1/Royal Irish Rifles. Working Party of 1 Officer & 140 other ranks.	
	30th		Company Commanders Conference. Coys at disposal of O.C. Coys. Same working parties found as yesterday.	

B.S.A.
1st October 1916

Signed 2/Lieut. & a/Adjt.
2nd Bn. The Rifle Brigade

8th, Division.

25th, Brigade.

2nd, Rifle Brigade.

October, 1916.

To. The D.A.G.
G.H.Q., 3rd Echelon
Base

Herewith War Diary for month of October 1916.
Please acknowledge.

B Wilson 2/Lieut. & Adjt.
for OC
2. Bn. The Rifle Brigade.

Army Form C. 2118.

2nd R. Berks
October 1916

WAR DIARY
or
INTELLIGENCE SUMMARY
(Erase heading not required.)

Place	Date	Hour	Summary of Events and Information	Remarks and references to Appendices
Hebuterne Reserve Trenches	October 1916 1st.		Daily working parties found as usual. Coys at disposal of O.C. Coys.	
	2nd.		Coys at disposal of O.C. Coys. Daily working parties.	
	3rd.		The Battalion relieved the 2nd. R. Berks Regt. on the left sub-section, Hebuterne Section.	
Front Line	4th.		The enemy were quiet. Rapid fire was opened at intervals during the night in accordance with a scheme for a raid by the 23rd & 24th Inf. Brigades on our right. 2 other ranks wounded.	
	5th.		1 other rank wounded. The enemy were again quiet.	
	6th.		2 other ranks wounded. Enterprise was carried out on our right by 23rd & 24th Brigades.	
	7th.		The Battalion was relieved by 2nd Bn. R. Berks Regt. and moved back to Brigade Reserve Trenches. 1 other rank wounded. Other Coy Rooms joined for duty.	
	8th.		Working parties of 2 Officers & 150 men found. Coys at disposal of O.C. Coys.	
	9th.		The C.O., Coy Commdr. & R.S.O. of 8th Leicesters went & Reconnoitred the trenches & Battalion area & all information possible given to them as they are to relieve the Battalion tomorrow.	
	10th.		The Battalion was relieved by the 8th Leicesters & marched from Brigade Support through HEBUTERNE–LES-MINES to HUCHIN CAMP where they spent the night.	

Army Form C. 2118.

WAR DIARY
or
INTELLIGENCE SUMMARY

(Erase heading not required.)

Instructions regarding War Diaries and Intelligence Summaries are contained in F. S. Regs., Part II. and the Staff Manual respectively. Title Pages will be prepared in manuscript.

Place	Date	Hour	Summary of Events and Information	Remarks and references to Appendices
	Oct 16 11th		The Battalion left HOUCHIN CAMP at 8.45 A.M. & marched through VAUDRICOURT and LABEUVRIERE - to ALLOUAGNE, arriving at mid-day.	
	12th		Coys at disposal of OC Coys. Maj. Genl. R.B. Stephens C.M.G. late Commander of the Battalion, made an unofficial visit.	
	13th		Coys at disposal of OC Coys. The M.O. gave a short lecture on the use of the First Field Dressing to each Company & the Lewis Gun Detachment.	
	14th		Coys at disposal of OC Coys at 11.30 p.m. Transport & Lewis Gun Detachment left ALLOUAGNE proceeding to LILLERS Station to entrain for PONT-REMY.	
	15th		The Battalion entrained at LILLERS at 3 A.M. and arrived at PONT-REMY at 11 A.M. and marched to AIRAINNES where the night was spent on billets.	
	16th		The Battalion paraded at 7 A.M. & marched about 1½ miles on the AIRAINNES-SOUES ROAD from this point it was conveyed in French Motor Busses, each on holding 30 men. The route was via AMIENS and the destination for the Busses was from this point the CITADEL. Battalion marched about 6 miles to Corps known at THE CITADEL.	
	17th		The C.O., 2nd in Command & Coy Commdrs. visited the forward a. a. of the QUEUCOURT LES BOEUFS are. Coys at disposal of OC Coys.	
	18th		The Earl of Cavan C.B. M.V.O., Commander of the XIV Corps to which the Battalion is now attached, visited the CITADEL CAMP & addressed all officers above including those of the rank of temporary Captain, belonging to 25th Inf. Brigade.	

WAR DIARY
or
INTELLIGENCE SUMMARY

Army Form C. 2118.

Place	Date	Hour	Summary of Events and Information	Remarks and references to Appendices
	19th		The Battalion left the CITADEL at 8 A.M. & marched through CARNOY, passing TRONES WOOD BIVOUAC at NOON, where they remained until 4 p.m. Incessant rain fell practically every minute of the day. The Bn. then moved off in single file along a pair of trench bounds & relieved the 11th Buffs near LES BŒUFS, one Coy in the front line on MISTY TRENCH, three Coys in support, Battalion headquarters in an old German dug-out, which had been used by Bavarian & Prussian Staffs. A big German dump had been here & lots of bunks, shovels & R.E. stores were used by the Battalion.	
	20th		The weather improved. The artillery on both sides continued to be very active. Capt. & Q.M. W. Aldridge was wounded by shrapnel on the sag which brought up the Battalions rations, stores, which had to be carried about 5 miles at track across, water had also to be brought in a similar manner.	
	21st		Sharp frost during the night. 1 deserter from 13th Prussian Infantry Regt. surrendered to the Coy in the front line. The day was very fine & bright throughout.	
	22nd		Sharp frost again during the night. 4 casualties to mid-day at 10 p.m. Battalion moved to its assembly trenches 1/2 of "D" Coy remaining in front line. "A" Coy occupied the assembly trench next to them, with "B" Coy immediately behind, followed by "C" Coy & remainder of "D" Coy. During these operations Capt. S.W. Murray D.S.O. was wounded by shell fire on the Trench & ankles. The Battalion spent the night in these trenches which were without dug-outs, also no fires were allowed, & remained there until ZERO hour the next day.	

WAR DIARY or INTELLIGENCE SUMMARY

Army Form C. 2118.

Place	Date	Hour	Summary of Events and Information	Remarks and references to Appendices
	Oct '16		At zero hour 2.30 p.m. "A" + "B" Coys advanced out of their assembly trenches leading on to the junction of ZENITH + ECLIPSE, with the 2 Lincolnshire Regt on their right, attacking ZENITH trench. The leading waves advanced close behind the creeping barrage in good order, but the right platoon failed to strike the strong point at the junction of ZENITH + ECLIPSE as the Battalion on their right were beaten back by Machine Gun fire. The remainder of the leading waves, however, succeeded in holding a line of shell holes from N.28.a.4.4. (Misty trench) for about 130 yards towards ECLIPSE trench. At zero hour "C" Coy + ½ of "D" Coy left RAINBOW trench + occupied assembly trenches vacated by "A" + "B" Coys and at 2.55 p.m. they advanced on the same line as "A" + "B" Coys had done, again the right platoon was beaten off from the strong point at ZENITH + ECLIPSE where Captain Mr. Sampson was killed, while attempting to force an entrance (the Battalion on the right not being able to make any headway) and eventually "C" Coy + ½ of "D" Coy reached the line A + B Coys had got up to, had to dig in. from up the shell holes + construct a strong point at the end of the new trench leading to ECLIPSE trench. The other ½ of "D" Coy who were in the N half of MISTY trench joined the new trench up to MISTY.	

WAR DIARY
or
INTELLIGENCE SUMMARY

Army Form C. 2118.

(Erase heading not required.)

Place	Date	Hour	Summary of Events and Information	Remarks and references to Appendices
	23 Oct '16 cont'd		Casualties were heavy not only in the advance, but more especially in consolidating the new trench. During the night Cpl. of 13th Prussian I.R. Regt. were captured at the String front & some nine deserters & other ration party who had lost their way, & 2 Officers & 50 O.R. was sent out with one German, who had of surrendered, & brought in 30 or more close under the parapet of PURPLE trench, but were heavily fired on keeping them back. Most of the casualties were caused by machine gun fire from PURPLE trench.	
			Casualties:- Captain His. Simpson – Killed Lieut. J.R. Collot ,, ,, 2/Lieut. J.R. Greathurst ,, ,, 2/Lieut. P.V. Godwin ,, ,, Captain Sir Murray D.S.O. Wounded 2/Lieut. G. Knowles ,, ,, 2/Lieut. J.A. Braham ,, ,, 2/Lieut. A.J. Brown ,, ,, +230 other ranks killed, wounded & missing.	
	24th		The Battalion held MISTY TRENCH and the NEW trench until 11 p.m. when they were relieved by the 2nd Sherwood Foresters. About 5 P.M. Br. H.Q. Busch was wounded in the NEW trench. Lieut. Col. Heaton R.D. and D.S.O. 2/Lt. Cremer, Lieutenant, & Inss Leekam were the only officers remaining unwounded.	
	25th		The Battalion bivouaced in the open during & heavy frost near the German Dump at WINDMILL from 3 am. to 10 A.M. When proceeded under heavy shell fire to C Camp TROMEF WOOD on arrival this camp was shelled. 2 other ranks wounded	
	26th		The Battalion remained at TROMEF WOOD Camp, no parades were possible, the men spent the day in drying & cleaning their clothes kit.	

WAR DIARY — ARMY FORM C2118
2 Rifle Bde Vol 2

PLACE	DATE Oct/16	HOUR	SUMMARY OF EVENTS AND INFORMATION	Remarks references appendices
TRONES WOOD	27		Weather fine until 4 p.m. when heavy rain flooded most bivouacs.	
	28		The Battalion returned to the Carnoy Dump occupied NEEDLE & deepening trenches, relieving 2nd Devons.	
	29		Artillery on both sides very active. 10th Rants wounded	
	30		The Battalion was relieved at about 10 by the 9th Border Regt & proceeded to Camp B. TROWES WOOD. Very heavy rain fell during afternoon & night.	
	31		The Battalion left TRONES WOOD & marched to CITADEL CAMP which was reached at 3 p.m. the condition of the cross country roads was beyond description, the mud being knee deep.	

Field
2/11/16

B.M.Priest 2/Lieut.
a/Adjt 2nd Bn. The Rifle Brigade.

8th, Division.

25th, Brigade.

2 nd, Rifle Brigade,

November, 1916.

The D.A.G.,
  3rd. Echelon

R.B.636.
1-12-16.

1. Herewith War Diary for month of November 1916.
2. Please acknowledge.

P Warner 2nd Lieut: &/adjt
  for O.C.
2nd Bn. The Rifle Brigade.

Army Form C. 2118

2 Rifle Brig Nov 25

WAR DIARY
or
INTELLIGENCE SUMMARY
(Erase heading not required.)

Instructions regarding War Diaries and Intelligence Summaries are contained in F. S. Regs., Part II. and the Staff Manual respectively. Title Pages will be prepared in manuscript.

Place	Date	Hour	Summary of Events and Information	Remarks and references to Appendices
CITADEL CAMP (SOMME)	NOVR 16 1st.		Battalion remained at CITADEL. Parades under O.C. Coys.	
	2nd		Field-Marshal. H.R.H. Arthur W.P.A. Duke of Connaught & Strathearn K.G., K.T., K.P, etc. Colonel in Chief of the Rifle Brigade, inspected the Battalion at BRAY-ALBERT crossroads.	
	3rd		The Battalion left the CITADEL at 9.30 a.m. & marched to billets at MEAULTE	
MEAULTE	4th		Major General H. Hudson, C.B., C.I.E. Divisional Commander, inspected the Battalion and presented D.C.M. to C.S.M. Mitchell for gallantry in the field at the HOHENZOLLERN Redt. on Sept. 26th. 1916. Lieut. E.D.S. Caswell rejoined from the Base.	
	5th		Church Parade - in Church Army Hut. MEAULTE. Working Parties consisting of 4 B.O.R. were found. Battalion had baths at VILLE. Draft of 180 O.R. joined for duty.	
	6th		The Commanding Officer inspected the new Drafts, which were afterwards inspected by Br. Genl. J.H.W. Pollard Cm'd'g 25th Inf't. Brigade. Parade under O.C. Coys.	
	7th		Parades under O.C. Coys. Working Parties of 62 O.R. were found.	
ON MARCH	8th		The Battalion left MEAULTE at 10.15 A.M. & marched through FRICOURT-MAMETZ-MONTAUBAN reaching CARNOY at 1.45 p.m. where they encamped in huts.	
CARNOY & TRENCHES	9th		The Battalion left CARNOY at 12.45 p.m. & marched through MONTAUBAN-GUILLEMONT-GINCHY - relieved 2nd Northampton Regt. Support Battalion in HOGS BACK TRENCH. Casualties - O.R's - 4 killed 7 wounded	

Army Form C. 2118

WAR DIARY
or
INTELLIGENCE SUMMARY
(Erase heading not required.)

Instructions regarding War Diaries and Intelligence Summaries are contained in F. S. Regs., Part II. and the Staff Manual respectively. Title Pages will be prepared in manuscript.

Place	Date	Hour	Summary of Events and Information	Remarks and references to Appendices
TRENCHES	Nov. 16. 10th		Remained in Brigade Support at HOGS BACK TRENCH. Enemy heavily shelled the trenches with 2.1 c.m. between 11.30 a.m. & 4 p.m. Casualties:- O.R. 1 killed, 1 missing, 9 wounded.	
	11th		Battalion left HOGS BACK TRENCH & relieved 2nd Bn. Lincoln Regt. in the right Bn. area of the Division in front of LESBOEUFS. 2 Coys were in the front line - BENNET-TRENCH, one in support on MIRAGE, one in reserve in GERMAN TRENCH. The Battalion was the right Battalion of the British Army, the 135th French Infantry Regt. being on their right. Relief 11 p.m. & 5 a.m. enemy fired a large number of Gas Shells in vicinity of Bn. H.Q. 1 Casualty from Gas. 6 killed, 9 wounded - Shell fire.	
	12th		"C" Coy relieved by "A" Coy in BENNET. "C" Coy marched to GUILLEMONT for one night. Casualties 8 killed 10 wounded	
	13th		"C" Coy returned to trenches, taking up reserve position, bringing Bn. rations. They were heavily shelled & had 19 Casualties - 4 killed 15 wounded	
	14th		Battalion relieved in front line by 2nd Lincoln Regt. & marched to Brigade Reserve, GUILLEMONT Camp. Casualties 2 missing, 4 wounded Shell fire.	
GUILLEMONT CAMP	15th		Rested in Camp. Working Party of 110. at 8 a.m. & 150 at 8 p.m. Casualties - 1 missing, 4 wounded.	
	16th		Bn relieved at GUILLEMONT by 1st R. Inniskilling Fusiliers & marched to SANDPITS - MEAULTE arriving at 8 p.m.	

Army Form C. 2118

WAR DIARY
or
INTELLIGENCE SUMMARY
(Erase heading not required.)

Instructions regarding War Diaries and Intelligence Summaries are contained in F. S. Regs., Part II. and the Staff Manual respectively. Title Pages will be prepared in manuscript.

Place	Date	Hour	Summary of Events and Information	Remarks and references to Appendices
SANDPITS.	May 16th 17th		Rested at SANDPITS. Coys at disposal of O.C. Coys.	
	18th		As for 17th.	
	19th		Battalion entrained at EDGE HILL Station near DERNANCOURT & detrained at AIRAINES & marched 3 miles to billets at WARLUS	
WARLUS.	20th		Parades under O.C. Coys for training.	
	21st		As for 20th: 2/Lts: H.G. Priestley, J.H. Bowker, S.H. Wells, W.F. Barker joined for duty.	
	22nd		As for 20th.	
	23rd		As for 20th. 2/Lieuts: R.R. Shaw & J. Nettleton joined for duty.	
	24th		As for 20th. Military Medal awarded to, Sgt. Dale Sgt. Riston, a/Cpl McDonald, Pl. Westrop, Pl. Nelson, Pl. Hyde, Pl. Lay.	
	25th		As for 20th. Capt. J.C. Maclean. R.A.M.C. attached to the Battalion, awarded Bar to Military Cross. a/Cpl Ball awarded Distinguished Conduct Medal	
	26th		Church Parade - 10 A.M.	
	27th		Parades under O.C. Coys. 2/Lieuts: A.E. Youssell joined for duty.	
	28th		Parades under O.C. Coys	

1875 Wt. W593/826 1,000,000 4/15 J.B.C. & A. A.D.S.S./Forms/C. 2118.

WAR DIARY or INTELLIGENCE SUMMARY

Army Form C. 2118

Place	Date	Hour	Summary of Events and Information	Remarks and references to Appendices
WARLUS	Nov: 16 29th		Parades under S.C. Coys.	
	30th		As for 29th.	

B.E.J.
30th November 1916

B Mason 2/Lieut: T/adjt.
for O.C.
2nd Bn. The Rifle Brigade.

8th, Division.

25th, Brigade.

2nd, Rifle Brigade.

December, 1916.

Army Form C. 2118

2 Rifle Bde 75/8
Vol 26

WAR DIARY
or
INTELLIGENCE SUMMARY
(Erase heading not required.)

Instructions regarding War Diaries and Intelligence Summaries are contained in F.S. Regs., Part II. and the Staff Manual respectively. Title Pages will be prepared in manuscript.

Place	Date	Hour	Summary of Events and Information	Remarks and references to Appendices
Wormhout (Regt Billets)	1915 1	9.00	Companies at disposal O.C. Companies	
"	2 "		Companies at disposal O.C. Companies	
			Lieut Colonel H W E FINCH commanding 25th Brigade inspected drafts which have arrived since 7/11/15	
"	3 "		Companies at disposal O.C. Companies. Parade service 10 a.m.	
"	4 "		Companies at disposal O.C. Companies	
"	5 "		Companies at disposal O.C. Companies	
"	6 "		Companies at disposal O.C. Companies	
"	7 "		Companies at disposal O.C. Companies	
"	8 "		Companies at disposal O.C. Companies. Capt J.C. Orr reported for duty.	
"	9 "		Companies at disposal O.C. Companies. Parade service	
"	10 "		Companies at disposal O.C. Companies	
"	11 "		Companies at disposal O.C. Companies	
"	12 "		Companies at disposal O.C. Companies	

Army Form C. 2118.

WAR DIARY
INTELLIGENCE SUMMARY

(Erase heading not required.)

Instructions regarding War Diaries and Intelligence Summaries are contained in F. S. Regs., Part II. and the Staff Manual respectively. Title Pages will be prepared in manuscript.

Place	Date	Hour	Summary of Events and Information	Remarks and references to Appendices
Waolow	1916 13 Dec		Companies at disposal O.C. Companies	
"	14 "		Companies at disposal O.C. Companies	
"	15 "		Companies at disposal O.C. Companies	
"	16 "		Companies at disposal O.C. Companies. Lieut L. Webb reported for duty	
"	17 "		Companies at disposal O.C. Companies. Parade Service	
"	18 "		Companies at disposal O.C. Companies	
"	19 "		Companies at disposal O.C. Companies	
"	20 "		Companies at disposal O.C. Companies	
"	21 "		Companies at disposal O.C. Companies	
"	22 "		Companies at disposal O.C. Companies	
"	23 "		Companies at disposal O.C. Companies	
"	24 "		Companies at disposal O.C. Companies	
"	25 "		Christmas Day celebrations	

Army Form C. 2118

WAR DIARY
INTELLIGENCE SUMMARY
(Erase heading not required.)

Instructions regarding War Diaries and Intelligence Summaries are contained in F. S. Regs., Part II. and the Staff Manual respectively. Title Pages will be prepared in manuscript.

Place	Date 1916	Hour	Summary of Events and Information	Remarks and references to Appendices
Warlus (Rest Billets)	Dec 26		Major General W. B. Hereeker. D.S.O. commanding 8th Division inspected the Brigade and presented Military Medal Ribbons to 7 men of the Battalion.	
	" 27		Coys at disposal of O.C. Coys.	
	" 28		The Battalion left Warlus at 7 A.M. and marched to AIRAINES where they entrained en route for the forward area. The Battalion detrained at EDGE HILL and marched to Camp 12 near Morlancourt - resting for the night - 2/Lt H.A. Troak joined the Battalion.	
	" 29		The Battalion left Camp 12 and marched to Camp 16 near BRAY, where they rested the night. 2/Lt E.J. Ratliff joined the Battalion.	
	" 30		500 of the Battalion moved by Motor Lorries to MAUREPAS from there marched to FREGICOURT, taking over from 2nd Battalion SEAFORTH HIGHLANDERS as support Battalion. The remainder of the Battalion marched to Camp X at MAUREPAS.	
	" 31		100 men were sent back from Support Line to MAUREPAS - 8 other ranks joined the Battalion from Base.	

[signature]
Lt & Actg Adjutant
2nd Bn. The Rifle Brigade

2nd Bn. Rifle Bde.
Jan - Dec 1917.

Army Form C. 2118

WAR DIARY
or
INTELLIGENCE SUMMARY
(Erase heading not required.)

Instructions regarding War Diaries and Intelligence Summaries are contained in F.S. Regs., Part II. and the Staff Manual respectively. Title Pages will be prepared in manuscript.

2 Rifle Bde

Place	Date	Hour	Summary of Events and Information	Remarks and references to Appendices
MAUREPAS FRÉGICOURT	JANY. 1917 1st.		Working Parties of 4 Officers + 200 other ranks from Maurepas to trenches.	
	2.		Working Parties as for 1st.	
	3.		On the night of 3/4th the Battalion was relieved in the Support-Line by the 7th. Bow. D.C.L.I. & moved back to Camp 14. near BRAY	
Camp 14.	4.		Coys at disposal of O.C. Coys. Working parties of 2 Officers & 80 other ranks made found for Camp Improvement.	
	5.		Coys at disposal of O.C. Coys. Brigade Conference was held at Headqrs. 1st Royal Irish Rifles at 11.A.M.	
	6.		Coys at disposal of O.C. Coys.	
	7.		Coys at disposal of O.C. Coys.	
	8.		As for 7th. ult	
	9.		The Battalion marched from Camp 14 to the BRAY-TOURIERS for AIRAINES.	

WAR DIARY
or
INTELLIGENCE SUMMARY

(Erase heading not required.)

Army Form C. 2118

Instructions regarding War Diaries and Intelligence Summaries are contained in F.S. Regs., Part II. and the Staff Manual respectively. Title Pages will be prepared in manuscript.

Place	Date	Hour	Summary of Events and Information	Remarks and references to Appendices
WARLUS	JANY 1917 10		The Battalion reached AIRAINES at 12.45AM & marched to billets in WARLUS. The Battalion paraded at 10AM. & the reorganization of the Battalion under the new system was started.	
	11.		New organization was again practised under Company arrangements.	
	13th to 18th		Company training continued	
	19		New organization practised by Battalion.	
	20.		Battalion training continued. 2/Lieut B.R. Everett joined for duty.	
	21		Battalion Training continued. Battle Patrol Platoons & 25K. Inf. Brigade gave demonstrations at METIGNY before Major General W.G.E. Wemeker D.S.O., Commdg. 8th Division. - Brig. General Coffin Commdg. 25th Inf. Brigade. - Battalion Commanders & Officers from 8th Divisional Schools.	
	22		Battalion Training continued.	

Army Form C. 2118

WAR DIARY
or
INTELLIGENCE SUMMARY
(Erase heading not required.)

Instructions regarding War Diaries and Intelligence Summaries are contained in F.S. Regs., Part II. and the Staff Manual respectively. Title Pages will be prepared in manuscript.

Place	Date	Hour	Summary of Events and Information	Remarks and references to Appendices
WARLUS	22.		Battalion training continued.	
	23.		Battalion marched to AIRAINES - Station entrained for EDGE-HILL from there the Battalion marched to Camp 12.	
	24.		Coys at disposal of S.E. Coy. for training under the new organization.	
	25.		Coy training continued. The Commanding Officer & Bombing Officer proceeded to RANCOURT to reconnoitre the line to be taken over by Bn.	
	26.		Battalion marched from Camp 12 to Camp 17. One Officer from each Coy & Bombing Officer proceeded to RANCOURT to take over stores & from 12th South Wales Borderers	
	27.		450 men of the Battalion marched from Camp 17 to the trenches & relieved the 12th South Wales Borderers in the RANCOURT Sector - Right Sub-Sector. Details were left at Camp 21 MAUREPAS RAVINE	
	28.		Casualties 1 other rank wounded - Shell fire. Draft of 31 other ranks joined details at MAUREPAS.	
	29.		Casualties 3 other ranks killed one wounded - Shell fire. Working Party 100 other ranks & 1 Officer found from MAUREPAS for work on ABODE-LANE	

1875 Wt. W593/826 1,000,000 4/15 J.B.C. & A. A.D.S.S./Forms/C. 2118.

Army Form C. 2118

WAR DIARY
or
INTELLIGENCE SUMMARY

(Erase heading not required.)

Instructions regarding War Diaries and Intelligence Summaries are contained in F. S. Regs., Part II. and the Staff Manual respectively. Title Pages will be prepared in manuscript.

Place	Date	Hour	Summary of Events and Information	Remarks and references to Appendices
	30.		Battalion was relieved at night by 1st. Royal Irish Rifles + marched to reserve camp MAUREPAS. Working party of 1 officer 100 other ranks at night.	
Camp MAUREPAS	31.		Coys at disposal of O.C. Coys. Working party of 30 other ranks by day + 2 officers + 230 other ranks by night. Camp slightly shelled. Casualties NIL.	

2nd February 1917

B C Prevot 2/Lieut & adjt
for O.C.
2nd Bn. The Rifle Brigade

Army Form C. 2118

2 Rifle Bde
Vol 28

WAR DIARY
or
INTELLIGENCE SUMMARY
(Erase heading not required.)

Instructions regarding War Diaries and Intelligence Summaries are contained in F.S. Regs., Part II. and the Staff Manual respectively. Title Pages will be prepared in manuscript.

Place	Date	Hour	Summary of Events and Information	Remarks and references to Appendices
MAUREPAS RAVINE	1-2-17		Coys at disposal of O.C. Coys for training. 130 O.R. allotted to A & B Coys. Working parties, 25 O.R. by day - 2 Officers and 230 O.R. by night. Camps shelled slightly, day and night.	
"	2-2-17		Coys at disposal of O's. Coys for training. B'n. re-allotted to C & D & H.Q. Coys. Working party of 1 Officer and 73 O.R. by day and 2 Officers & 230 O.R. by night. Camp shelled slightly during day and night.	
"	3-2-17		Coys at disposal of O.C. Coys for training. Brigadier Genl. Coffin inspected camp. Battalion marched from MAUREPAS RAVINE Camp and relieved the 1st K.R.R. in the trenches at RANCOURT. RIGHT SUB-SECTOR. Details kept at MAUREPAS RAVINE CAMP. Working parties of 444 O.R. by day.	
"	4-2-17		Casualties 6 O.R. wounded by shell fire. Working party 1 Officer & 100 O.R. found for attack at MAUREPAS RAVINE CAMP for work on ABODE LANE. Support and Reserve Coys engaged at night carrying R.E. material to front line.	
"	5-2-17		Working parties as for 4th. O.R. Coys relieved by A & B Coys in the front line. Casualties 2 O.R. killed in pillbox 1 O.R. wounded by shell fire.	
"	6-2-17		Working parties as for 5th. 1 O.R. accidentally wounded whilst at work or digging.	
"	7-2-17		Battalion relieved in front line by 1st R.I.R. and moved back to support position at LEFOREST. Working parties as for 6th.	
"	8-2-17		Detail Camp shelled at night. Casualties NIL. Battalion engaged in working and carrying parties. Working party 5 Officers & 400 O.R. found by detail from MAUREPAS CAMP.	

B.Caror
2nd Bn. Rifle Brigade
Lt & Adjt

Army Form C. 2118

WAR DIARY
or
INTELLIGENCE SUMMARY
(Erase heading not required.)

Instructions regarding War Diaries and Intelligence Summaries are contained in F.S. Regs., Part II. and the Staff Manual respectively. Title Pages will be prepared in manuscript.

Place	Date	Hour	Summary of Events and Information	Remarks and references to Appendices
MAUREPAS CAMP	9-2-17		Working Party 50 O.R. from Battalion. Battalion engaged in carrying parties.	
"	10.2.17		The Commanding Officer and 1 Officer & 2 N.C.Os. attended a Lecture at Camp 21 on the Small Box Respirator. Working Parties as for 9th.	
"	11.2.17		The Battalion was relieved in the Support position by the 17th Welsh Regt and entrained at MAUREPAS corner for Camp 13 G.H.Q. Reserve middle area.	
Camp 13 BRAY-CORBIE(R)	12.2.17		Coys.under O.C. Coys. for training. 1 Officer attended lecture at ETINEHEM on Censorship.	
"	13.2.17		The Battalion engaged on Battalion training. Battle Patrol Platoon engaged in conjunction with Brigade B.P.Ps. for training under the supervision of Brig-Genl C Coffin D.S.O.	
"	14.2.17		The Battalion engaged in training under new organisation.	
"	15.2.17		Battalion Training cont(d). The Commanding Officer, all available Officers and 45 N.C.Os attended a Lecture at Camp 12, Subject Aerial Contact Patrol. 1 O.R. accidentally wounded during working parties.	
"	16.2.17		Battalion training cont(d) by day and night	
"	17.2.17		Battalion Training Cont(d). Baths at Camp 12 allotted to C & D Coys. No one set in after Hucks frost.	
"	18.2.17		Divine Service. Baths allotted to "A", "B" & "B" Coys.	

P Mason Lt.Col
C.O. O.C.
2nd Bn. the Rifle Brigade.

1875 Wt. W593/826 1,000,000 4'15 J.B.C. & A. A.D.S.S./Forms/C. 2118.

WAR DIARY
or
INTELLIGENCE SUMMARY
(Erase heading not required.)

Army Form C. 2118

Instructions regarding War Diaries and Intelligence Summaries are contained in F.S. Regs., Part II. and the Staff Manual respectively. Title Pages will be prepared in manuscript.

Place	Date	Hour	Summary of Events and Information	Remarks and references to Appendices
Camp 13 BRAY-CORBIE ROAD	19.2.17		Battalion Training Cont'd. The Commanding Officer, all available officers and all Platoon Sergeants attended a demonstration by the Battle Patrol Platoons of the 2nd Rifle Brigade and 2nd Royal Berks. before G.O.C. 4th Army, 8th Division, + 25th Inf. Bde.	
"	20.2.17		Rain fell most of the day. Coys under O.C. Coys for training.	
"	21.2.17		The Battalion moved from Camp 13 to Camp 17 and stayed there one night. 2/Lt Helm A.P.S.A. Keppel, 2/Lt G.H. Southall + 2/Lt W.B. Batchelor and A & B.O.R. joined for duty.	
Camp 17 SUZANNE	22.2.17		The Battalion moved by Bus from Camp 17 to front line to relieve 2 Coys of 2/W.Ridings + 2 Coys of 1/Hants Regt. in the QUARRY FARM Sector. A party of 50 O.R. remained at Schaik Camp CURLU with 3 Officers. A party of 2 Officers and 135 O.R. marched to LITTLE-DALE DUMP as permanent party for loading and pushing stores on the Light railway forward.	
QUARRY FARM SECTOR BOUCHAVESNES	23.2.17		1 O.R. despatched to England for Temporary Commission. Conditions in front line uncomfortable - much mud and water. Enemy quiet.	
"	24.2.17		Working party of 1 N.C.O and 10 men from Schaik Camp were employed working on the Camp morning and afternoon. Enemy quiet. Casualties 2 Killed. 4 Wounded. - 2 admitted to Hospital trench feet.	
"	25.2.17		Working party detailed yesterday was found to day. The Battalion was relieved in the line by 2/Linc. Regt. and moved back to Support at BOUCHAVESNES - Casualties, Wounded. 6 admitted to Hospital. Sick 2/Lt A. Baxter admitted to Hospital trench feet.	

B Marion Lt + Adjutant
2nd Bn the Rifle Brigade

Army Form C. 2118

WAR DIARY

INTELLIGENCE SUMMARY

(Erase heading not required.)

Instructions regarding War Diaries and Intelligence Summaries are contained in F. S. Regs., Part II. and the Staff Manual respectively. Title Pages will be prepared in manuscript.

Place	Date	Hour	Summary of Events and Information	Remarks and references to Appendices
BOUTHAVESNES JUNCTION WOOD	26.2.17		Working party found as on 25th. - 52 other ranks admitted to Hospital with trench feet. Enemy quiet.	
"	27.2.17		Working party found as usual. 2/Lt C.E. Coote and 2/Lt W. Brown joined for duty. Enemy Quiet. 10 other ranks admitted to Hospital. Trench feet.	
" "	28.2.17		The Battalion was relieved by 1st R.I.R. and moved back to Reserve - 3 Coys JUNCTION WOOD and 1 Coy MESSINES. Working party found as usual. Captain & Quartermaster J.H. Alldridge, R.C. joined for duty.	

B Marcel Lt. & Adjutant
for O/C
2nd Bn. The Rifle Brigade.

1875 Wt. W593/826 1,000,000 4/15 J.B.C. & A. A.D.S.S./Forms/C. 2118.

To: D.A.G.
   3rd Echelon.
   Base.

R.B. 162.
2.4.17.

Herewith War Diary for month of March 1917.

[signature]
Captain
A/Adjutant
for O.C.
2nd Bn Rifle Brigade

WAR DIARY or INTELLIGENCE SUMMARY

Army Form C. 2118

2 Lin Lin B.C. N/8

WE 29

Place	Date	Hour	Summary of Events and Information	Remarks and references to Appendices
CURLU.	1.3.17		Battalion less 2 Coys moved back from JUNCTION WOOD to LINGER CAMP, CURLU.	
JUNCTION WOOD.	2.3.17		The Battalion took up positions previously occupied on February 26th	
	3.3.17		The Battalion moved to LOCK BARRACKS (3 Coys and Bn Hd Qrs) and 1 Coy moved to LOCUST SUPPORT.	
BOUCHAVESNES SECTOR.	4.3.17		At 5.15 A.M. the 2nd Bn. R. Berks Regt attacked FRITZ and PALLAS TRENCH in conjunction with the 2nd Brigade on the left, all the objectives were gained with out strong opposition and enemy's retaliation was negligible. 2nd Bn. Lincolnshire Regt. reported nothing up and carrying parties 1 Coy moved up to support 2nd R. Berks Regt. and took up positions to Coy in our old front line and 1 Coy in the captured trenches. 1 Coy by gradual following casualties. 2 Officers and 20 other ranks being heavily shelled previous to taking up its position. The officers were 2/Lt Piddy and 2/Lt Brown. A collecting post for prisoners of 1 Officer 2/Lt Lettich and 20 other ranks was found and about 20 prisoners passed through the hands of this party. She further lost 1 other rank killed and 3 wounded during the day. 2/Lt ... the Cpl 1 Coy was employed carrying R.E. stores to the R Berks Regt. for consolidating the captured position. To night 1 Coy was sent up to wire the first line at Bouleux Ridge. One Coy took over a portion of our front line on the right of the captured trenches and took the position vacated by the Bn supports. She Battalion suffered 1 O.R. killed and 6 O.R. wounded today.	
	5.3.17		Carrying party of 1 Coy was heavily shelled by LT. PIDSLEY was seriously wounded and two other ranks wounded by 1 Coy of the Kings Liverpool Regt supply party was found of 20 O.R. under 2/Lt. BOWLER.	
	6.3.17		Carrying party of 1 Company was found today 1 Officer 2/Lt RATLIFF and 50 O.R. at present 2/Lt ... 2nd DUMP supply and attacked the attack, the Battalion lost 1 Officer and 90 Other ranks wounded and 1 wounded LITTLEDALE Carrying party of 18 Other ranks supplied the Battalion in the front line from DUMP. At night the Battalion relieved the 1/9/R. Royal Irish Rifles in the front line in position B by FRITZ TRENCH 1 Coy in the support 1 Coy holds...	
	7.3.17		Night that 2 Lieutenants an 20 other rank and the relieved was carried out without any incident	
	8.3.17		In our old front line 1 Officer 2/LT. CATES wounded & 1 OR killed 2 OR ...	
	9.3.17		some shelling took place during the day which was ... ... now took place 20 O.R. ... ... 2/Lt CATES died of wounds and one transferred ... No B. A 24	

Army Form C. 2118

WAR DIARY
or
INTELLIGENCE SUMMARY
(Erase heading not required.)

Instructions regarding War Diaries and Intelligence Summaries are contained in F. S. Regs., Part II. and the Staff Manual respectively. Title Pages will be prepared in manuscript.

Place	Date	Hour	Summary of Events and Information	Remarks and references to Appendices
BOUCHAVESNES SECTOR.	10.3.17		Shelling was rather heavier than usual 3 OR accidentally wounded.	
	11.3.17		2nd LT WELLS joined 2nd Bn Battn. On amph. last dull kirk firesin rear of our lines and one of our machines was hit and came down (direction of) RANCOURT. 10 R was wounded.	
	12.3.17		2nd LT. REDFERN joined for duty cas. the 2 O R wounded.	
	13.3.17		Trench from working saps carried out by Battalion. Battalion relieves part of I R Berks and K.R.I.R in the trenches in front of BOUCHAVESNES. Casualties 14 O R wounded.	
	14.3.17		Own and other Artillery did much fire on many front line trenches. Battalion activity was to take over a extended part from their present position in front of BOUCHAVESNES. Casualties 1 OR Killed 5 wounded.	
	15.3.17		Enemy reported retiring on our left. Shrapnel Bombers entered enemy trenches in two places. Battle Patrol Pluton joined from LITTLEDALE DUMP. Sent into front line for patrolling duty. 8 NCO's & OR joined for duty at "Details camp". LT CASSWELL reported for duty. Both aeroplanes active. Action pushed by O of Battalion.	
JUNCTION WOOD. N.R.CLERY.	16.3.17		Active patrolling and night Raid by F LANCS A. I.R. inflicted many French casualties Battalion bivid. by 13 K.I.R. a moved up to line & bivouacs at Junction Wood. 13 by 13	
			MARGATE 3 WOOD Brigade H. Q. moved. Battn. ACTION NOTES: LANGTON BROWN'S Enemy reported running away as follows FRITZ BRENNER Rgt. op. GLS ATHEVE from 3 a.m. 16th, 3rd Army Corps, WARDJUNCTION WOOD to 4 a.m. 17th, FRITZ ALLEY to French Junction S.Cov.	
	17.3.17		MIZ LION with FRITZ ALLEY & French Junction S.Cov.	
	18.3.17		Battalion relief at GRAY RUINS 4 moved to billeting area at CLERY.	
			Battalion engaged clearing up about GRA ELLIS	
MOISLAINS	19.3.17		Work was carried out at LOCK PADDACKS & many ref. to other details attached R I Rondel Relieved MOISLAINS 1 Bg ob ANGBACH joined 1 Sgt 84 ONG NCO and FRITZ Burks 1 Bn etc	
			BERTRA wher will Bay ob 28 pork as and LIVERPOOL Yh. N. YORKS Regt. 23rd Brigade and all advanced guard casualties nil	
BOUCHAVESNES	20.3.17		Battalion on leave at 11 am and move back to BOUCHAVESNES for rest making one company leaving at LIVERPOOL and one of front line.	
	21.3.17		Battalion ... casualties ...	

1875 Wt. W593/826 1,000,000 4/15 J.B.C. & A.M A.D.S.S./Forms/C. 2118.

Army Form C. 2118.

WAR DIARY
or
INTELLIGENCE SUMMARY

(Erase heading not required.)

Instructions regarding War Diaries and Intelligence Summaries are contained in F. S. Regs., Part II. and the Staff Manual respectively. Title Pages will be prepared in manuscript.

Place	Date	Hour	Summary of Events and Information	Remarks and references to Appendices
ROICHAVESNES	22.3.17		Battalion employed road making	
	23.3.17		ditto	
	24.3.17		Battalion employed road making. In afternoon Battalion moved to FRIEZ FARM. Draft of 68 O.R. and 1 Officer 2/Lt. C. Mackenzie reported, also 2/Lt. H. Barker rejoined, (strength) 2/Lt. H. Mackenzie reported sick.	
MOISLAINS	25.3.17		Battalion marched to Moislains and did church work on roads	
	26.3.17		Battalion bathed at Manencourt and fitted with small box respirators	
EQUANCOURT	27.3.17		The Battalion relieved the 2nd Lincs Reg't in the outpost line in front of EQUANCOURT Wood	
	28.3.17		Still in line. Battle Patrol Platoon pushed forward posts on to the FINS - NURLU road.	
	29.3.17		Still in line. "C" Coy pushed out patrols and occupied village of FINS night of 29th/30th and together with "D" Coy occupied a line of outposts East of FINS and along FINS-NURLU road, joining up with posts of Battle Patrol Platoon 1 Guthered 1 Rgl. wounded.	
FINS-NURLU				
DESSART WOOD. FINS-EQUANCOURT.	30.3.17		Attack on DESSART WOOD. Orders were issued to "B" Coy to advance covered by patrols of the Battle Patrol Platoon, from sunken road N.W. of FINS at 4.P.M. On emerging from the road the leading wave were met by heavy M.G. fire from the right front, but as soon as the number of men advancing was seen by the enemy, they fled and were captured with their gun by a platoon of Royal Irish Rifles on our right. The Battle Patrol Platoon & B. Coy supported by A. Coy advanced with little opposition through DESSART WOOD and after throwing out patrols and advanced Lewis Guns they dug themselves in about 200 yards to the N.E. of the Wood getting into touch with the 60th Cyclists on the GOUZEAUCOURT-FINS road to the right and the 59th Brigade of 20th Division on the left. It is worthy of note that both and Battalions of this Regiment were in line in the attack, and Battalion on the	

2449 Wt. W14957/M90 750,000 1/16 J.B.C. & A. Forms/C.2118/12.

Army Form C. 2118.

WAR DIARY
or
INTELLIGENCE SUMMARY

(Erase heading not required.)

Instructions regarding War Diaries and Intelligence Summaries are contained in F. S. Regs., Part II. and the Staff Manual respectively. Title Pages will be prepared in manuscript.

Place	Date	Hour	Summary of Events and Information	Remarks and references to Appendices
DESSART WOOD. FINS. EQUANCOURT.	30.3.17		right, and the 10th & 11th Battalions of the 109th Infantry Brigade on the centre and left respectively. Casualties. 2/Lt H.G. Adams slightly wounded at duty. 3. O.R. killed. 10. O.R. wounded. G.O.C. 8th Division telegraphed his congratulations on "an altogether successful operation." The 1st Battalion R.I.Rs. of tr the capture of DESSART WOOD advanced and occupied the ridge south of our line.	
NURLU MOISLAINS RIVERSIDE WOOD.	31.3.17		On night of 30th 31st - Battalion moved back to Billets in Riverside Wood which they took over from R.I.Rs.	

Lasallis?
Captain
A/Adjutant
for O.C.
2nd Bn. Royal Irish Brigade.

WAR DIARY or INTELLIGENCE SUMMARY

Army Form C. 2118.

2 Rifle Bde
April 1917

Place	Date	Hour	Summary of Events and Information	Remarks and references to Appendices
RIVERSIDE WOOD	1/4/17		"D" Coy front was confronted by a listening line on No. 1 & 2 Posts. Rest of Bn & other ranks formed in battalion	
"	2/4/17		Nothing hostile found in front line.	
GOUZ-LE-PRAND	3/4/17		Battalion moved up and took over outpost line from 1/4 H.L.I. in position SOREL LE GRAND. During the night "B" & "C" Coys pushed forward strong patrols to establish what hostile held 1300 yards in advance of our front line. They became unable to occupy the mill buildings on the FINS-GOUZEAUCOURT road on the high ground on our right flank. Connection was established with the 2nd 13th Brigade on the right.	
GOUZEAU-COURT	4/4/17		An attack was ordered to be carried out at 2am by 2 Royal Scots on the right, whose objective was the East end of GOUZEAUCOURT WOOD, and by this battalion against the high ground N. & West of GOUZEAUCOURT moved with a view to the WOOD and the vicinity of getting the buildings in time. The attack was ordered to take place at 2.15 a.m. At 2.15 a.m. 3 Platoon of "C" Coy advanced from the main road to capture the high ground N.E. & nearly all to get forward about 500 yards when they came under enfilade M.G. fire from the wood in front of which and a little to the N. the Royal Scots were held up. "C" Coy suffered about 17 casualties and as no further advance could be made until the right flank was secured, they dug themselves in on the ground already gained. About 5.30 a.m. when it was received that the 2nd Division had captured METZ EN COUTURE and were moving eastwards and others were moved for the battalion to capture their objective by standing patrols afterwards. The battle outpost platoon was moved up after dark and half of them were able to occupy the high ground on our left flank and orders were then given for "C" Coy to advance and establish a post in front of the left objective to the East. "D" Coy succeeded on the FINS road. This was accomplished without loss. The other half of the Second Patrol Platoon under 2/Lt Adams was sent forward to hunt up the FINS road and occupy the mill on a strong point. They succeeded in pushing forward and	

Army Form C. 2118.

WAR DIARY
or
INTELLIGENCE SUMMARY.
(Erase heading not required.)

Instructions regarding War Diaries and Intelligence Summaries are contained in F.S. Regs., Part II. and the Staff Manual respectively. Title pages will be prepared in manuscript.

Place	Date	Hour	Summary of Events and Information	Remarks and references to Appendices
PN1 GOUZEAU-COURT	4/4/17		wind, and its Whistling themselves, close to the German post. All were killed up by rifle and machine gun fire and 2/Lt Adams was hit and received casualties in attempting to capture the post. B Coy also attempted to occupy the high ground on our right flank but was unable to occupy the crest though they gained several hundred yards.	Wapped 2/Lt. A/Aghander 2/Lt. A/Azzeguie
ditto.	5/4/17		A Sist Coy was brought up to join in the attack at 10 a.m. and after about 30 recruits had been fired Sgt Crow in charge of the 2 platoons of the Battle Patrol Platoon worked their way forward and drove the Germans out of the Strong Post and pushed on down the slope and caused the enemy many casualties in the bog ground. The enemy retaliated by bringing heavy shell fire on their troops in exposed condition and after dark Sgt Crow after suffering 5 or 6 casualties brought his detachment back to the enemy trench or the crest by the Mill buildings. 2/Lt Southall in charge of B Coy Platoons on our right flank again attempted to occupy the crest but was himself wounded and 2 or 3 casualties, and it was not till after dark that this ground was occupied. Our casualties during the operations of 4th & 5th April totalled 2/Lt Southall wounded 2/Lt Southall wounded and 10 other ranks killed, 23 wounded.	
	6/4/17		The Battalion were in and organized the captured ground & they were relieved at dusk by the 13th Yorkshire Regt (40th Div) on the left and by the 2 Scottish on the right. The latter moved into Support at LIERAMONT.	
LIERAMONT	7/4/17		The Battalion rested.	
"	8/4/17		Church Parade. Captain Hon E. Coke M.C. and 2/Lt Sherman joined for duty.	

Army Form C. 2118.

WAR DIARY
or
INTELLIGENCE SUMMARY.
(Erase heading not required.)

Instructions regarding War Diaries and Intelligence Summaries are contained in F. S. Regs., Part II. and the Staff Manual respectively. Title pages will be prepared in manuscript.

Place	Date	Hour	Summary of Events and Information	Remarks and references to Appendices
LIERAMONT	9/4/17		The Battn. bathed at MONS BOIS and changed clothing	
"	10/4/17		Training at LIERAMONT.	
"	11/4/17		The Battn. moved to AIZECOURT-LE-BAS. relieving the 2nd Devon	
AIZECOURT-LE-BAS	12/4/17		Battn. finding working party	
"	13/4/17		Do. Do.	
"	14/4/17		Do. Do.	
"	15/4/17		The Battalion moved to HEUDICOURT and relieved the Sherwood Foresters. Ramoved if at 5pm by 4 Coys. At 5 minutes interval. C.O. left for battld. H.Qrs. Conference.	
HEUDICOURT	16/4/17		Battalion doing carrying work - 2nd Lindroos and 2nd Lieut. S.F. G.O.R. joined the Battn.	
"	17/4/17		Battalion resting and carrying for Royal Scots.	
"	18/4/17		Battalion relieved the IRISH RIFLES in the Outpost Line	
"	19/4/17		Battalion engaged in working on improvement to existing trenches	
"	20/4/17		At 12 midnight the 2/Leinsters Regt on our right were ordered to push forward patrols to note + endeavour to capture GONNELIEU. The Battn. was to cooperate, keeping in touch with the left of the 2/Leinster and the right of the 2/R.W.K. on our left. The 19/R.W.F. who were to cooperate with our patrols of the 2/Leins. R. pushed forward supported by their Arty. Corps. our patrols keeping in touch with them. The 2/Leins. R. patrols reached the outskirts of GONNELIEU but being unable to push through it without a still bigger gap being caused. They then called to the 2/Leins. R. Coys. to proceed through the our patrols + touch GONNELIEU withdrew to the Outpost line as ordered. The 19/R.W.F. patrols withdrew and a gap between 19/R.W.F.	

Army Form C. 2118.

WAR DIARY
or
INTELLIGENCE SUMMARY.

(Erase heading not required.)

Instructions regarding War Diaries and Intelligence Summaries are contained in F. S. Regs., Part II. and the Staff Manual respectively. Title pages will be prepared in manuscript.

Place	Date	Hour	Summary of Events and Information	Remarks and references to Appendices
COUZEAUCOURT GONNELIEU	21/4/17		Brief Summary of orders issued to Battalion prior to the attack on GONNELIEU. Known as the 2/Line R had captured the village, and military objectives near, no other information shewed that the objective had gained that Battn. would move forward and secure the line R.27.d.3.2 to R.27.d.5.5 protecting & covering the flank of the Brigade by keeping in touch with the 19/R.W.F. on the left and making a line of posts between their final objective and the Right flank of the 19/R.W.F. The following positions would be taken up on arrival before ZERO. The Battle Orbat Station would take up a position at point R.32.a.0.8. – The 2 Leading Coys on a line R.26.c.0.6 T R.32.c.0.3. The flanking Sgt at R.25.d.8.7. The reserve Coy remained at the Quarry R.31.d.3.4. Plan of attack. The Battle Patrol Platoon would advance in 4 strong patrols on a front between the CAMBRAI road and the COUZEAUCOURT – GONNELIEU road, keeping in touch with 2/Quicks & 19/R.W.F. on right respectively. D Coy (Left attacking Coy) would advance in Support of R.B.P.P. between the CAMBRAI road and the COUZEAUCOURT – GONNELIEU road at R.32.a.0.9. A Coy (Right attacking Coy) would also Support the B.P.P. moving forward from a line R.32.c.0.9 & R.32.a.0.4 both Coys keeping in touch with each other. C Coy would move forward from their present positions to the Quarry and make a Support line between R.26.c.7.9 T R.32.a.9.7, as soon as the objective had been gained. Progress of the operation.—(a) At 4.40 am no very lights had been seen & no any information received that the 2/Line R. had captured the village (b) At 4.50 AM information received that H.Very lights had been seen to be fired from the village. Immediately ordered my Adjutant to proceed to the Advanced Signal Station at R.32.a.0.9. so that he might personally direct the operations on our my orders and Adjut. me informed of the progress of the operation. (C) At 5.10 AM I received information that my Companies had commenced to move in accurate with my instructions but that the leading Coys were suffering casualties from hostile M.rifle in village and that the B.P.P were being held up by heavy machine gun and rifle fire, from a German trench R.26.c.0.4 – R.26.d.0.2 (d) Seeing that to continue the strong frontal attack would involve heavy casualties, otherwise I ordered that the B.P.P should hold on & their present position & as accurate every effort to gain a footing in the village. In the meanwhile that the left Coy should attack the trench from left flank, sending strong patrols to attack Lot R.26.d.0.4 & R.26.d.0.2	

[A7091.] W. W12839/M1293. 75. 10. 6. 1/17. D. D. & L., Ltd. Forms/C.2118/14.

Army Form C. 2118.

WAR DIARY
or
INTELLIGENCE SUMMARY.

(Erase heading not required.)

Instructions regarding War Diaries and Intelligence Summaries are contained in F. S. Regs., Part II. and the Staff Manual respectively. Title pages will be prepared in manuscript.

Place	Date	Hour	Summary of Events and Information	Remarks and references to Appendices
GOUZEAUCOURT – GONNELIEU	2/4/17		(3) At the same time I directed that the right attacking Coy. should enter the village with their patrol at R32.d.0.8. and to take both machine guns and infantry holding the trench in that sequence.	
			(B) Both these situations were successful and the enemy now almost surrounded, were forced to surrender and 46 prisoners and 2 machine guns were captured.	
			(2) This maneuver enabled the B.P.P. to enter the village from the N. and to clear the N.W. end of it.	
			(R) The B.P.P. were then ordered to take up a position in front of the final objective to secure the Leading Coys. from the danger of a counter attack.	
			(4) The two Leading Coys. supported by 2 platoons of the Firing Coy. then pushed forward to the final objective & established a line of posts. These joined at T. 1 & R.27.a.2.8. & this line is a long to cut the GOUZEAUCOURT – CAMBRAI road at R.26.B. & R.35.35.	
			(R) Remaining 2 platoons of the Flank Coy. together with the Support Coy. (less 1 Platoon of Support) commenced to dig a support line behind the Germans were between R.26.C.7.9 and R.32.a.9.P. and also man a post to protect our flank between our left post at R.26.d.4.4 and the right post of the 19 R.W.F. at R.26.a.8.5.	
			(6) When these positions had been established immediately the B.P.P. who had been bivouac in the Street fighting in GONNELIEU.	
			The success of this operation was due to the initiative and courage of the 5th Patrol Platoon which held on to ground gained under heavy fire, and the quickness with which the other Coy. acted although suffering casualties on flank of the enemy position.	
			The enemy must have suffered heavy casualties in Killed though their actual numbers known. At 5.30 a.m. when I saw that the trench & M.G. crews of the village could not hold out much longer & that the machine guns had not yet been silenced I decided to call off the fire of the Stokes Trench Battery and called them off. Unfortunately these were overrun & too late to be of any assistance in capturing the village. The Battalion felt most regretted was carried on by Lieut. H. R. Hall Shell fire, Major L. R. B. Webb. M.V.O. as his Co. a short while just previous	

Army Form C. 2118.

WAR DIARY
or
INTELLIGENCE SUMMARY.
(Erase heading not required.)

Instructions regarding War Diaries and Intelligence Summaries are contained in F. S. Regs., Part II. and the Staff Manual respectively. Title pages will be prepared in manuscript.

Place	Date	Hour	Summary of Events and Information	Remarks and references to Appendices
FONZEAUCOURT-	21/4/17		to view the progress of the Companies. Captain Jno. S. Cooke M.C. resumed the command & continued the attack. Our losses on this day were. Killed 2Lt Holland + 2 others. Wounded Major Jno A. Ellis. Captain S.G. Holland. 2Lt Horsfall 2Lt Bell + 45 other ranks. Prisoner & stretcher bearers men from the 97th S.I. Reg. and 4 complete machine gun crews. The Battalion was relieved in the Outpost line by 1/R.I.R. and moved into Support.	
CONNELIEU				
"	22/4/17		Battalion digging & wiring in the BROWN LINE.	
"	23/4/17		do do	
"	24/4/17		The Battalion relieved the 11/R.I.R. in the Outpost line. The 1/R.I.R. had advanced the outpost near the CAMBRAI Road. We improved the outpost & support lines and started a wiring. 4 Enemy patrols were found by R.I.R. We sent out wiring patrols, who although not encountering the enemy brought back very useful information.	
	25/4/17		Lieut C.H. Curtis and 23 other ranks joined the Bn. Two strong patrols were sent out with a view of capturing a sniper's post. The post was however found to be evacuated. Information was obtained of an enemy position which was successfully bombed, destroyed by our artillery.	
	26/4/17		Battalion was relieved by 11/R.I.R. and moved on to Support. 2/Lt L.H. Bland 2/Lt Brand 2/Lt Stewart assumed command of the Battalion.	
	28/4/17		Battalion employed on the W.L. + 6 + R. Subpost line	

Army Form C. 2118.

WAR DIARY
or
INTELLIGENCE SUMMARY.

(Erase heading not required.)

Instructions regarding War Diaries and Intelligence Summaries are contained in F. S. Regs., Part II. and the Staff Manual respectively. Title pages will be prepared in manuscript.

Place	Date	Hour	Summary of Events and Information	Remarks and references to Appendices
GOUZEAUCOURT	2/4/17		Battalion employed on digging in Support Line	
"	3/4/17		Battalion employed on digging in Support Line	

Army Form C. 2118.

WAR DIARY
or
INTELLIGENCE SUMMARY.
(Erase heading not required.)

Instructions regarding War Diaries and Intelligence Summaries are contained in F. S. Regs., Part II. and the Staff Manual respectively. Title pages will be prepared in manuscript.

2 Rfle Bn Vol 31

Place	Date	Hour	Summary of Events and Information	Remarks and references to Appendices
SOREL – FINS-GOUZEAUCOURT	1-5-17		The Battalion bathed at Sorel.	
	2-5-17		Companies under O.C's Coys for training.	
	3-5-17		Corps Commanders inspected the Battalion and presented Medals to the following members of the Battalion. 2/Lt. J.H.BOWLER. MILITARY CROSS. Sgt. A.Cross. Distinguished Conduct Medal. A/Cpl. E.Phillips. Military Medal. Sgt. H.Souster. Distinguished Conduct Medal. Divisional Commander congratulated all ranks of the Battalion, on their smart turnout and soldierly bearing, on the Corps Commanders inspection. 2/Lt G.H. 2/Lt.G.C.Chatfield and 8 other ranks joined for duty.	
	4-5-17		Battalion working on Light Railway, between Fins and Gouzeaucourt. Southall awarded Military Cross, for gallantry and devotion to duty	
	5-5-17		Battalion working on Light Railway between Fins and Gouzeaucourt. 2/Lt.W.A.Martin joined for duty.	
	6-5-17		Battalion working on Fins-Gouzeaucourt Light Railway.	
	7-5-17		ditto.	
	8-5-17		ditto.	
VILLERS-GUISLAINS	9-5-17		Battalion relieved 2nd East Lancs Regt in Outpost Line, East of Villers Guislains. Work on improvement of positions. Casualties . 2. other ranks. 1 Troop of the Corps Cavalry Regt. (Royal Wilts Yeomanry) attached for instruction in reconnaissance, patrols etc.	

Army Form C. 2118.

WAR DIARY
or
INTELLIGENCE SUMMARY.
(Erase heading not required.)

Instructions regarding War Diaries and Intelligence Summaries are contained in F. S. Regs., Part II. and the Staff Manual respectively. Title pages will be prepared in manuscript.

Place	Date	Hour	Summary of Events and Information	Remarks and references to Appendices
VILLERS-GUISLAINS	10-5-17		Patrols reported Honnecourt Wood strongly held and the enemy busy in improving his defences. Casualties. 3 other ranks.	
	11-5-17		2/Lt C.E.Pegram and 9 other ranks joined for duty.	
	12-5-17		Battalion (less 1 Company) was relieved by 1st R.I.R's and moved into Brigade Reserv S.W. of Villers Guislains. Battalion worked all night on 2nd line defences.	
	13-5-17		Battalion worked all night on second line defences.	
NURLU	14-5-17		Battalion was relieved by 21st Middlesex Regt, and moved into Corps reserve at Nurlu. Casualties. 1 other rank.	
	15-5-17		Battalion bathed at Sorel. Refitting of Clothing & necessaries.	
	16-5-17		Training was begun under Platoon arrangements.	
	17-5-17		Training of the Battalion continued. Draft of 2/Lt G.H.Jackson M.C.and 23 other ranks joined for duty. Sports were held in the evening.	
	18-5-17		Training continued. Sports held in the evening.	
	19-5-17		The Battalion carried out firing on the range.	
	20-5-17		Church Parade.	
	21-5-17		Training continued. The Divisional Commander presented Medal ribbons to C.S.M. F.Birtwistle (Distingusined Conduct Medal)	
	22-5-17		Training during the day was prevented by rain. A night march by compass was carried out.	
	23-5-17		Training as usual. Captain A.H.Pelham Burn, and 33 other ranks joined for duty.	

Army Form C. 2118.

WAR DIARY
or
INTELLIGENCE SUMMARY.
(Erase heading not required.)

Instructions regarding War Diaries and Intelligence Summaries are contained in F. S. Regs., Part II. and the Staff Manual respectively. Title pages will be prepared in manuscript.

Place	Date	Hour	Summary of Events and Information	Remarks and references to Appendices
NURLU	24-5-17		Musketry Training.	
	25-5-17		Training continued.	
	26-5-17		Training continued. 30 yards range in the Camp was completed.	
	27-5-17		Church Parade.	
	28-5-17		Battalion training continued. 2/Lts W.Brown. L.H.Hillman, and J.M.L.Renton joined for duty.	
	29-5-17		The Battalion marched from Nurlu Camp to Aizecourt-le-Haut, taking over from 1st Sherwood Foresters.	
AIZECOURTLE HAUT	30-5-17		Battalion Training continued.	
	31-5-17		The Battalion marched from Aizecourt-le-Haut to Camp 17 in the morning. Bathing parades took place during the afternoon.	

2nd June 1917.

J. Brand
Lieutenant-Colonel,
Commanding 2nd Battn.The Rifle Brigade.

WAR DIARY
or
INTELLIGENCE SUMMARY.
(Erase heading not required.)

Army Form C. 2118.

2 Rfl Bde Y/1/32

Place	Date	Hour	Summary of Events and Information	Remarks and references to Appendices
HIZECOURT-LE-HAUT	1/6/17		The Battalion marched from HIZECOURT-LE-HAUT to VAUX-SUR-SOMME arriving therein and was billeted in the outskirts of the village. The weather was hot & sultry throughout the march.	
VAUX-SUR-SOMME	2/6/17		The Bat. was scattered in various small groups being trained under canvas.	
" "	3/6/17		The Rifle bn. less one Coy. & one Coy of 1st Kings Royal Rifles entrained at HEILLY & on arrival these the Battalion marched to CROIX ROUGE and the one Coy. which remained at rear joined 2moro on the 5.	
CROIX ROUGE	4/6/17		The Company which remained at VAUX-SUR-SOMME entered the Battalion Lines at the village rejoined. About 1 noon. Musketry training and bayonet fighting carried out by the Coy. who also attached at CROIX ROUGE on the 3d inst.	
	5/6/17		Training of Specialists, Musketry and bayonet fighting continued. Kitcl. and Burman and 20 other ranks joined the Battalion for duty.	
	6/6/17		Training continued. as on 5th inst. during the afternoon 2 officers were allotted to Coys	
	7/6/17		Training continued. 2Lieut. J. Lewis and 52 other ranks joined the Battalion for duty.	
	8/6/17		Training continued	
	9/6/17		Training continued. 12 other ranks wounded in duty.	
	10/6/17		Training continued	

Army Form C. 2118.

WAR DIARY
or
INTELLIGENCE SUMMARY.
(Erase heading not required.)

Instructions regarding War Diaries and Intelligence Summaries are contained in F.S. Regs., Part II. and the Staff Manual respectively. Title pages will be prepared in manuscript.

Place	Date	Hour	Summary of Events and Information	Remarks and references to Appendices
ROUGE CROIX	11/6/17		The Battalion marched from ROUGE CROIX to billets situated near P.27.d.1.4. in S. Belgium & France. (Ref 27). 16 other ranks joined for duty.	
"	12/6/17		Training continued. The Battle Patrol Platoon was used to assist N.C.Os recently returned to their Companies.	
S.W. of CAESTRE	13/6/17		Training continued. The Battalion marched to new area S.W. of CAESTRE at noon P.31.W.1.Y.4.T. (P.31) Weather fine and very hot. 247.W.O. Field and 35 other ranks joined for duty.	
S.E. of POPERINGHE	14/6/17		Battalion marched to new area 3 miles S.E. of POPERINGHE (map reference BELGIUM and FRANCE (F.23.A.8.3.). The 2nd Battalion was about 2 miles away (S.E. 2670) & kindly joined for duty.	
"	15/6/17		Training continued.	
"	16/6/17		Training continued.	
"	17/6/17		2nd Lt. Church Grundy was Adjutant during past week very free and hot. The Battalion marched to Baths (about 3 miles N.E.)	
"	18/6/17		Training continued. 8 other ranks joined for duty.	
E. of STEENVOORDE	19/6/17		Battalion marched back to new area. Map reference Sheet 27 BELGIUM and FRANCE. R.34 and 35 (about 2 miles E. of STEENVOORDE).	
"	20/6/17		Training continued.	
"	21/6/17		Battalion Training (Attack).	

Army Form C. 2118.

WAR DIARY
or
INTELLIGENCE SUMMARY.

(Erase heading not required.)

Instructions regarding War Diaries and Intelligence Summaries are contained in F. S. Regs., Part II. and the Staff Manual respectively. Title pages will be prepared in manuscript.

Place	Date	Hour	Summary of Events and Information	Remarks and references to Appendices
Ei STEENVOORDE	22/6/17		Training continued. 1 Officer and 140 Other Ranks sent to Summer Rest Camp for 14 days.	
"	23/6/17		Battalion training (Attack)	
"	24/6/17		Sunday. Weather unfavourable, no church parade.	
"	25/6/17		Battalion training etc. Inspection of Companies at work by Corps Commander	
"	26/6/17		Lieut Elliot Jacob R.C.B. Training continued.	
"	27/6/17		Training continued.	
"	28/6/17		Training continued.	
POPERINGHE	29/6/17		B of C, 1, 2 and 3 Platoons of D Co marched to Headquarters 171st Tunnelling Coy at F.21.d (Sheet 27) & will be attached to 171st Tunnelling Coy & working parties	
DOMINION CAMP VLAMS-POPERINGHE	30/6/17		The Battalion less B, C & D Coy marched to DOMINION CAMP (G.23.8. Central Sheet 28).	

R. Brand Lieut- Colonel
Comdg 2nd Bn...

A5834 Wt. W4973/M687 750,000 8/16 D. D. & L. Ltd. Forms/C.2118/13

D.A.G.
3rd Echelon

Herewith War Diary for
July 1917 made up to 30th
only, under instructions of
25th Infantry Brigade.

C. Mackern 2/Lieut
for Lt. Colonel
Comdg 2nd Rifle Brigade

Army Form C. 2118.

2 Rfl Bde
Vol 33

WAR DIARY
or
INTELLIGENCE SUMMARY.
(Erase heading not required.)

Instructions regarding War Diaries and Intelligence Summaries are contained in F. S. Regs., Part II. and the Staff Manual respectively. Title pages will be prepared in manuscript.

Place	Date	Hour	Summary of Events and Information	Remarks and references to Appendices

A5834 Wt. W4973/M687 750,000 8/16 D. D. & L. Ltd. Forms/C.2118/13

Army Form C. 2118.

WAR DIARY
or
INTELLIGENCE SUMMARY.

(Erase heading not required.)

Instructions regarding War Diaries and Intelligence Summaries are contained in F. S. Regs., Part II. and the Staff Manual respectively. Title pages will be prepared in manuscript.

Place	Date	Hour	Summary of Events and Information	Remarks and references to Appendices

A 5834   Wt. W4973/M687   750,000   8/16   D. D. & L. Ltd.   Forms/C.2118/13

Army Form C. 2118.

WAR DIARY
or
INTELLIGENCE SUMMARY.
(Erase heading not required.)

2 RB   Vol 34

Instructions regarding War Diaries and Intelligence Summaries are contained in F. S. Regs., Part II. and the Staff Manual respectively. Title pages will be prepared in manuscript.

Place	Date	Hour	Summary of Events and Information	Remarks and references to Appendices
VLAMERTINGHE	1/8/17		The Battalion arrived at HALIFAX Camp at about 10.30.am.	
	2/8/17		Re-organising etc.	
OUDERDOM	3/8/17		Parades under O.C. Coys. 2/Lt. O.R. joined for duty. Captain W. Stock R.A.M.C. joined for duty as Medical Officer vice Captain J. C. Maclean invalided	
	4/8/17		Parades under O.C. Coys.	
STEENVOORDE	5/8/17		Sunday. Church Parade at 11 am. Battalion proceeded by Bus to billets in and around STEENVOORDE. Latter part of week, weather very bad.	
	6/8/17		Battalion Training.	
	7/8/17		Training. 5 1 O.R. joined for duty.	
	8/8/17		Training.	
	9/8/17		Training.	
	10/8/17		The Battalion left STEENVOORDE by Bus at 8.15 pm and debussed near HALIFAX Camp, marched to SWAN CHATEAU and took over dugouts there.	
VLAMERTINGHE – OUDERDOM.	11/8/17		Had message to say Operations postponed, and marched back to HALIFAX CAMP in evening.	
YPRES – OUDERDOM.	12/8/17		Marched up to YPRES in the afternoon and took over tunnels in the ramparts at "The Esplanade" and "Lille Gate". Lt.Col. Hon R Brand being supernumary-Brigade Commander in case of a casualty. Major J.J.B.Cole had temporary command of the Battalion.	
WESTHOEK.	13/8/17		2/Lt. Everett went up to the line on WESTHOEK Ridge with guides so as to lead the Battalion up in the evening. Head of Battalion marched out of MENIN Gate at 8.10.pm. with 200 yards distance between double platoons. We picked up two Brigade guides at BIRR Cross roads, and set off over a very badly shell pitted country deep in mud. Battn closed up in single file. After going about ½ hour the enemy opened a heavy barrage of 4.2" and we all round, and we stopped under what cover we could for about 20 minutes till it calmed down. The guides next lost their way, and it was nearly 2 O'clock in the morning before we had entirely taken over the line from the 8th Cheshire Regt.	

Army Form C. 2118.

WAR DIARY
or
INTELLIGENCE SUMMARY.
(Erase heading not required.)

Place	Date	Hour	Summary of Events and Information	Remarks and references to Appendices
EAST OF YPRES	23/6/17		A & D Coys in the firing line under Captain Milne and Captain Curtis, H.Q. & C Coy (Capt. Pegram) in support in JAFFA Trench on the top of the WESTHOEK Ridge, and B Coy (Capt. Heaton-Ellis) in reserve in BELLEWARDE Ridge. The Lincolns (25th Bde) held on our right and the Scottish Rifles (23rd Bde) on our left. The Support trench was more or less continuous though entirely demolished in many places, but the front line was only held in short lengths of trench and posts.	
	24/6/17		Three enemy aeroplanes appeared low over our trenches in the early morning firing their machine guns but causing no casualties. A good deal of shelling during the day, and in the evening about 8.45 pm a very heavy barrage was put down on our support line during which 2/Lt. & A/Adjutant C.Mackeson was severely wounded while sending up S.O.S. Signals at the request of the Lincolns on our right. He lived all that night in the H.Q. Dugout and was removed in a stretcher the next day, apparently better. However, he most unfortunately died later at BRANDHOEK, after an operation. Patrols active during the night.	
	25/6/17		Plenty of work by C & B Coys in carrying fatigues. B had a particularly hard time of it and worked very well. The front line trenches were shelled and sniped, some of our own 6" shells falling between our front and support lines. Luckily a Major of R.F.A. was in our O.P. at the time, and we got off his corroborative evidence by pigeon straight to the Corps. The gunners couldnt then say " The - Infantry always say its us when they are shelled". During the day 2/Lt. Nettleton made a reconnaissance of the country with guides to lead up the Royal Irish Rifles to their position of attack. 2/Lt Everett was to have done this but he took over A/Adjt. when 2/Lt Nett Mackeson was hit. After dark we were going to advance out line down to the road 300 yards W of HANNEBEEK but the Division on our right were driven back sligtly, so that the Lincolns had to withdraw their their right Company. Our gunners also put down a light barrage this side of the road so that the scheme fell through and we remained in our old front line position, but cleared up all ground to the road by patrols. 2/Lt. H.Barker arrived about 7 pm amd joined D Coy for duty in the front line about 10.30 pm.	

Army Form C. 2118.

WAR DIARY
or
INTELLIGENCE SUMMARY.
(Erase heading not required.)

Instructions regarding War Diaries and Intelligence Summaries are contained in F.S. Regs., Part II. and the Staff Manual respectively. Title pages will be prepared in manuscript.

Place	Date	Hour	Summary of Events and Information	Remarks and references to Appendices
EAST OF YPRES	16/8/17		The Battalion was in support to the Royal Irish Rifles and Royal Berkshire Regt. the Lincolns being in reserve. We had to find 2 Coys (A & D) as an immediate support to the R.I.R. with orders to advance at Zero plus.20 and take up a position 100 yds E of the HANNEBEEK and wait there for orders ready to act on any emergency. Zero was fixed for 4.45.am.and at Zero minus 50 minutes A & D Coys had to retire back to the support trench (a distance of about 300 yds) only leaving out 4 small posts which were withdrawn at Zero minus 30 minutes. At Zero minus 50 orders were sent to B Coy in reserve to join the Battalion, taking cover in JAFFA Avenue as near JAFFA Trench as possible. This message failed to reach them, though the Coy joined the Battalion later. At Zero minus 40 minutes we were ordered by Brigade to furnish one Coy to mop up for the R.I.R. as their mopping up Company had nearly all become casualties. D Coy who had mopped up on the 31st July was detailed for this job and Captain Curtis was hurriedly given an idea of the ground and what he had to do. The attack started well and at Zer plus 1 hr 15 mins I had a message from A Coy that they had reached their objective 100 yds E of the HANNEBEEK. From about 8.30. am I could see that everything was not going quite right in front, and was rather worried as my support Coy C who had been out carrying all night had not yet returned. There were only 8 Lewis Guns with 2 men each, and ½ of B Coy with me in the support trench. At 9.45 am I saw that the attack was on our right front on the ridge about J 7 c had failed and the Germans had counterattacked successfully, driving the Regiment there back and taking some prisoners. Numbers of stragglers of various regiments were now filtering back right up to the support line so I advanced with every available man I could find to our old front line trench. Here I found Capt Milne with ½ A Coy and various men of other regiments. The Battalion did good execution among the bosches wh were advancing from shell-hole to shell hole down the opposite slope of the valley during the rest of the morning and early afternoon. At 4.15 pm Captain Curtis got to Bn. H.Q. with ½ dozen riflemen, he having been till then in shell holes E of the HANNEBEEK with a mixed lot of R.B. R.I.R. and West Yorks and only retired when out of ammunition and practically surrounded. D Coy had killed about 20 Germans during their mopping up and sent back over 40 prisoners, but when advancing to support the troops in front who had been heavily counter-attacked and driven back, they suffered very heavy casualties themselves. All of C Coy who had got lost on the BELLEWARDE Ridge the night before had by now joined up so that when a message came down from Brigade to advance with every possible man to Repel a threatened German counter attack and to counterattack	

WAR DIARY
or
INTELLIGENCE SUMMARY.

(Erase heading not required.)

Army Form C. 2118.

Instructions regarding War Diaries and Intelligence Summaries are contained in F. S. Regs., Part II. and the Staff Manual respectively. Title pages will be prepared in manuscript.

Place	Date	Hour	Summary of Events and Information	Remarks and references to Appendices
EAST OF YPRES.	16/8/17		counter-attack them in turn with the sword, we were able to put about another 50 men into the firing line. Captain Curtis being slightly wounded since the 14th and very exhausted, was left behind at old Bn. H.Q. with 2/Lt. Nettleton who had been blown up and rather shaken by a shell, to help him. 2/Lt. Pinnock with his 5 Signallers & 4 runners were also left to look after communications. On the whole the telephone line between firing line and Bn. H.Q. in the support trench line worked very well, greatly owing to the efforts of A/C Colter. About 6 pm Genl. Coffin came along the front line to our bit of the trenches making a reconnaisance of the position. He told us that we were to be relieved that night by the 8th Sherwood Foresters and would be withdrawn to an old support line in JAFFA trench. Half the Battalion were relieved that night by 11 pm but 2 Coys of the Sherwood Foresters lost themselves on that trackless and shell pitted ground between BELLEWARDE and WESTHOEK Ridge so that A & C had to be relieved during daylight on the 17th. This was successfully done by 9.20 .a.m.	
	17/8/17		10 Signallers joined for duty. Cleaned up dead out of the trench, salvaged rifles, ammunition etc made it more of a continuous trench and handed over to the Lincolns at 10 pm.while we went back into reserve on the BELLEWARDE Ridge. Just before relief the Bosch put down a heavy barrage of H.E. and gas shells 200 yards behind us and down wind.	
	18/8/17		Had a quiet day on BELLEWARDE Ridge cleaning up in the sun and watching the batteries and working parties near BIRR X Roads have a very bad time of it from the enemy's heavies. Marched back at 6 pm - BIRR X Roads- MENIN Gate - YPRES Cloth Hall - Esplanade - KRUISTAAT - Belgian Battery Corner - Groenen Jager -X Roads to Camp at HALIFAX where the Colonel and Captain Alldridge were waiting for us with a hot meal. Casualties during tour of duty in trenches and battle of 16th August:- 2/Lt. C.Mackeson died of wounds Capt. H.H Elliott R.A.M.C. wounded at duty. 2/Lt. H.Barker missing Other Ranks 10 killed 2/Lt. R.H.Robinson Died of wounds 72 wounded 2/Lt. E.F.Ratliff wounded 50 missing Capt. A.H.Curtis wounded at duty 6 wounded at duty 1 died of wds.	

Army Form C. 2118.

WAR DIARY
or
INTELLIGENCE SUMMARY.
(Erase heading not required.)

Instructions regarding War Diaries and Intelligence Summaries are contained in F.S. Regs., Part II. and the Staff Manual respectively. Title pages will be prepared in manuscript.

Place	Date	Hour	Summary of Events and Information	Remarks and references to Appendices
OUDERDOM - AMERTINGHE	19/8/17		Church Parade and Baths in the morning at HALIFAX Camp. In the afternoon the Battalion moved back to BORRE by bus. The Transport preceded the Battalion being brigaded under the Brigade Transport Officer. Billetted that night at BORRE.	

CAESTRE AREA	20/8/17		Companies under Company Commanders reorganising and refitting.
			Military medals awarded to:
			1152 -A/Cpl. G.Stone (Bar to M.M.) 3631 A/Cpl. H.Salter
			15441 Rfn. W.Nelson 200893 Sgt. V.Scrivener
			971 Rfn. H.Bullen 15960 Rfn. H.Warner
			2866 Rfn. W.Tomlinson 14851 Rfn. A.Tippen
			1821 A/Cpl. J.Stayton 200627 Rfn. G.Goddard
			3183 Rfn. J.Vince
			Reinforcements joined as under:-
			    2/Lt. H.A Barker
			    " H.F Cranswick
			    " E.B.Tangtie and 289 other ranks.	

	21/8/17		The men were of good physique and above the average standard. The Division was inspected by the Commander in Chief, being drawn up in 3 sides of a square. Captain C.W.H.Baillie Ox & Bucks L.I. took up the duties of Acting Adjt. vice 2/Lt. C.Mackegson.	
BORRE	22/8/17		Parades under Company Commanders. C.O. inspected drafts received since 31-7-17. 9764 C.W. M.Sgt. A.E Trueman appointed to permanent Commission as 2/Lt. in Regular Army and posted to the Battalion for duty.	
	23/8/17		Parades under O.C.Coys. Reorganising the Coys with 4 Platoons.	

	24/8/17		The Brigade paraded for C.of E Service conducted by the Rev A.S.Crawley, Senior Divisional Chaplain, assisted by the Rev J.A.Kitson The Service was attended by the II Anzac Commander, Major General Sir A J Godley K.C.B. K.C.M.G. and the Divisional Commander. Reinforcements joined as under:- 2/Lt. C.H.Cooke
			    " D.A.Gibbs
			    " R.C.Cook
			    " G. Gamble
			    " H.A. Sutton	

Army Form C. 2118.

WAR DIARY
or
INTELLIGENCE SUMMARY.

(Erase heading not required.)

Instructions regarding War Diaries and Intelligence Summaries are contained in F. S. Regs., Part II. and the Staff Manual respectively. Title pages will be prepared in manuscript.

Place	Date	Hour	Summary of Events and Information	Remarks and references to Appendices
BORRE —	24/8/17		Lt. Col. the Hon. R.Brand.D.S.O. took over Command of Brigade the Brigadier proceeded on leave.	
CAESTRE AREA.	25/8/17		Regimental Birthday. No Parades, but Sports were held under Coy arrangements. A Concert was held in the evening.	
	26/8/17		No Parades. Voluntary Services (C of E) held at Coy billets.	
	27/8/17		The Battalion under Major J.J.B.Cole M.C. marched from BORRE at 6 am to KORTEPYP Camp near NIEPPE. The 25th Brigade relieving a New Zealand Brigade forming Divisional Reserve. Honours and awards granted to Officers, N.C.Os and men as under:- D.S.O. Capt I.C.Maclean M.C. RAMC Military Cross. Capt(A/Major) J.J.B.Cole 2/Lt.(A/Capt) H.R.Price. 2/Lt. N.Redfern(Attd 25th T.M.Battery) D.C.M. 6197. R.SM. J.Furey 5822 Rfn. P.Blazeby Military Medal 26586 Rfn.Sgt F.Barnes. 3954 Cpl. C.Lacon 9202 Rfn. J.Cartwright. 678 Rfn. H.Lane. Parchment Certificate 4765 Sgt. E.Leege.	
KORTEPYP. CAMP. NR NIEPPE.	28/8/17		Training under Coy Commanders.	
	29/8/17		Training under Coy Commanders.	
	30/8/17		Commanding Officer (Major J.J.B.Cole M.C.) with 4 Coy Commanders, and L.G.Offr. reconnoitred the front system of trenches but unable to proceed to actual front line by day.	

A5834 Wt.W4973/M687 750,000 8/16 D. D. & L. Ltd. Forms/C.2118/13

Army Form C. 2118.

WAR DIARY
or
INTELLIGENCE SUMMARY.
(Erase heading not required.)

Instructions regarding War Diaries and Intelligence Summaries are contained in F. S. Regs., Part II. and the Staff Manual respectively. Title pages will be prepared in manuscript.

Place	Date	Hour	Summary of Events and Information	Remarks and references to Appendices
KORTEPYP CAMP. NR NIEPPE.	31/8/17		Training under Coy Commanders. Parchment Certificates awarded by Divisional Commander for gallantry and devotion to duty East of YPRES between 15th & 16th August 1917. 397 Cpl. J. Spellman. 2766 Rfn. W. Farrell 385000 Rfn. H. Bint.	
	2-9-17.			

[signature] Major.
Commanding 2nd Bn. The Rifle Brigade.

Army Form C. 2118.

2 Rifle Brigade
Vol 35

WAR DIARY
or
INTELLIGENCE SUMMARY.
(Erase heading not required.)

2nd BN. THE RIFLE BRIGADE
No.
Date
8th DIVISION

Instructions regarding War Diaries and Intelligence Summaries are contained in F. S. Regs., Part II. and the Staff Manual respectively. Title pages will be prepared in manuscript.

Place	Date	Hour	Summary of Events and Information	Remarks and references to Appendices
CAMP NEUVE-EGLISE	1-9-17		Companies under Company Commanders for Training	
	2-9-17		Church Parade.	
	3-9-17		Companies under Company Commanders for Training. 15 O.R. joined for duty.	
	4-9-17		Companies under Company Commanders for Training. Lieutenant Colonel the Hon. R.Brand D.S.O. awarded BAR TO DISTINGUISHED SERVICE ORDER for gallantry and devotion to duty EAST of YPRES 31st July – 1st August 1917.	
	5-9-17		Companies under Company Commanders for Training	
	6-9-17		-----------do----------	
	7-9-17		-----------do----------	
NEAR KORTEPYP	8-9-17		No.4215 Rifleman W.Johnson of A Company awarded MILITARY MEDAL for gallantry and devotion to duty near YPRES between 15th & 18th August 1917.	
			Companies under Company Commanders for Training. 12 O.R. joined for duty.	
	9-9-17		Voluntary C. of E.Service. The following awards granted for gallantry and devotion to duty EAST of YPRES between 15th & 17th August 1917:– THE MILITARY CROSS– Captain A.H.Curtis – Captain H.H.Elliott R.A.M.C. – 2/Lt. E.F.Ratliff. BAR TO DISTINGUISHED CONDUCT MEDAL 6602 Company Sergeant Major F.Birtwistle. THE MILITARY MEDAL – No.Z/281 Lance Corporal C.Colter. 2/Lt. W.Bridgeman joined for duty.	
	10-9-17		Companies under Company Commanders for Training.	
RED LODGE NEAR PLOEGSTEERT WOOD	11-9-17		Battalion moved into Brigade Support at RED LODGE (Sheet 28 S.W. T.18.d.7.4.) relieving 1st Bn. Sherwood Foresters.	
	12-9-17		Company Training and Refitting of Clothing.	

Army Form C. 2118.

WAR DIARY
or
INTELLIGENCE SUMMARY.
(Erase heading not required.)

Instructions regarding War Diaries and Intelligence Summaries are contained in F. S. Regs., Part II. and the Staff Manual respectively. Title pages will be prepared in manuscript.

Place	Date	Hour	Summary of Events and Information	Remarks and references to Appendices
RED LODGE NEAR PLOEGSTEERT WOOD	13-9-17		Battalion found Working parties for R.E.	
	14-9-17		------do------	
	15-9-17		------do------. 9 O.R. Joined for duty.	
	16-9-17		------do------	
	17-9-17		------do------	
	18-9-17		MERITORIOUS SERVICE MEDAL awarded to No.1522 Sgt. C.Ransted for gallantry and devotion to duty near ROMARIN during bombing practice on 15th September 1917.	
ST YVES SECTOR.	19-9-17		The Battalion relieved the 2nd. Bn. Royal Berkshire Regt. in the trenches. A & B Coys *in front line* C Coy in support and D Coy in reserve, Headquarters at ST YVES WARNTON SECTOR.	
	20-9-17		Quiet day with occasional shelling on support line. C Company found working parties to assist A & B Coys on work in front line. D Coy found carrying parties.	
	21-9-17		2/Lt. C.H.Cooke and 1 O.R. killed and 3 O.R. wounded by shell fire at dawn. The remainder of the day was quiet. Work as on previous night. 2/Lts J.B.Lund,D.F.Thuillier A.J.Sluman and C.B.Matheson joined for duty.	
	22-9-17		Slight shelling in early morning and evening. Work as on previous night.	
PLOEGSTEERT	23-9-17		Inter Company relief C. Coy relieved A, and D Coy relieved B. The enemy attempted to raid one of our posts in front of LA BASSE VILLE, on being discovered cutting our wire they tried to rush the trench by throwing bombs. 2Lt. C.B.Matheson was killed and 2/Lt. G.Gamble subsequently died of wounds. 2 Sergeants killed and 5 O.R. wounded The bodies of 5 Germans were found in front of our trench. No German reached our trench. A great deal of shelling at night, 2/Lt. H.A.Barker being wounded. Total casualties 5 O.R. killed and 12 O.R.wounded.	
WARNETON	24-9-17		Slight Shelling. 2 O.R. killed and 3 O.R.wounded. Work as on previous days.	

Army Form C. 2118.

WAR DIARY
INTELLIGENCE SUMMARY.
(Erase heading not required.)

Instructions regarding War Diaries and Intelligence Summaries are contained in F. S. Regs., Part II. and the Staff Manual respectively. Title pages will be prepared in manuscript.

Place	Date	Hour	Summary of Events and Information	Remarks and references to Appendices
ST. YVES. WARNETON SECTOR.	25-9-17		Slight shelling and a few minenwerfers fell on our front line. Captain A H Curtis wounded. 1 O.R. killed and 10 O.R. wounded.	
	26-9-17		Heavy shelling about midday on Support line. 6 O.R. killed and 12 O.R. wounded. 4 O.R. joined for duty.	
	27-9-17		Inter Brigade relief. Battalion relieved by 1st Bn. Worcester Regt. and marched back to Camp. at DE SEULE Following awards granted for gallantry and devotion to duty EAST of YPRES between 15th & 17th August 1917:- BAR TO THE MILITARY MEDAL - No.2/922 Sergeant A Dale- No.3585 Rfn. J.Vince. MILITARY MEDAL: No.2561 L/Sgt. O.Gerrard- No. 2278 Rfn. J.Tracey- No.19907 Rfn. J.Berry - No.1583 Sgt. W.Small- No. Z/696 Rfn. A Derrington No.25735 Rfn. W.Moore- No.1754 Rfn. T.Masters- No.2491 Rfn. G.Hendle No.3289 L/Cpl. J.Webster- 29624 Rfm. A.Addison- No.1534 Cpl. T.Rogers- No.25847 Sgt. W.Partridge.	
DE SEULE CAMP BAILLEUL-ARMENTIERES ROAD 	28-9-17		Companies under Os C Coys. 2/Lt. E.F.Ratliff joined for duty.	
	29-9-17		Companies under Company arrangements.	
	30-9-17		Church Parade at 10.a.m.	
	2/10/17.			

Lieutenant-Colonel
Commanding 2nd. Battalion The Rifle Brigade.

Army Form C. 2118.

WAR DIARY
or
INTELLIGENCE SUMMARY.
(Erase heading not required.)

Instructions regarding War Diaries and Intelligence Summaries are contained in F. S. Regs., Part II. and the Staff Manual respectively. Title pages will be prepared in manuscript.

2 Rfl Bde Vol 56

Place	Date	Hour	Summary of Events and Information	Remarks and references to Appendices
BAILLEUL - NIEPPE DE SEULE CAMP ROAD	1-10-17		Companies under Company Commanders for Training.	
	2-10-17		Companies under Company Commanders for Training.	
	3-10-17.		Companies under Company Commanders for Training, 3 Companies worked under R.E. at night.	
	4-10-17		Companies under Company Commanders for Training. No.5701 Rfn. H.Barnard awarded the MILITARY MEDAL for gallantry and devotion to duty on night 23-9-17 at LA BASSE VILLE. Working party of 250 under R.E.	
	5-10-17		Companies under Company Commanders for Training. 2/Lt.D.P.Jones joined for duty. Working party of 250 under R.E.	
	6-10-17		Companies under Company Commanders for Training. Working-party of 250 under R.E.	
	7-10-17		Parade Service (C.of E.) at 10 am. Baths for Battalion.	
	8-10-17		Companies under Company Commanders for Training. Working party of 250 under R.E.	
	9-10-17		Companies under Company Commanders for Training. No.3339 Sergeant R.Doveton awarded DISTINGUISHED CONDUCT MEDAL for gallantry and devotion to duty at LA BASSE VILLE on night of 23/24-9-17.	
	10-10-17		Companies under Company Commanders for Training. Working party of 200 under R.E.	
	11-10-17		Companies under Company Commanders for Training.	
	12-10-17		Companies under Company Commanders for Training. Working party of 200 under R.E. Divisional Commander presented Medal Ribbons to Officers, N.C.Os and men for gallantry in action E.of YPRES	

Army Form C. 2118.

WAR DIARY
or
INTELLIGENCE SUMMARY.

(Erase heading not required.)

Instructions regarding War Diaries and Intelligence Summaries are contained in F. S. Regs., Part II. and the Staff Manual respectively. Title pages will be prepared in manuscript.

Place	Date	Hour	Summary of Events and Information	Remarks and references to Appendices
ROMARIN CAMP NEAR PLOEGSTEERT.	13-10-17		25th Infantry Brigade relieved 24th Infantry Brigade, and Battalion moved into Brigade Reserve at ROMARIN, relieving 1st. Battalion Sherwood Foresters. 2/Lt. F.E.A.Fulford joined for duty. Casualties:- 1 Other rank wounded.	
	14-10-17		Parade Service (C.of E.) at 10.30.am. Battalion found working parties of 215 for work at night under R.E. and Pioneers.	
	15-10-17		Companies under Company Commanders for Training. Working parties as for 14th.	
	16-10-17		Companies under Company Commanders for Training. Working parties as for 14th.	
	17-10-17		Companies under Company Commanders for Training. Working parties of 175 for work at night under R.E.& Pioneers. Baths for Battalion.	
	18-10-17		Companies under Company Commanders for Training. Working parties as for 17th.	
	19-10-17		ditto	
	20-10-17		ditto.	
WARNETON FRONT LINE SECTOR	21-10-17		Battalion relieved 2nd. Bn. Lincolnshire Regt. in front line, WARNETON Sector. C & D Coys in front line, B Coy in Support, C Coy in Reserve, Battn. H.Q. ST.YVES	
	22-10-17		Intermittent shelling. Work:- A and part of B Coy. carried. Remainder of B Coy assisted front line Coys with work. Casualties- 1 other rank wounded by shell fire.	
	23-10-17		Continual shelling and Trench Mortar fire on LA BASSE VILLE and front line. Casualties- 2 other ranks killed, 12 wounded. Work- As for 22nd. Following Officers joined for duty:- 2/Lts. A.G.Tyndal, J.Brooker and G.E.Collins.	
	24-10-17		Intermittent shelling and Trench Mortar fire. Casualties- 3 other ranks wounded. 2/Lt. D.F.W.Baden-Powell joined for duty.	

(A7092) Wt W12859/M1293. 75,000. 1/17. D.D. & L., Ltd. Forms/C.2118/14.

WAR DIARY
or
INTELLIGENCE SUMMARY.

Army Form C. 2118.

(Erase heading not required.)

Instructions regarding War Diaries and Intelligence Summaries are contained in F. S. Regs., Part II. and the Staff Manual respectively. Title pages will be prepared in manuscript.

Place	Date	Hour	Summary of Events and Information	Remarks and references to Appendices
FRONT LINE WARNETON SECTOR	25.10.17.		Less shelling than two previous days. Casualties- 1 other rank wounded.	
	26.10.17.		A quiet day. On the night of 25/26th 2/Lt. J.E.Lund took out a patrol of 2 men between BASSEVILLE and WARNETON to investigate an enemy trench. He left the men of his patrol about ¾ of the way across No man's land and proceeded alone to the enemy wire. When on the wire, 2 Germans passed inside the wire within ten yards of him, one of whom he wounded with a revolver shot. This alarmed the garrison consisting of about 12 men, who, after a moments panic, commenced to bomb 2/Lt. Lund who maintained his position, and though sligh tly wounded in the wrist by a German bomb returned the enemy's fire with Mills bombs and revolver. He succeeded in pitching one bomb in amongst a party of four men, but could not see the effect. Owing to the danger of being separated from his men, he with- drew after some time. Quiet day. no casualties	
	27.10.17. 28.10.17.		A Quiet day, e xcept for Trench Mortar fire. At 9 pm. 2/Lt.E.B.Anstie and a party of 25 other ranks raided the enemy trenches under artillery barrage. They succeeded in entering enemy trenches, and killing one German, but the remainder of the- garrison of the post raided, ra n away while our party was getting through the wire. Our casualties w ere in the raid were:- 5 other ranks slightly wounded, 1 other rank missing(believed blown up by shell) Other casualties during the day 3 other ranks killed by trench mortar fire in a front line post.	
	29.10.17.		After dawn, e xceptionally quiet day. 3 other ranks wounded by shell fire. Battalion was relieved by 1st Bn. Worcester Regiment, and moved into.DE SEULE Camp. Following Officers joined for duty:- 2/Lts. H.Coles, C.F.Sidney and A.F.A. Woodward.	
DE SEULE CAMP BAILLEUL - NIEPPE ROAD.	30.10.17.		Insp ections and refitting clothing of Coys and Detts. Baths for Battalio n.	
	31.10.17.		Companies under Company Commanders for Training.	

(signed) W.H. Maude
Captain 1st /16. Colonel.
Comdg. 2nd Bn. The Rifle Brigade.

NO. 27.
MESSAGE MAP.
German Trenches Corrected to 24-10-17.

Div. Boundary
Front Line ......
Batt'n Boundary
Company Boundary
Barrage Zero +?
Barrage Zero +?
Front line after attack.

Scale 1:10,000.

Printed by an Advanced Section, A.P.&S.S.

MESSAGE FORM.

To:—   NO.

1. I am at........................ { Note:—Either give Map Reference or mark your position by a 'X' on the Map on back.

2. I have reached limits of my Objective.

3. My Platoon / Company is at........................and is consolidating.

4. My Platoon / Company is at........................and has consolidated.

5. Am held up by (a) M.G. / (b) Wire at........................(Place where you are).

6. Enemy holding strong point........................

7. I am in touch with........................on Right / Left. at............

8. I am not in touch with........................on Right / Left.

9. Am shelled from........................

10. Am in need of:—

11. Counter Attack forming at................

12. Hostile (a) Battery
           (b) Machine Gun   } active at........................
           (c) Trench Mortar

13. Reinforcements wanted at........................

14. I estimate my present strength at............rifles.

15. Add any other useful information here:—

                                        Name........................
                                        Platoon......................
Time............m.   Company......................
Date............1917.   Battalion....................

(A). Carry no maps or papers which may be of value to the Enemy.

(B). Give no information if captured, except the following, which you are bound to give:—
        Name and Rank.

(C). Collect all captured maps and papers and send them in at once

D.A.G.
3rd Echelon
Base

Herewith War Diary of this
Battalion for month of
November 1917.

[signature]
Lieut
for Captain
Comdg 2nd Bn Rifle Brigade

Army Form C. 2118.

WAR DIARY
or
INTELLIGENCE SUMMARY.
(Erase heading not required.)

Instructions regarding War Diaries and Intelligence Summaries are contained in F. S. Regs., Part II. and the Staff Manual respectively. Title pages will be prepared in manuscript.

Place	Date	Hour	Summary of Events and Information	Remarks and references to Appendices
SEULE CAMP BAILLEUL - ARMENTIERES ROAD.	1-11-17		Companies under Coy.Commanders for Training.	
	2-11-17		Companies under Coy.Commanders for Training. R.C. Church Parade Service at BAILLEUL to commemorate soldiers of Allied Forces who have fallen in the War.	
	3-11-17		Companies under Coy. Commanders for Training.	
	4-11-17		C.of E. Parade Service at 10 am. 21 other ranks joined for duty.	
	5-11-17		Companies under Coy. Commanders for Training.	
	6-11-17		Companies under Coy. Commanders for Training. The following were awarded the MILITARY MEDAL for gallantry and devotion to duty near WARNETON on 28th Oct.1917. 24308 L/Cpl. J.Jordan 21908 Rfn. G.Ball.	
	7-11-17		Companies under Coy. Commanders for Training.	
	8-11-17		Companies under Coy. Commanders for Training. Baths for Battalion.	
	9-11-17		Companies under Coy. Commanders for Training.	
	10-11-17		Companies under Coy. Commanders for Training. Final of Brigade Boxing Tournament results - FEATHERS Runner up. Cpl Lewsey- Welter Winner A/Cpl. Dorow- MIDDLE Runner up. Sgt. Rye- HEAVY Winner. C.Q.M.Sgt. Bingham 2/Lt:g G.H.C.Anderson, J.B.Macgeorge, and W.Morrison joined for duty. C. of E. Parade Service at 10 am. 10 other ranks joined for duty.	
NEAR VIEUX-BERQUIN	11-11-17		Battalion moved into billets in the RUE DU BOIS and RUE VERTE, VIEUX BERQUIN. 2/Lt. B.R.Everett struck of strength of Battalion from 7-9-17. 'sick'	
	12-11-17			
	13-11-17		Companies under Coy. Commanders for Training.	

Army Form C. 2118.

WAR DIARY
or
INTELLIGENCE SUMMARY.

(Erase heading not required.)

Instructions regarding War Diaries and Intelligence Summaries are contained in F. S. Regs., Part II. and the Staff Manual respectively. Title pages will be prepared in manuscript.

Place	Date	Hour	Summary of Events and Information	Remarks and references to Appendices
NEAR VIEUX-BERQUIN	14-11-17		Companies under Coy. Commanders for Training. No.6197 R.S.M. J.Furey M.C. joined for duty.	
	15-11-17		Companies under Coy. Commanders for Training.	
	16-11-17		The Battalion marched to CAESTRE where they entrained. The Battalion detrained at YPRES and marched into bivouacs at C Camp. WIELTJE.	
WIELTJE Near YPRES.	17-11-17		The Battalion moved into the line N.W. of PASSCHENDAELE relieving the 47th Canadian Inf. Battn.- 1st Division on the left, 2nd. Lincolnshire Regt. on right. Heavy shelling on Battalion front during relief and throughout the night.	
PASSCHENDAELE SECTOR YPRES FRONT	18-11-17		Battalion remained in the line and were heavily shelled, the enemy several times putting down intense barrages. During the night the Battalion advanced their line in the centre, straightening out a re-entrant, without any opposition.	
	19-11-17		Heavy shelling of our front and support lines and communications throughout the day. The Battalion were relieved at night by the 2nd. East Lancashire Regt. During the tour the Battalion experienced heavier shelling than on any previous occasion. CASUALTIES:- 2/Lts. A.G.Tyndall and A.F.A.Woodward killed- 2/Lt. J.B.Lund wounded. Other Ranks. 77 killed, 87 wounded. 22 missing	
	20-11-17		The Battalion entrained at WIELTJE and proceeded to "B" Camp BRANDHOEK.	
POPERINGHE - VLAMERTINGHE Rd	21-11-17		Companies under Coy. Commanders for Training. Baths for Battalion.	
	22-11-17		Companies practised in forming up for the attack.	
	23-11-17		Companies practised in forming up for and advancing to the attack. 2/Lt. King-Harman joined for duty.	
BRANDHOEK	24-11-17		Battalion Training by day- Company Training by night.	
	25-11-17		Brigade Training by day- Battalion Training by night.	
	26-11-17		Brigade Training by day - Brigade Training by night.	

A5834 Wt.W4973/M687 750,000 8/16 D. D. & L. Ltd. Forms/C.2118/13.

Army Form C. 2118.

WAR DIARY
or
INTELLIGENCE SUMMARY.
(Erase heading not required.)

Instructions regarding War Diaries and Intelligence
Summaries are contained in F. S. Regs., Part II.
and the Staff Manual respectively. Title pages
will be prepared in manuscript.

Place	Date	Hour	Summary of Events and Information	Remarks and references to Appendices
BRANDHOEK	27-11-17		Battalion Rested.	
POPERINGHE-VLAMERTINGHE ROAD	28-11-17		Companies paraded in Battle Order for Inspection by the Commanding Officer. Baths for Battalion.	
ST. JEAN area.	29-11-17		Battalion moved to "F" Camp ST. JEAN. 2/Lt. C.B. Keppie joined for duty.	
Near YPRES.	30-11-17		Battalion, less details, moved to CAPRICORN Camp.	

3/12/17.

J.H. Hill
Lieut.
for Captain
Comdg. 2nd/7 Bn. W. Yorks Brigade.

WAR DIARY
INTELLIGENCE SUMMARY.
(Erase heading not required.)

Army Form C. 2118.

Place	Date	Hour	Summary of Events and Information	Remarks and references to Appendices
N.E. PASSCHENDAELE – ST. JEAN. (NR YPRES)	1st Dec. 1917		At dusk the Battalion marched by road to WATERLOO and then by track No. 5 N. to assembly positions N.E. of PASSCHENDAELE. Lt. Colonel Hon R. Baird D.S.O. wounded. Lt. G.H.Q. Anderson M.C. took over command of the Battalion.	
	2nd "		At 1.55 AM. A, B, and C Coys advanced to the attack on a frontage of 370 yards. D Coy remained in the original front line. The attacking waves came immediately under intense machine-gun fire and suffered heavy casualties. They succeeded in advancing about 100 yards beyond the front line, where they dug themselves in, but were unable to reach their objectives or to capture the redoubt, known as VENISON TRENCH, in the centre of the Battalion front. Before 9 p.m. and 2 midnight the Battalion was relieved by a 5th Battalion and marched to HASLAR CAMP, ST JEAN. Casualties:— Capt. E.J. Ratcliff M.C. } Killed 2/Lt. 75 Morrison. } " J. Brooker } 2/Lt. G. Thos George } " R.P. Jones } " E.M. King-Harman } Wounded " R.F.W. Sladen-Powell } " H.F. Cranswick } " W. Bridgeman } O.R. 21 Killed - 72 wounded - 21 missing	
WIZERNES – ACQUIN	3rd "		The Battalion proceeded by buses from ST. JEAN to WIZERNES and marched to billets at ACQUIN. Captain C.W.H. Baillie took over command of the Battalion.	

Army Form C. 2118.

WAR DIARY
INTELLIGENCE SUMMARY.
(Erase heading not required.)

Instructions regarding War Diaries and Intelligence Summaries are contained in F. S. Regs., Part II. and the Staff Manual respectively. Title pages will be prepared in manuscript.

Place	Date	Hour	Summary of Events and Information	Remarks and references to Appendices
ACQUIN (TRAINING AREA)	4th Dec 1917		Battalion inspected by the Corps Commander. Battalion bathed. The following Awards granted for gallantry and devotion to duty near PASSCHENDAELE between 19th and 19th Nov 1917.	
			B₁ R₁ to Military Medal.	
			MILITARY MEDAL	
			No. 4012 Sgt. A. Shepland. No. 6429 Sgt. A. Smith. No. 1522 Sgt. J. Ranwell " 4819 "Cpl. J. Whiting " 1767 Rfn. J. Gibson " 11858 Rfn. J. H. Whittaker " 643 " C. Halcomb	
			Battalion reorganised on 8 double-Platoons	
	5th Dec		Coys under O.C. Coys for training and Reorganization. 28 O Rs joined for duty.	
	6th Dec		Coys under O.C. Coys for training.	
	7th "		Coys under O.C. Coys for training.	
	8th "		Coys under O.C. Coys for training. Major J.J.B. (86 M.G. Coys) over command of the Batt?	
	9th "		C. of 'E' Parade Service at 11 a.m. Captain S. A. Hadland - 2/Lt S. Logan - P. T. Dent - W. H. Kearn M.C/M.M. 2/L. C. J. Eyston - 27 O Rs joined for duty.	
	10th "		Coys under O.C. Coys for Training	
	11th "		Coys under O.C. Coys for Training.	
	12th "		Coys under O.C. Coys for Training.	
	13th "		Coys under O.C. Coys for Training. Lt. P.C.S. Stevenson joined for duty.	
	14th "		Coys under O.C. Coys for Training. Following Awards granted by Divisional Commander for gallantry and devotion to duty near PASSCHENDAELE between 20th Nov and 2nd Dec 1917.	

WAR DIARY
INTELLIGENCE SUMMARY.

(Erase heading not required.)

Army Form C. 2118.

Place: ACQUIN (TRAINING AREA.)

Date	Hour	Summary of Events and Information	Remarks and references to Appendices
14th Dec 1917 (Cont'd)		PARCHMENT CERTIFICATE No. B/723 Rfn. F.C.A. Hignton No. 28322 Rfn. W. Sims No. 15448 Rfn. F.L. Golledge " S/28497 " E. Derrick " S/14464 " H. Southall " 2/67 " T.H. Bate " 2/40 " S. Swinsoe	
15th Dec		Coys under O.C. Coys for Training. Divisional Cross Country run. Bat'n Team 6th	
16th Dec		C. of E. Parade Service at 11 a.m.	
17th "		Coys under O.C. Coys for Training. Brigade Cross Country run. Bat'n Team 1st & 16 O.R. joined for duty. Transport inspected by O.C. 8th Div Train	
18th "		Coys under O.C. Coys for Training. Following Awards granted for gallantry and devotion to duty near PASSCHENDAELE between 20th Nov & 3rd Dec. 1917. MILITARY MEDAL No. 397 Cpl. (A/Sgt.) now Sgt. L. Spelman No. 2753 A/Cpl. now Cpl. (A/Sgt.) R. Davis " S988 A/Cpl. now Cpl. T. Stainer. 743 Sgt. R. Bloodworth " 4984 Rfn. B. Pearce. 3831 Rfn. W. McEvoy	
19th "		Coys under O.C. Coys for Training. Battalion bathed.	
20th "		Coys under O.C. Coys for Training.	
21st "		Coys under O.C. Coys for Training.	
22nd "		Inter-platoon Auto Matching and Miniature Range shooting Competition 1st 7 & 8 Platoon 2nd 11-12 Platoon	
23rd "		Christmas Day celebrated on this date throughout the Brigade Church Parade (C. of E.) 10 a.m. Finals of Divisional Boxing Competition RESULT: Light weight Cpl. Brooks HEAVYWEIGHT Sgt/Cpl Bingham	
24th "		Battalion bathed.	

WAR DIARY / INTELLIGENCE SUMMARY

Army Form C. 2118.

Place	Date	Hour	Summary of Events and Information	Remarks and references to Appendices
ACQUIN.	24th Dec '17 (Contd)		Following awards granted for gallantry and devotion to duty at PASSCHENDAELE between 2nd Nov. & 3rd Dec 1917:— **MILITARY CROSS** Capt. J.C. PASCOE M.C. 2/Lt. (Acting) C.P. Pegram 2/Lt. (now Lieut.) G.H.S. Anderson M.C. 2/Lt. A.H. Burman **DISTINGUISHED CONDUCT MEDAL** No.1522 Sgt. C. Ransted. No.26847 Sgt. W.C. Partridge 8 O.Rs joined for duty	
	25th Dec		1st Line Transport moved from ACQUIN to YORK CAMP, BRANDHOEK.	
	26th Dec.		Battalion marched to WIZERNES STATION, proceeded thence by rail to ST JEAN and then marched to JUNCTION CAMP.	
JUNCTION CAMP. ST JEAN. NR YPRES.	27th Dec		Coys. under O.C. Coys for Training.	
	28th Dec.		B.C. & D Coys paraded for work under R.E. and 22nd Bn. D.L.I. The Camp was shelled during the morning and afternoon. 1 O.R. wounded.	
	29th Dec		Coys under O.C. Coys for Training.	
	30th Dec		Battalion relieved the 19th Bn. Sherwood Foresters in support at BELLEVUE.	
NR PASSCHEN- DAELE	31st Dec		Battalion found carrying parties to the Front Line. Quiet day. 2 O.R. wounded.	

2nd January 1918

J. [signature]
Lieutenant
for Lt. Colonel
Commanding 2nd Bn. The Rifle Brigade.

SECRET.

Report of the part played by the 2nd Batt: The Rifle Brigade
in the recent operations at PASSCHENDAELE
Reference attached photo. Map.

1. ASSEMBLY. This was carried out with comparative easy.
Neither the enemy's artillery nor machine guns were particularly active.

2. FORMING UP. Little interference from the enemy with the exception
of close-range sniping from TEAL COTTAGE. Owing to the latter
being in the enemy's possession it was found necessary to throw back
the left flank from the point where the tapes ended on the left
(i.e. about 250 yards from the MOSSELMARKT – WALLEMOLEN
road) to join hands with the 32nd Division.

3. ADVANCE. Very intense machine-gun fire commenced immediately
after ZERO and continued until ZERO +60. Two machine guns
were seen firing from TEAL COTTAGE and three from the front
of the Northern Redoubt (which was strongly held) but there
were certainly others firing direct from the flanks and
probably many more. Carry out indirect fire from the line
WRANGLE FARM – WROTH FARM. Intermittent bursts of
machine-gun fire continued from ZERO + 60 until dawn.
The advance was checked for the following reasons:-
(a) The number of casualties rendered further progress impossible.
(b) The front trench of the Northern Redoubt and shell-holes
in front of and to the flanks of this position were strongly
held by enemy who had been pushed out in front of our barrage.
(c) The 32nd Division having failed to take TEAL COTTAGE our
left was in the air and it was necessary to throw back
a defensive flank.

4. CONSOLIDATION. Posts of from 3 to 6 men each were formed
in shell-holes.

5. HOLDING THE LINE. The enemy's attitude throughout the day
following the attack was aggressive. Several attempts were made
to raid our posts but these were driven off. There was also
a considerable amount of bombing and rifle bombing from the
enemy's forward posts. Except for a few hours during
the morning, it was practically impossible, owing to h...
and accurate sniping, to get from post to post. T...
was never established with the units on our left

2.

6. <u>RELIEF.</u> All posts were taken over by the relieving units. Relief was carried out individually by small bodies of men and few casualties were sustained.

7. <u>COMMUNICATIONS.</u> Throughout the operations communication from the front to the support-line and thence to Batt. HQ was entirely by runner.

8. <u>GENERAL REMARKS.</u> Visibility in the moonlight was up to 500 yards. The moon was behind us. It seems obvious that the enemy observed our forming up, but instead of interfering with it, pushed forward posts and machine-guns in front of our barrage-line. Consequently when our barrage commenced the machine-gun fire increased rather than lessened.

It was very noticeable that there was practically no enemy barrage on our front or support line, their artillery fire being practically confined to the back areas and the ground between the support line and MOSSELMARKT. Even in these areas it was not very heavy.

From our new line the ground slopes very slightly to the Northern Redoubt and thence steeply to the N.E.

There was a considerable number of enemy dead between our advanced posts and the Northern Redoubt.

J.H. Anderson
Lt.
a/adjt. 2nd Batt. Rifle Bde

6th December 1917.

Headquarters 25th Infantry Brigade.   SECRET

In reply to your No. BS/77, herewith information as required:-

(a) **BARRAGE**. 1. Very efficient.
   2. Not many shorts.
   3. Pace was found suitable.

(b) **ASSEMBLY**. Carried out with only slight interference from the enemy, although from their subsequent action, the forming up on the tapes was apparently observed by them.

(c) **ENEMY FIRE**. 1. No enemy barrage on our front or support lines. Searching fire from about 200 to 0 in rear of support line.
   2. Machine gun fire particularly deadly. Machine guns firing low — about 2 feet from the ground.

(d) **FORMING UP**. 1. Under the circumstances (ie. Teal Cottage being in the hands of the enemy) the tapes were all that could be desired.
   2. The direction tapes proved useful in the absence of any apparent landmarks.

(e) **EQUIPMENT**. 1. The men were not overloaded in any case.
   2. There was no shortage, except of Very lights.

                                    S. Anderson
                                    Lt.
                                    a/Adjt.
                                    2nd Battn. Rifle Brigade.

6th December 1917.

4th Copy.

History

Army Form C. 2118.

WAR DIARY
—or—
INTELLIGENCE SUMMARY.
(Erase heading not required.)

Instructions regarding War Diaries and Intelligence Summaries are contained in F.S. Regs., Part II. and the Staff Manual respectively. Title pages will be prepared in manuscript.

Place	Date	Hour	Summary of Events and Information	Remarks and references to Appendices
BELLEVUE – PASSCHENDAELE SECTOR	1.1.18		Battalion still in support at BELLEVUE, carrying to front line – Casualties nil. Quiet day.	
	2.1.18		Battalion still in support at BELLEVUE carrying – Enemy Aircraft showed some activity. 2/Lt. A.G.Sutton killed. 1 O.R.Killed. 2 O.Rs wounded.	
	3.1.18		Battalion were relieved on night of 2nd/4th by the 2nd Devon Regt. and moved by train from WIELTJE to BRANDHOEK. – Shelled slightly during relief – Casualties 2 O.Rs wounded.	
"B" CAMP, BRANDHOEK	4.1.18		Battalion at BRANDHOEK. Cleaning up and Bathing.	
POPERINGHE – VLAMERTINGHE ROAD	5.1.18		BRANDHOEK. Training under Company arrangements.	
	6.1.18		BRANDHOEK. Church Parade. Following HONOURS & AWARDS published in the London Gazette. MENTIONED IN DESPATCHES. December 18th 1917. Lt-Col. The Hon. F.Brand.D.S.O. 2/Lt. B.E.Everest. 2/Lt. J. Nettleton. 2/Lt. C. Mackeson. (died of wounds) 2876. C.S.M.H. Spencer. 8478. C.M.S.A. Foreman. 8589. C.Q.M.S.G. Bingham. 8/655. Sergt.H. Steele.O.B.E. S/461. Cpl.J.Potterton. (attd.A.P.M.) DECEMBER 21st 1917. Captain.I.V.MacLean.D.S.O. M.C. (R.A.M.C.) late attd. PROMOTED FOR DISTINGUISHED CONDUCT IN THE FIELD January 1st, 1918. To be Hon.Major. Honorary Conduct in the Field Captain & Quartermaster.J.H.Alldridge.M.C. AWARDED MILITARY CROSS. 2/Lt. H.H.Darby. 5571.C.S.M. A.E.Richardson.	

A.534 Wt.W4973/M687 750,000 8/16 D.D.&L.Ltd. Forms/C.2118/13

Army Form C. 2118.

WAR DIARY
INTELLIGENCE SUMMARY.
(Erase heading not required.)

Instructions regarding War Diaries and Intelligence Summaries are contained in F.S. Regs., Part II. and the Staff Manual respectively. Title pages will be prepared in manuscript.

Place	Date	Hour	Summary of Events and Information	Remarks and references to Appendices
WIELTJE - ST JEAN	7.1.18		Battalion moved to WIELTJE-ST JEAN area. H.Q. and A.& B. Companies at JUNCTION CAMP. C.& D.Companies at CALIFORNIA CAMP.	
	8.1.18		Battalion finding Working Parties.	
	9.1.18		Battalion on Working Parties.	
	10.1.18		ditto. Draft of 9 O.Rs joined for duty.	
WIELTJE - ST JEAN AREA	11.1.18		Battalion on Working Parties. 2/Lt. G.E.Collins killed by shell fire. 1 O.R. ditto.	
	12.1.18		Battalion on Working Parties. Following Officers joined for duty. 2/Lt. B.E.Everett, Lt. L.S.Chamberlen,M.C. 2/Lt. R.T.Parkin, 2/Lt. W.M.Gardiner, 2/Lt. H.M.Small, 2/Lt. G.E.Lascelles, 2/Lt. D. Gault.	
	13.1.18		H.Q. A.& B.Companies moved from JUNCTION CAMP to join remainder of Battalion at CALIFORNIA CAMP. Working Parties. 1 O.R. wounded.	
	14.1.18		Working Parties. Casualties. 2 O.Rs killed 4 wounded.	
BELLEVUE - PASSCHENDAELE SECTOR	15.1.18		The Battalion relieved 2nd.Bn. The Devon Regt at BELLEVUE. Casualties Lt-Col J.J.B. Cole M.C. wounded by Shell Fire. Relief carried out in a heavy snow storm. Captain F.D.R.Milne took over command.	
	16.1.18		Battalion relieved the 1st Royal Irish Rifles in the line (left sub-sector). Condition of posts was extremely bad. Enemy activity slight. Casualties caused by our own artillery. 2/Lt. W.M. Gardiner killed. 2 O.R. killed 6 O.Rs wounded. 7 O.Rs missing	

Army Form C. 2118.

WAR DIARY
INTELLIGENCE SUMMARY.

(Erase heading not required.)

Instructions regarding War Diaries and Intelligence Summaries are contained in F. S. Regs, Part II. and the Staff Manual respectively. Title pages will be prepared in manuscript.

Place	Date	Hour	Summary of Events and Information	Remarks and references to Appendices
PASSCHENDAELE SECTOR	17.1.18		Battalion holding the line. - working on improvement of posts at night - conditions continued very bad. Enemy Artillery inactive. Slight shelling of Battalion H.Q. (Pill Box 83.) Casualties 1 O.R.wounded.	
E. OF STEENVOORDE	18.1.18		Battalion holding the line - relieved at night by the 2nd Battn. Royal Fusiliers (29th Division). Enemy inactive - a quiet day. On relief, Battalion marched out to WIELTJE and thence entrained to ABEELE - whence they were conveyed by lorry to Billets at K.28, K.29, K.74, K.75. East of STEENVOORDE	
STEENVOORDE	19.1.18		Battalion established in Billets. H.Q.at K.75.a.7.9. Major S.A.Hedland took over Command of the Battalion. Battalion specially mentioned in Brigade Orders of 16th inst. "The work done during the last week by the 2nd Battalion The Rifle Brigade "on the Divisional Reserve line, is reported by Lt.-Col.Sherbrooke D.S.O. "1st Sherwood Foresters (attached H.Q.8th Division) to be extremely good "particularly the work done by the Company commanded by Captain H.Heaton-"Ellis. The Brigade Commander is very pleased to have received "this excellent report, and wishes to congratulate all ranks of the 2nd "Battalion, The Rifle Brigade."	
	20.1.18		Battalion resting and cleaning up.	
EAST OF STEENVOORDE	21.1.18		Battalion resting - cleaning up and re-fitting.	
	22.1.18		Training under company arrangements. ditto. Following extract from report of inspection of Transport dated 19.1.18. "General Condition excellent. The Turnout of Transport of 2nd Bn. "The Rifle Brigade was exceptionally good." No other unit was individually mentioned.	
	23.1.18		Training under Company arrangements. Following Officers joined for duty. 2/Lt. H.F.C.Moore. 2/Lt. D.F.Thuillier. and draft of 146 Other Ranks.	

Army Form C. 2118.

WAR DIARY
INTELLIGENCE SUMMARY.
(Erase heading not required.)

Place	Date	Hour	Summary of Events and Information	Remarks and references to Appendices
STEENVOORDE	24.1.18		Battalion training under company arrangements.	
	25.1.18		ditto. The Battalion played 2nd Bn. The Lincolnshire Regt in the first round of the Brigade Football Competition and won by two goals to none.	
	26.1.18		Training under Company arrangements. Sports held in the afternoon. Commanding Officer inspected the new draft.	
EAST OF	27.1.18		Battalion Resting. Church Parades. Battalion beat 25th Trench Mortar Battery in the 2nd round of the Brigade Football Competition. 6 goals to nil.	
	28.1.18		Battalion Training. 7 O.Rs joined for duty.	
	29.1.18		Training continued. Boxing competition held.	
	30.1.18		Training continued. 1.O.R.joined for duty.	
	31.1.18		Training continued.	

P.R. Preston
2/Lieut.
for Major.
Commanding 2nd Battalion. The Rifle Brigade.

WAR DIARY
or
INTELLIGENCE SUMMARY

Army Form C. 2118

(Erase heading not required.)

Place	Date	Hour	Summary of Events and Information	Remarks and references to Appendices
STEENVOORDE AREA Sh.27.K.28 K.29.35	31.1.18		Battalion Training.	
	1.2.18		Battalion Training. Draft of 36 other ranks joined.	
	2.2.18		Battalion marched via STEENVOORDE - ABEELE Road to POPERINGHE being billetted in the RUE de BRUGES. Battan. Headquarters 9 Rue de Bruges. relieving the 2nd. Battn. Scottish Rifles.	
	3.2.18		Battalion finding working parties of 70 men, 50 men, and 50 men, with 2 Officers with each party. Working in Army Battle Zone.	
POPERINGHE	4.2.18		Battalion finding working parties same as yesterday. Captain J. Maclean D.S.O, M.C. rejoined Battn. for duty as Medical Officer.	
	5.2.18		Battalion finding Working parties same as yesterday. 2/Lieut. D. Gault struck off strength, upon being evacuated to England "Sick".	
	6.2.18		Battalion finding Working parties same as yesterday. 2/Lieut. W.H. Brann joined for duty. Battalion played Divl. M.G. Battn. in semi-final of Divl. Football Competition. Result.- lost 0.- 5.	
	7.2.18		Battalion finding Working parties.	
	8.2.18		Battalion finding Working parties. Nothing of interest to report.	
	9.2.18		Battalion finding Working parties same as previously during tour in billets in POPERINGHE.	
	10.2.18		Battalion finding Working parties as usual.	
	11.2.18		Same as yesterday. Nothing of interest occurred.	
	12.2.18		Battalion finding Working parties as usual. Remainder of Battn. moved by march route to "B" Camp, BRANDHOEK, where working parties rejoined Battn. in the evening. Transport moved to YORK CAMP. Casualty 1 O.R. S.I.W.	

Army Form C. 2118.

WAR DIARY
or
INTELLIGENCE SUMMARY.
(Erase heading not required.)

Instructions regarding War Diaries and Intelligence Summaries are contained in F. S. Regs., Part II. and the Staff Manual respectively. Title pages will be prepared in manuscript.

Place	Date	Hour	Summary of Events and Information	Remarks and references to Appendices
"B" Camp BRANDHOEK	13.2.18		Battalion training under Company arrangements. Battalion bathed.	
	14.2.18		Battalion training under Company arrangements. Baths at POPERINGHE. Major H.S.C. PEYTON M.C. joined for duty and took over command of the Battalion. Details moved to BRAKE CAMP.	
(FRONT LINE)	15.2.18		Battalion moved by rail to MANOPS JUNCTION, and thence by march route to Front line, relieving 2nd. DEVON Regt. A. & D. Coys. occupied Front line system from (approximately) D.6.d.9.8. to V.29.a.7.65. B. and C. Companies in Support on GOUDBERG - MOSSELMARKT line. Front Line system under command of O.C. D. Coy. Headquarters VIPILE FARM. Support line under command of O.C. B. Coy. H.Q. VINECO T Battalion Headquarters at BELLEVUE. Weather fine and dry. A good relief. 1 O.R. wounded.	
	16.2.18		Battalion holding Front line, being centre Battalion of Divisional Front. Heavy hostile barrage put down on our front and support lines between 9.30 and 11.30 a.m. otherwise a quiet day and night. Casualties 3 O.R. killed 6 O.R. wounded. BELLEVUE shelled at intervals with 5 minute concentrations. - H.E. and Gas mixed. Companies working in front and support line systems. Two platoons of 2nd. Royal Berkshire Regt. carrying R.E. material for Front line. Captain W.G. GABAIN M.C. joined for duty.	
near PASSCHENDAELE	17.2.18		Battalion holding line as before. A quiet day in front line and support. BELLEVUE shelled at intervals, - considerable quantity of gas shell sent over - identified by Divl. Gas Officer as Blue Cross. Casualties 2 O.R. wounded. Weather dry and cold.	
	18.2.18		Battalion holding line as before. Enemy M.G. and artillery inactive during the day on front and support lines. BELLEVUE shelled but not so much, owing to retaliation by our artillery. During the night enemy attempted to raid a post on D. Company's frontage. - they were repulsed. Otherwise a quiet night, save for occasional bursts of machine gun fire. Weather continuing fine and dry. 3 O.Rs wd.	

Army Form C. 2118.

WAR DIARY
or
INTELLIGENCE SUMMARY.

(Erase heading not required.)

Instructions regarding War Diaries and Intelligence Summaries are contained in F. S. Regs., Part II. and the Staff Manual respectively. Title pages will be prepared in manuscript.

Place	Date	Hour	Summary of Events and Information	Remarks and references to Appendices
PASSCHENDAELE near (Front & Support Lines)	19.2.18		Battalion holding line as before. A quiet day. BELLEVUE shelled at intervals. Battalion relieved in the evening by the 2nd. Bn. Middlesex Regt. Relief being reported complete at 10.30 p.m. Battalion marched by Companies to OXFORD ROAD NORTH and entrained there and proceeded by light railway to HAGLE DUMP, detraining there for "B" Camp, which was reached at 2.50 a.m. on the 20th. Casualties 1 O.R. killed 3 O.Rs. wounded. During whole of this tour in the line, the weather was fine and cold, - bright moon at night.	
"B" CAMP	20.2.18		Battalion at "B" Camp resting and cleaning up.	
BRANDHOEK	21.2.18		Battalion at "B" Camp. Baths at VLAMERTINGHE. Changing clothing.	
	22.2.18		Battn. at "B" Camp. Training under Company arrangements.	
	23.2.18		Battn. entrained at HAGLE DUMP Siding at 2.0 p.m. and proceed by rail to MANORS JUNCTION, and thence by route march to the trenches, relieving the 2nd. Battn. Middlesex Regt. in the same sector as last tour in the line. Relief was effected without casualties. Battalion working on line of trenches in front and support. "B" and "C" Companies were in front line with "A" and "D" Companies in Support on GOUDBERG line. Battn. H.Q. at BELLEVUE.	
PASSCHENDAELE SECTOR	24.2.18		Battalion holding line as yesterday. Enemy inactive generally during day. Machine Guns active at night. BELLEVUE shelled at intervals with short concentrations.	
	25.2.18		Battalion holding line as before. 2nd. Lieut. S.K. Moore killed by rifle fire in early morning. A quiet day. inter-company relief carried out in the evening. "A" Company relieved "B" Coy. and "D" relieved "C" Company in front line. Enemy machine guns active at night. BELLEVUE shelled with 12 shell. Otherwise enemy artillery inactive.	
	26.2.18		Battalion holding line and working on front and support systems. Quiet day. Casualties 1 O.R. Killed. 1 O.R. wounded.	

A5834 Wt.W4973/M1687 750,000 8/16 D. D. & L. Ltd. Forms/C.2118/13

Army Form C. 2118

WAR DIARY
or
INTELLIGENCE SUMMARY
(Erase heading not required.)

Instructions regarding War Diaries and Intelligence Summaries are contained in F. S. Regs., Part II. and the Staff Manual respectively. Title Pages will be prepared in manuscript.

Place	Date	Hour	Summary of Events and Information	Remarks and references to Appendices
NEAR PASSCHENDAELE	27.2.18		Battalion holding line as before, - were relieved at night by the 2nd. Middx. Regt. and marched out to OXFORD ROAD NORTH where they entrained and proceeded by rail to "B" Camp, detraining at HAGLE DUMP. During this tour the weather kept fairly dry, - rain began falling during relief which was carried out without losses. Major A.E. WASS M.C. joined for duty as second in command on the 26th inst. and took over command of the Battalion from this date.	
"B" CAMP BRANDHOEK	28.2.18		Battalion at "B" Camp resting and cleaning up.	

3rd March, 1918.

B. R. Inglis
for Major.
Comdg. 2nd Battalion The Rifle Brigade.

25th Inf.Bde.
8th Div.

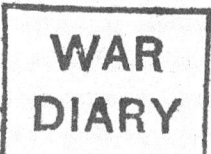

2nd BATTN. THE RIFLE BRIGADE.

M A R C H

1 9 1 8

Army Form C. 2118.

WAR DIARY
or
INTELLIGENCE SUMMARY.
(Erase heading not required.)

Instructions regarding War Diaries and Intelligence Summaries are contained in F. S. Regs., Part II. and the Staff Manual respectively. Title pages will be prepared in manuscript.

2 Rif. Bgde.

Place	Date	Hour	Summary of Events and Information	Remarks and references to Appendices
STEENVOORDE	1-3-18		Parades under Company arrangements.	
	2-3-18		Parades under Company arrangements	
ESCHEN DREUKENABEEK	3-3-18		Battalion relieved 2nd. Bn. West Yorks Regt. in the Support Line and were employed on carrying parties etc.	
	4-3-18		Battalion employed on carrying parties, etc.	
	5-3-18		-------do--------	
	6-3-18		-------do-------- Casualties 7 O.R. killed 6 O.R.Wounded.	
STEENVOORDE	7-3-18		Battalion relieved and moved by bus to STEENVOORDE Area. Battalion billetted in STEENVOORDE.	
	8-3-18		Coys at disposal of O.C.Coys for cleaning up etc. Battalion inspected by the Commanding Officer in billets. 86 O.R. joined for duty.	
	9-3-18		Baths for the Battalion. Church Parade.	
	10-3-18		Coys. at disposal of Os.C. Coys.	
TILQUES	11-3-18		Battalion moved to TILQUES Area by road and rail. Battalion billetted in TILQUES.	
	12-3-18		Companies paraded for Squad Drill Arm Drill etc. under Company arrangements. 108 O.R. joined for duty.	
	13-3-18		Companies under Os.C.Coys for Musketry and elementary practise in the Assault.	
	14-3-18		Coys.for training on Assault Course - Entended order drill- Artillery Formation. Boxing Tournament held in afternoon Battalion V 2nd. Bn. E.Lancs.	
	15-3-18		Coys under Os.C. Coys for Training.	

Army Form C. 2118.

WAR DIARY
or
INTELLIGENCE SUMMARY.
(Erase heading not required.)

Instructions regarding War Diaries and Intelligence Summaries are contained in F. S. Regs., Part II. and the Staff Manual respectively. Title pages will be prepared in manuscript.

Place	Date	Hour	Summary of Events and Information	Remarks and references to Appendices
TILQUES	16-3-18		Battalion Route March.	
	17-3-18		Church Parade. 2/Lt. L.W.J.Pinnock despatched to England for 6 months tour of duty.	
	18-3-18		Battalion Training. Battalion bathed at ST.OMER.	
	19-3-18		Battalion practised in A.R.A. Competition.	
	20-3-18		Battalion Training.	
	21-3-18		Battalion passed through Gas Test. Battalion Training.	
	22-3-18		Battalion marched to ARQUES, where they entrained.	
	23-3-18		Battalion proceeded by train to ROSIERES :EN SANTERRE detrained and marched to CHAULNES, and were conveyed in lorries to MORCHAIN. Opened out into artillery formation and advanced to PARGNY, coming under heavy shell fire, while crossing the high ground above the river. Took over line of river from N. of PARGNY bridge to S. of FONTAINE LES PARGNY with A.B.& C Coys.in the line, D Coy in support. Shortly before midnight patrol of enemy succeeded in rushing bridge-head, and penetrated between front and support lines. These were ejected by immediate counter-attack, 8 of the enemy being killed, 2 taken prisoners, and 2 machine-guns captured.- Casualties.- Killed.- 2/Lt. E.B.Anstie Wounded.- 2/Lt. R.T.Parkin Lt. L.S.Chamberlen.M.C. 2/Lt. C.B.Keppie. 2/Lt. A.J.Sluman. about 60 other ranks killed & wounded.	
	24-3-18		Shortly after dawn the enemy commenced to bomb the posts on the river bank, succeeded in fording the river to the right, and left of the line held by the Battalion, and started to work round our flanks. Situation became very precarious and withdrawal was ordered. This was effected in good order, but with very heavy casualties. Battalion taking up line of sunken road 500 yards E of MORCHAIN. Remained here for about 1 hour, and then withdrew about another 300 yards to a position on N.E. outskirts of village. Here the Battalion remained until about 4 pm. with no other troops in sight, enemy passing in large numbers on sunken road and in hollow behind wood about ¼ mile eastwards. Finally ordered to withdraw	

Army Form C. 2118.

WAR DIARY
or
INTELLIGENCE SUMMARY.
(Erase heading not required.)

Instructions regarding War Diaries and Intelligence Summaries are contained in F. S. Regs., Part II. and the Staff Manual respectively. Title pages will be prepared in manuscript.

Place	Date	Hour	Summary of Events and Information	Remarks and references to Appendices
	25-3-18		to line of trenches astride MOECHAIN-PERTAIN Road, N. of POTTE where rest of Division had already formed up. Casualties.- Killed.-Captain S.A.Hadland- 2/Lt. R.T.Dent- 2/Lt. G.E.Lascelles- 2/Lt. D.A.Gibbs. Died of wounds.-Lt.Col. H.S.C.Peyton M.C. Wounded at duty.-2/Lt. W.H.Brann.-Wounded. 2/Lt. B.R.Everett- Captain C.E.Pegram M.C. Wounded & Missing.- 2/Lt. E.F.C.Moore- 2/Lt. T.C.Lewis- Missing.- Captain I.C.MacLean D.S.O.M.C.- Captain W.G.Gabain M.C. About 300 other ranks killed, Wounded and missing. Major A.E.Wass M.C. took over command of the Battalion.

About 4 a.m. Battalion Headquarters and a party of 80 men under Captain F.D.R. Milne were despatched to LICOURT to take part in action, timed to commence at 9 a.m. in conjunction 160 men of 2/Royal Berks. Regt., elements of the 24th Brigade, 24th Division and 3rd French Corps, which had as its object the re-capture of lost ground to line of SOMME Canal. Remainder of Battalion under Captain E.W.Cremer, in trenches W. of MORCHAIN. At about 8 am enemy penetrated our line on a wide front and advanced rapidly towards DRESLINCOURT and PERTAIN - Battalion became scattered into about 5 groups, each under an Officer or N.C.O., which took up a number of positions, retiring gradually in a N.W. direction. Headquarter Party held on to trench on S. outskirts of LICOURT until enemy within 200 yards, and all other British troops out of sight, withdrew with difficulty to PERTAIN (which they found occupied by the enemy) thence to a position 1 mile N.W. of that village, remaining there for 2 hours, thence to line of OMIECOURT-MARCHELEPOT road, holding on there for 4 hoursand finally to HYENCOURT-MARCHELEPOT railway where remainder of Division was already in position. Casualties.- Wounded. Captain F.D.R.Milne - 2/Lt. H M.Small- 2/Lt. C.H.Sidney- 2/Lt. A.A.Sutton. About 500ther ranks killed, Wounded and missing. | |
| | 26-3-18 | | About 2 a.m. Battalion was ordered to march to bivouacs in W. outskirts of LIHONS- MEHARICOURT road and S of CHAULNES-ROSIERES Railway. Remained there till 5.30 p.m. when enemy had entered LIHONS, orders were received to withdraw through line held by 23rd and 24th Brigades. to bivouacs W. of ROSIERES. | |

Army Form C. 2118.

WAR DIARY
or
INTELLIGENCE SUMMARY.
(Erase heading not required.)

Instructions regarding War Diaries and Intelligence Summaries are contained in F.S. Regs., Part II. and the Staff Manual respectively. Title pages will be prepared in manuscript.

Place	Date	Hour	Summary of Events and Information	Remarks and references to Appendices
	27-3-18		At about 10 am the Battalion was ordered to counter-attack through S outskirts of ROSIERES in the direction of the Sugar Rifinery. Battalion advanced in artillery formation, coming under fairly haevy shell fire, but on arrival at objective found line intact. Reinforced 8th D.L.I. and 2/Worcester R.gt. in front line. About 20 other ranks killed and wounded.	
	28-3-18		About 1 am, no enemy attacks having developed on our front, Battalion was withdrawn to bivouacs W of ROSIERES. At about 9 am proceeded to position in mobile reserve on railway line 1½ miles W of VRELY. When troops in front withdrew, Battalion took up line of trenches ⅔ W. of this point. At about 3.30. pm. ordered to march to MOREUIL to hold bridgehead at all costs. On arrival at MOREUIL, bridgehead was found to be held by French. Battalion went into billets at MORISEL.	
	29-3-18		Battalion remained in billets. At about 2 pm Battalion ordered to take up position in S. corner of large wood N.E. of MOREUIL. Fairly heavily shelled. At about 5.pm. French commenced to withdraw S.W. 19th Corps N.W. Battalion carried out rearguard action to cover right flank of latter. About 10 pm Battalion dug in 300 yards N. of wood and facing it, on right of 19th Corps.	
	30-3-18		At 4 am orders were received to abandon this line. Battalion marched via CASTEL to wood N.W. of ROUVREL where they remained bivouacked till evening. About 6 pm Battalion marched to CASTEL coming under heavy shell fire in valley W of village, and t ok up position to protect bridgehead, supporting 23rd and 24th Brigades. Casualties.- About 20 other ranks Killed and Wounded.	
	31-3-18		Battalon remained in position W. of CASTEL, protecting bridgehead.	

5-4-18.

[signature]
Major.
Commanding 2nd. Battn. The Rifle Brigade.

The date of Peyton's first Commission is March 25th 1911. Joined 2nd Bn. and killed March 24th 1918, Commanding that Battalion on last day of his 6th year of Service.

25th Brigade.

8th Division.

2nd BATTALION

THE RIFLE BRIGADE

APRIL 1918.

Army Form C. 2118.

WAR DIARY
or
INTELLIGENCE SUMMARY.
(Erase heading not required.)

2nd Bn The ~~RIFLE~~ BRIGADE

Place	Date	Hour	Summary of Events and Information	Remarks and references to Appendices
THENNES - COTTENCHY - LE MESGE	1-4-18		At about 10 am Battalion moved into position about 500 yards S of THENNES in readiness to counterattack, and remained there all day. At dusk relieved by elements of 3rd Cavalry Brigade in line S.E. of THENNES.	
	2-4-18		The Battalion was relieved in the Line by a Company of the 133rd French Regt. and marched to billets in COTTENCHY. Battalion paraded at 2 pm. and marched to SAINS_EN_AMIENOIS where they embussed and proceeded to billets at LE MESGE.	
	3-4-18		Coys under Os.C.Coys. for cleaning and reorganization	
	4-4-18		Coys. under Os.C.Coys. for cleaning and reorganization. Battalion bathed. Lieut. J.P.F.Kennedy joined for duty, and took over command of "C" Company.	
	5-4-18		Coys. under Os.C.Coys for training in Arm Drill & Squad Drill. Captain R.C.S.Stevenson took over command of "A" Company. Draft of 73 Other ranks joined for duty.	
	6-4-18		Coys. under Os.C.Coys for training in Musketry and Extended order drill. 144 Other ranks joined for duty.	
	7-4-18		Church Parade. 85 Other ranks joined for duty.	
	8-4-18		Coys. under Os.C.Coys. for training in Musketry and & Close order Drill. 20 Other ranks joined for duty.	
	9-4-18		Coys. under Os.C.Coys. for training. 146 Other ranks joined for duty.	
	10-4-18		Coys. under Os.C.Coys. for Musketry, Section. Platoon, and Company Drill. 115 Other ranks joined for duty.	
	11-4-18		Coys. under Os.C.Coys. for training, Miniature Range and Drill. Captain R.A.Mostyn-Owen takes over Command of the Battalion this date, and is permitted to wear the badges of rank of Major. 30 Other ranks joined for duty.	

Army Form C. 2118.

WAR DIARY
or
INTELLIGENCE SUMMARY.
(Erase heading not required.)

Instructions regarding War Diaries and Intelligence Summaries are contained in F.S. Regs., Part II. and the Staff Manual respectively. Title pages will be prepared in manuscript.

Place	Date	Hour	Summary of Events and Information	Remarks and references to Appendices
LE MESGE - CAMON	12-4-18		Coys. under Os.C.Coys for Training. Miniature Range & Artillery Formations. Lt.(A/Capt)B.C.Pascoe M.C. appointed Brigade Major 25th Infantry Brigade Captain R.H.C.Ward . Lt.J.S.Gribbon, 2/Lt.J.D.Aitken and 2/Lt. P.G.McCubbin joined for duty.	
	13-4-18		Battalion paraded on SOUS-REINCOURT Road to march to entraining point at HANGEST. The Battalion detrained at ST. ROCHE, AMIENS. The Battalion was billeted in the RIVERY-CAMON Area.	
	14-4-18		Battalion rested.	
	15-4-18		Parades under Company arrangements for Musketry & Squad Drill 2/Lt.H.E.Mitchell, 2/Lt. W.Loftus & 2/Lt. W.A.Seaman joined for duty.	
	16-4-18		Coys. under Os.C.Coys for Musketry, Clse Order Drill and Miniature range.	
	17-4-18		Coys. under Os.C.Coys. for Artillery Formation and training in the attack. Capt. (A/Major) R.A.Mostyn-Owen is permitted to wear the badges of rank of Lieut-Colonel pending the official announcement in the London Gazette.	
	18-4-18		Companies under Os.C.Coys. for training in Artillery Formation, practice in the Attack, Bayonet Fighting and Physical Training. 2/Lt. Oddy A.E. 2/Lt. W.H.Harris M.C. W.H. F.C.March - T.McGee - W.Mackechnie - H.Young - J.Doyle - K.J.Guerrier - J.M.Simon joined for duty. The Divisional Commander has awarded Parchment Certificates to the undermentioned N.C.Os and men for gallantry and devotion to duty WEST of the SOMME between 21st March and 2nd April 1918. 5431 Cpl.(A/Sgt) M.Molloy - Z/402 Rfn. F.Wilcox - 2435 Rfn. R.Collins - 4569 Cpl.(A/Sgt.) E.Butler - 28322 A/Cpl. W.Simms.- 25722 A/Cpl. A.Davids.- 28155 Rfn. W.Matthews - 1443 A/Cpl. W.Hughes - 2070 Rfn. A.Windebank - S/10534 Cpl. F.Pamplin - 27310 Rfn. A.Barnes - 19863 Rfn. J.Taylor.- 2383 A/Cpl. R.Farrell.- 6/315 Rfn. A.Bloomfield.- 34104 Rfn. E.Goldsmith.- 4663 A/Cpl. M.O'Keefe - 9887 A/Cpl. A.Burwood - 4463 C.Q.M.Sgt. L.Williams - 1522 Sgt. C.Ransted. D.C.M. M.M.- 26878 Cpl. A.Lambkin - 8453 A/Sgt. T.Braund.- 11957 A/Sgt. C.Price - 564 A/Cpl. S.Roper - 203226 Rfn. G.Phillips - 13872 Rfn. A.Nichols.	

Army Form C. 2118.

WAR DIARY
or
INTELLIGENCE SUMMARY.
(Erase heading not required.)

Instructions regarding War Diaries and Intelligence Summaries are contained in F. S. Regs., Part II. and the Staff Manual respectively. Title pages will be prepared in manuscript.

Place	Date	Hour	Summary of Events and Information	Remarks and references to Appendices
CAMON — BLANGY TRONVILLE — VILLERS-BRETONNEUX	19-4-18		Companies under Os.C. Coys. for Gas Drill Musketry and Squad Drill. The Battalion. (less Details) moved from CAMON to billets at BLANGY TRONVILLE.	
	20-4-18		The Battalion relieved elements of the 55th & 56th Battalions of the 14th Australian Brigade. "B" Company front line- (left), "C" Company front line (right) "A" Company Support, "D" Company Reserve. The night was exceedingly quiet and the relief was carried out without a casualty.	
	21-4-18		Very quiet all day. No casualties. A considerable amount of work was done improving posts and constructing a continuous apron of wire in front of front line.	
	22-4-18		A very quiet day. No casualties. Work as on 21st. "A" Company took over one Company front on the right up to, but not including the VILLERS BRETONNEUX WARFUSEE Road from one Company 2/East Lancs. Regt. this relief was carried out without casualties. Lieutenant Colonel H.S.C.Richardson took over Command of the Battalion vice Lieutenant Colonel R.A.Mostyn-Owen posted to Command of 13th Battalion the The Rifle Brigade.	
	23-4-18		A Patrol, consisting of 2/Lt. P.G.McCubbin and Other ranks left our lines at 2 am. 23rd inst to reconnoitre the right of our front. One Rifleman, wounded, reported at Battalion Headquarters at about 3 am that 2/Lt. McCubbin had been wounded, also some members of the Patrol. Another Patrol was immediately sent out no trace of the first patrol, which seems to have walked into an enemy post could be found. 2 unwounded members of the first patrol eventually returned to our lines. 2/Lt. McCubbin was "missing". 2/Lt. J.Farrell joined for duty. Reports received that enemy would attack at dawn obtained from prisoners captured on the right of our Sector. No attack developed, probably owing to wet morning. A quiet day. Work done improving our line and wiring posts continued A new M.G.Post made in our line near Battalion Headquarters. Some enemy Gas- shells at night. Reports again received late VILLERS BRETONNEUX would attack at dawn on 24th. Enemy observed working in WARFUSEE Road fired on by our Lewis guns and rifles from our line. Reported to Division by Brigade Major.	27/24th

Army Form C. 2118.

WAR DIARY
or
INTELLIGENCE SUMMARY.

(Erase heading not required.)

Instructions regarding War Diaries and Intelligence Summaries are contained in F. S. Regs., Part II. and the Staff Manual respectively. Title pages will be prepared in manuscript.

Place	Date	Hour	Summary of Events and Information	Remarks and references to Appendices
VILLERS-BRETONNEUX	23rd/24th April 1918		Heavy enemy barrage came down at 3.45.am.This continued until it became less intense, and chiefly covered ground between Reserve Line and Battalion Headquarters. Barrage included a large proportion of Gas Shells. Continual reports received from O.s.C.Companies that barrage was not on Front Line or Close support Companies during the above hours. During the night 23/24th ½ D Company had been moved into close support on the right and half on the left by order of G.O.C. 25th Infantry Brigade. The morning was very misty and the enemy put down a heavy smoke barrage at dawn, making it impossible to see for more than 20 yards. About 7 am. a runner from "A" Company reported at Battalion Headquarters that the enemy had got round the right flank of the Company, and was attacking them and the support platoons of D Company from flank and rear, and was moving towards "C" Company. At 8 am "B" Company was ordered to form a defensive flank, joining with support platoons of D Company and remains of "C" Company, from B Company's right to Reserve Line. Battalion H.Q. details moved forward to continue the line covering Battn. Headquarters and in touch with 2nd. R.Berkshire Regt. on the right, N.W. of VILLERS-BRETONNEUX. 2/Lt. Gurrier and elements of A C & D Coys joined this line during the morning. At 9 am enemy Very lights were seen going up on N.W. outskirts of VILLERS-BRETONNEUX and enemy Machine guns opened fire on vicinity of Bn. Headquarters. Reserve line, and vicinity of new line joining with 2nd. Royal Berkshire Regt. was shelled at intervals all day. B Company on the left was subjected to heavy Trench Mortar fire at intervals, the enemy advanced several times on the right of this Company, but was each time driven off by rifle and machine gun fire. It was afterwards ascertained that the enemy, after breaking through SOUTH of VILLERS BRETONNEUX WARFUSEE Road, had turned in Northwards, between our front and support lines and also in rear of the latter, being unobserved owing to the dense mist and smoke barrage. A & C Companies taken unawares in the rear were overwhelmed after a sharp fight by superior numbers of the enemy, the whole of the two Companies with few exceptions being killed or captured. Very little was ascertained as to their exact fate, but it is known that one platoon of D Coy. fought to their last man, and was completely wiped out. 2/Lt. J.Doyle, was dangerously wounded while commanding this Platoon,was found on the night of 24/25th during the counter-attack by the Australians. The remainder of the day passed without further attack on our front, with the exception of half-hearted	

Army Form C. 2118.

WAR DIARY
or
INTELLIGENCE SUMMARY.
(Erase heading not required.)

Instructions regarding War Diaries and Intelligence Summaries are contained in F. S. Regs., Part II. and the Staff Manual respectively. Title pages will be prepared in manuscript.

Place	Date	Hour	Summary of Events and Information	Remarks and references to Appendices
VILLERS BRETONNEUX	24/25th		attempts to turn the right flank of B Company which were frustrated by the effective firebrought to bear on them by this Company.	
	25-4-18		On the night 24/25th a counter-attack on VILLERS BRETONNEUX and ground S.W. of the village, was carried out by an Australian Brigade, which surrounded the village establishing itself on the Eastern outskirts asfar as the Old Hangars on the VILLERS BRETONNEUX -WARFUSEE road, with its right flank thrown back. Its left covered the Northern and North Western parts of the village, and was extended to the right flank of our B Company, where this Company bent back, forming our defensive flank. The Australian left at this time was not in touch with B Companies Right, but the gap was covered by the continuation of our line joining up with the 2nd. Royal Berkshire Regt. Our lines were shelled at intervals throughout the night. The lines held by the Battalion were not attacked on the 25th inst. Readjustments of our lines were carried out early on night 25/26th, B Company front line 2 Platoons of D Company in Support in positions occupiedby A Companywhen the line was taken over. 1 Platoon of D Company and an amalgamated Platoon formed of remains of A & C Coys in Reserve in old Reserve line. On the night 25/26th the Battalion moved to counter-attack position W. of VILLERS BRETONNEUX.	
	26-4-18		Situation on the S.E. outskirts of VILLERS BRETONNEUX being obscure, orders received from Division were brought to Battalion headquarters by Brigade Major, 25th Infantry Brigade that a reconnaissance was to be carried out to clear this part of the village if neccessary, and make sure of the situation. This was carried out by 2 Platoons of B Company under 2/Lt. McGee, accompanied by the Brigade Major, 25th Infantry Brigade, who carried out the reconnaissance meeting with considerable resistance outside the village. Several casualties were inflicted on the enemy, 2 machine gun teams being put out of action by our fire. The party returned at 2 pm, having suffered casualties.- 2/Lt. McGee killed- 26 Other ranks killed and wounded. The rest of the day passed without further incident.	
	27-4-18		A quiet day. The Battalion remained in counter-attack position andc was not called upon to take part in active operations. Casualties Nil. Casualties sustained by Battalion between 23/26th April .-1 Officer killed- 3 Officers wounded- 2 Officers wounded & missing-9 Officers Missing.	

Army Form C. 2118.

WAR DIARY
or
INTELLIGENCE SUMMARY.
(Erase heading not required.)

Instructions regarding War Diaries and Intelligence Summaries are contained in F. S. Regs., Part II. and the Staff Manual respectively. Title pages will be prepared in manuscript.

Place	Date	Hour	Summary of Events and Information	Remarks and references to Appendices
	28-4-18		Other ranks.- Killed 18- Wounded 96- Missing 268. At 10.30.am. orders were received to evacuate the position occupied by the Battalion and the Battalion moved by march route to billets at BOUTILLERIE,S. of AMIENS.	
	29-4-18		In billets at BOUTILLERIE.Companies under Os.C.Coys for re-organization and Baths.	
	30-4-18		The Battalion moved in busses to billets in AUCHENNEVILLE near ABBEVILLE Battalion Headquarters in Chateau. Reinforcements 176 Other ranks. Captain E.Boughton-Leigh. 2/Lt. E.P.Morgan joined for duty.	
BOUTILLERIS — AUCHENNVILLE			10-5-18.	

N.C.Richardson
Lieut-Colonel
Commdg. 2nd. Battn. The Rifle Brigade

WAR DIARY
or
INTELLIGENCE SUMMARY.

(Erase heading not required.)

Army Form C. 2118.

2nd Rifle Brigade

May 1918

Place	Date	Hour	Summary of Events and Information	Remarks and references to Appendices
	1.5.18		Parades under Os.C. Companies for Training.	
	2.5.18		The following message from Major General W.G.Henneker C.B. DSO. was received "I desire to thank Captain Pascoe MC. and the platoon of the 2nd. Bn. Rifle Brigade with him, for their splendid work on April 25th inclearing the houses and railway line S.E. of VILLERS BRETONNEUX. The operation was carried out with rare dash and gallantry, and fully achieved its object" The Divisional Commander awarded Parchment Certificates to the following.- 2/Lt. W.H.Brann - 2/Lt. A.A.Sutton.	
SALOUEL - HUCHENNEVILLE	3.5.18		The Battalion, less Transport, moved by bus from HUCHENNEVILLE to SALOUEL.	
	4.5.18		60 Other ranks joined for duty.	
	5.5.18		Battalion entrained at SALEUX Station and detrained at FERE_EN_TARDENOIS, and marched to billets at LHUYS.	
	6.5.18		Parades under Os.C. Companies for Training.	
LHUYS	7.5.18		Parades under Os.C.Companies for Drill and Musketry. Following telegram received from Colonel – in – Chief in reply to a telegram sent on the occasion of his birthday.% "My best thanks to all ranks, and my heartiest congratulations on their splendid services in the recent fighting, of which I and the whole Regiment are proud"	
	8.5.18		Parades under Os.C.Companies for Progressive Training. A & B Coys. Musketry.	
	9.5.18		Parades under Os.C.Companies for Progressive Training. A.& C Coys Musketry. The following decorations were awarded to the undernamed Officers for gallantry and devotion to duty West of the SOMME between 22nd March and 2nd April 1918. DISTINGUISHED SERVICE ORDER Captain G.H.G.Anderson MC. – BAR TO THE MILITARY CROSS Major A.E.Wass MC. – THE MILITARY CROSS Captain F.D.R.Milne & 2/Lt. A.J.Sluman.	

Army Form C. 2118.

WAR DIARY
or
INTELLIGENCE SUMMARY.
(Erase heading not required.)

Place	Date	Hour	Summary of Events and Information	Remarks and references to Appendices
VENTELAY – COURLANDON	10-5-18		The Battalion moved from LHUYS to COURLANDON by march route.	
	11-5-18		The Battalion moved from COURLANDON to VENTELAY by march route.	
	12-5-18		Church Parade at 9 am. The Battalion relieved 358th French Infantry Regiment on night 12/13th May. Relief was carried out quietly and no casualties suffered.	
	13-5-18		Battalion in front line. All quiet and no casualties suffered. Patrols were carried out at night.	
	14-5-18		Battalion in front line. Everything very quiet. No casualties.	
	15-5-18		Battalion in front line. All quiet. No casualties.	
	16-5-18		Battalion in front line. All quiet. On night of 16/17th May Battalion was relieved by 2nd. Essl Lancs. Regt. Relief was carried out without casualties, and Battalion moved into billets at GUYENCOURT.	
	17-5-18		Battalion rested and cleaned up. 81 Other ranks joined for duty.	
	18-5-18		Parades under Os.C.Companies for training. Decorations awarded to the following for gallantry and devotion to duty at VILLERS BRETONNEUX between 24th and 28th April 1918. THE MILITARY MEDAL – 40893.Rfn. E.Walker – 41083 Rfn. J.Coit. The Divisional Commander awarded Parchment Certificates to the following for gallantry and devotion to duty West of the SOMME between 22nd. March and 2nd. April 1918. Lieut. L.S.Chamberlen MC. 18160 Rfn. J.Ditch – 26490 Rfn.H.Harris. Promotion 2nd. Bn. Rifle Brigade. 2/Lt.(A/Capt) G.H.G.Anderson D.S O. MC (now Acting Adjutant) to be Adjutant and to retain his Acting rank vice Lt(A/Capt B.C.Pascoe MC.	
	19-5-18		Church Parade at 10 am.	

Army Form C. 2118.

WAR DIARY
or
INTELLIGENCE SUMMARY.
(Erase heading not required.)

2/ Rifle Brigade

May 1918

Place	Date	Hour	Summary of Events and Information	Remarks and references to Appendices
BERRY-AU-BAC	20.5.18		Parades under Os.C.Companies for Training. 18 other ranks joined for duty. On the night of 20/21st May the Battalion relieved the 2nd. Bn. R.Berks.Regt. in the right sector of 25th Infantry Brigade front. Relief was completed successfully and the front was very quiet.	
	21.5.18		Battalion in front line, all very quiet, no casualties.	
	22.5.18		Battalion in front line, all very quiet, 1 other rank killed while on patrol.	
	23.5.18		Battalion in front line, all very quiet. Casualties- 1 other rank wounded. 3 other ranks joined for duty.	
	24.5.18		Battalion in front line, very quiet, no casualties	
	25.5.18		Battalion in front line, All quiet, no casualties.	
	26.5.18		Battalion in front line All quiet , no casualties.	
GUYENCOURT	27.5.18		German attack started. Barrage opened at 1 am. and Battalion front was heavily gassed and Trench Mortared at 4 am. The enemy attacked, using Tanks. The Battalion suffered very heavy casualties during the preliminary bombardment and attack. The remnants retired to the 2nd Line and thence over the AISNE by GERNICOURT and held that village till forced to retire towards GUYENCOURT. Lieut-Colonel Richardson was wounded. Captain D.Heaton-Ellis killed. 2/Lts. Hoare., Denison, Lowder and Halford wounded. 60 Details (Lewis Gun) went up at 12 noon under 2/Lt. R.C.Ellis,who was killed. 44 other ranks went up under Capt. E.Boughton-Leigh and 2/Lt. J.Nettleton at 9.pm	

Army Form C. 2118.

WAR DIARY
or
INTELLIGENCE SUMMARY.
(Erase heading not required.)

2/Rifle Brigade

Place	Date	Hour	Summary of Events and Information	Remarks and references to Appendices
CHUNGRY - SARCY - CHAMPLAT	23-5-18		Remnants of Battalion still in the line. Casualties estimated at 27 Officers and 680 other ranks.	
	24-5-18		Remaining 60 other ranks and 7 Officers under Major A.E.Wass MC went to CHAMPLAT to form a Composite Battalion of 25th Infantry Brigade. Major A.E.Wass MC and /Lt. C.J.Eyston attached to 23rd Brigade to form a Battalion. The men in Composite Battalion of 25th Infantry Brigade marched to SARCY they went on and held a line N. of BOULEUSE. Casualties estimated at 3 Officers and 47 other ranks from remainder of Battalion and men in Composite Battalion.	
	30-5-18		3 Officers and 16 other ranks still with Composite Battalion of 23rd & 25th Inf. Brigades withdrew to South of SARCY.	
	31-5-18		3 Officers and 16 other ranks went to CHUNGRY and thence to NANTEUIL with remainder of Composite Battalion.	

A. E. Wass
Major
Commdg. 2nd. Bn. The Rifle Brigade

Army Form C. 2118.

WAR DIARY
or
INTELLIGENCE SUMMARY

(Erase heading not required.)

2 Rifle Bn

Instructions regarding War Diaries and Intelligence Summaries are contained in F.S. Regs., Part II. and the Staff Manual respectively. Title Pages will be prepared in manuscript.

Place	Date	Hour	Summary of Events and Information	Remarks and references to Appendices
GRAUVES-SOULLIERES	1-6-18		Men with Composite Battalion went to MARFAUX.	
	2-6-18		Captain E.Boughton-Leigh, 2/Lt. I.M.Simon with 9 other ranks went up to 2/8th Composite Battalion from Details.	
	3-6-18		Transport and remainder of Details moved from GRAUVES to SOULLIERES.	
	4-6-18		Training of men in Musketry, Close Order Drill- 3 Officers and 61 other ranks away with Composite Battalion.	
	5-6-18		Training of men in Arm Drill- Gas and Musketry.	
	6-6-18		Training of men in Guard Mounting- Musketry and Close Order Drill.	
	7-6-18		Training in Extended Order Drill- Arm Drill & Musketry.	
	8-6-18		Men paraded to make a Rifle Range.	
BANNES	9-6-18		Transport & Details moved to BANNES.	
	10-6-18		Training in Musketry and Extended Order Drill - Arm Drill.	
	11-6-18		Training in Platoon Drill- Musketry & Gas.	
	12-6-18		(Training in Musketry & Platoon Drill. (2/Lt. W.H.Brann and 13 other ranks rejoined from No.1 Composite Battalion.	
	13-6-18		The Battalion entrained at FERE-CHAMPENOISE.	
HOCQUINCOURT	14-6-18		The Battalion detrained at LONGPRE and marched into billets at HOCQUINCOURT.	
	15-6-18		Battalion employed in cleaning up and refitting clothing & equipment.	
	16-6-18		Church Parade at 10 am.	

Army Form C. 2118.

WAR DIARY
or
INTELLIGENCE SUMMARY

(*Erase heading not required.*)

Instructions regarding War Diaries and Intelligence Summaries are contained in F.S. Regs., Part II. and the Staff Manual respectively. Title Pages will be prepared in manuscript.

Place	Date	Hour	Summary of Events and Information	Remarks and references to Appendices
HOOQUINCOURT.	17-6-18		Training continued in Close Order Drill-Musketry and extended order Drill under Company Commanders .2/Lt. A.Laithwaite and 2/Lt. A.J.Guerrier joined for duty.	
	18-6-18		Companies under Company Commanders for Training. Draft of 637 Other ranks joined from Base. Lt. E.Davies (2nd.K.O.Y.L.I) joined for duty.	
	19-6-18		Details of Battalion bathed. Remainder under Company Commanders for Training and Organisation. The following Officers joined for duty.-Captain J.C.Wood 2/Lts: A.Henderson-J.C.Simpson-C.L.Corner-J.Wheler-A.C.Russell-H.W.Shearcroft-A.G.McBryde-J.W.Congdon-J.S.Lamb.-A.N.Cunningham-S.Halliday. Officers & 49 other ranks rejoined from 2/8th Composite Battalion.	
	20-6-18		Battalion inspected by G.O.C. 8th Division.	
	21-6-18		Training in Musketry-Section&Platoon under Company Commanders. G.O.C. 2,th Infantry Brigade inspected Reinforcements at 12 noon. Baths for Details of No.2 Composite Battalion.	
	22-6-18		Battalion moved to BUIGNY by road.	
WOIGNARUE - BUIGNY	23-6-18		Battalion moved to WOIGNARUE by road. Honours & Awards.- To be BrevetLt.Colonel. Brevet Major the Hon R.Brand D.SO Awarded the MILITARY CROSS Captain E.W.Cremer. Awarded the MERETORIOUS SERVICE MEDAL No.1051R.Q.M.S. G.Watkins -Z/635 Sgt.H.Steele Mentioned in Despatches May 24th1918. Lt.Colonel the Hon. R.Brand D.S.O. Lt.Colonel. J.J.B.Cole M.C.2/Lt.Major A.E.Wass M.C. 2/Lt.L.W.J.Pinnock MM. No.1683 Rfn. J.Moncur MM.	
	24-6-18		Cleaning and re-organisation of Companies- 2 Other ranks joined for duty.	
	25-6-18.		Training under Company & Platoon Commanders in morning- Specialists Training in afternoon.	

Army Form C. 2118.

WAR DIARY
or
INTELLIGENCE SUMMARY
(Erase heading not required.)

Instructions regarding War Diaries and Intelligence Summaries are contained in F.S. Regs., Part II. and the Staff Manual respectively. Title Pages will be prepared in manuscript.

Place	Date	Hour	Summary of Events and Information	Remarks and references to Appendices
WARLOIGNE.	26-6-18		Training as for 25th. The following Officers were taken on strength of the Battalion having joined for duty on 24th inst.:- Lt.C.V.Palgreen -Lt.F.P.Raven - Captain B.H.Bennett-2/Lts. S.L.Read-W.E.Gillespie-G.W.S.Brown-C.E.Goody-O.J.Lyne-E.T. Witherden-A.Macnamara- B.R.Everett. 24 Other ranks joined for duty.	
	27-6-18		Training as for 25th with addition of Shooting on 30 yds. Range.	
	28-6-18		Training under Company Commanders. Platoon & Section Drill and firing on range. Baths for the Battalion.	
	29-6-18		Training under Company Commanders. Platoon Schemes with ball ammunition. Lt.Col. R.H.Leyland joined Battalion and took over Command.	
	30-6-18		Divine Service -Church of England at 10 am.	

(signature)
Lt- Colonel.
Comdg. 2nd. Bn. The Rifle Brigade.

Army Form C. 2118.

WAR DIARY
or
INTELLIGENCE SUMMARY.
(Erase heading not required.)

WAR DIARY

JULY 1918

2nd Bn The Rifle Brigade

45

Army Form C. 2118.

WAR DIARY
or
INTELLIGENCE SUMMARY.
(Erase heading not required.)

Instructions regarding War Diaries and Intelligence Summaries are contained in F. S. Regs., Part II. and the Staff Manual respectively. Title pages will be prepared in manuscript.

Place	Date	Hour	Summary of Events and Information	Remarks and references to Appendices
WOIGNARUE	1-7-18		Training under Coy Commanders. Each Coy firing 1 hour on 200x range.	
	2-7-18		Training under Platoon Commanders for block on Hill. Schedule of Platoon formations and Fire Control & simple Field Firing Scheme carried out by each Platoon.	
	3-7-18		Companies under Coy Commanders for Block order Drill. Detailed Skill Company formations and Field Firing Scheme. 2½" S.A.A. Ration & 245 GB Rifle issued for duty. Lieut V.G. Greene posted for duty to M.O.	
	4-7-18		Battalion moved to WOINCOURT by MT & Bus. New billets reached by 1 p.m. Remainder billets.	
WOINCOURT	5-7-18		Companies under Coy Commanders for Training. B Coy on Coy range. C Coy on 30x range.	
	6-7-18		Companies under Company Commanders. Two Coys on 30x range. Battalion sports in the afternoon.	
	7-7-18		Divine Service Coy E at 9 am. Battalion Boxing and Wrestling. Football match. Battalion v Brigade Royal Winchester Regt. In afternoon (Rain).	
	8-7-18		Companies under Coy Commanders. A & C Coys on Training area for Coy attack practice. D Coy on 30x range. B Coy on Musketry competition.	
	9-7-18		Companies under Coy Commanders for Training. C & D Coys on 500x range. B Coy attack practice. A Coy 20x range.	
	10-7-18		Companies under Coy Commanders for Training. Coy Attack Practice. 1 Coy on 30x range Sports. Brigade Sports in afternoon.	
	11-7-18		Recruits joined for duty. Brigade Sports in afternoon. Coys under Coy Commanders for Training. A&B Coys 600x range. D Coy 30x range. C Coy on Training Area "A" Brigade Sports final also. LIEUTS. CM BEAZLEY and JM WEST joined for duty.	
	12-7-18		Coys under Coy Commanders had usual drill.	

Army Form C. 2118.

WAR DIARY
or
INTELLIGENCE SUMMARY.
(Erase heading not required.)

Instructions regarding War Diaries and Intelligence Summaries are contained in F.S. Regs., Part II. and the Staff Manual respectively. Title pages will be prepared in manuscript.

Place	Date	Hour	Summary of Events and Information	Remarks and references to Appendices
	13-7-18		Companies under Coy Commanders for Training. B.O.R. Coy. A. 2.00 P.M. G.2. A+B Coys. Gunnery Store. Divisional Horse Show. 2-17 R.H. Doy. & E. & Q. 10. Cwt joined for duty.	
	14-7-18		Divisional Horse Show. Divine Service C.of E. 9.15 A.M. Gunnery transferred from XXIII to XXI Corps.	
	15-7-18		Battalion moved by road to MENIN HERES.	
	16-7-18		Companies under Coy Commanders for training. Company Rear Guard Skeet.	
	17-7-18		Battalion Attack Practice.	
	18-7-18		Company Attack practice on 600 Range. Gas and Bombing. Brigade Sec. Starting & ARA Competition.	
	19-7-18		Battalion moved by rail from CAMICHE'S area to PERNES and thence by road to BARRIN. 6 Officers left to join various Battalions of the London Regiment.	
	20-7-18		Battalion arrived at OLHAIN WOOD. Brigade H.Q. in BARRIN. Divine Service C.of E. 11:15 A.M.	
	21-7-18			
	22-7-18		Battalion moved by road to MONT. ST. ELOY. 2 Officers left to join the London Regt.	
	23-7-18		Training under Company Commanders. Honours gained as follows a 1 Good Conduct Medal with gratuity. No.4463 C.Q.M.S. L. William. No. 4765 Sgt. E. Eastl.	
	24-7-18		The Battalion is in VIII Corps Reserve at MONT ST. ELOY. Training under Coy Commanding Lectures on Lewis Reading, H. O'R joined for duty.	
	25-7-18		Battalion turned in Field trenching order for inspection by Commanding Officer followed by training and Lectures under Company Commanders. Helmets saluted officially abolished.	

Army Form C. 2118.

WAR DIARY
of
INTELLIGENCE SUMMARY.
(Erase heading not required.)

Instructions regarding War Diaries and Intelligence Summaries are contained in F. S. Regs., Part II. and the Staff Manual respectively. Title pages will be prepared in manuscript.

Place	Date	Hour	Summary of Events and Information	Remarks and references to Appendices
	26-7-18		Battalion in Battle Line Attack Practice by 4 Coy & Bn H.Q. which Bn H.Q. on rejoining is Bn. H.Q. and Back Line – 1450 B Coy Cty and 2 officers and 20 O.R. joined for duty	
	27-7-18		Training under Company Commanders including return C.O. & 2nd in command resumed reserve line. Bn Training for this Coy – 1 Officer & 4 O.R. joined for duty	
	28-7-18		G.S.N.C.O. Reserve C.S.E. 11.45am Battalion Reached Canada Luff 6th Corner of 6th Coast Kings Canadians	
	29-7-18		Company in the day Commanders for Training by attack Practice	
	30-7-18		Companies in the day Commanders for Training – Drill & P.T. Lectures on range. 3. O.R. joined for duty.	
	31-7-18		Battalion Practised attack Practice tactics and a General Bn Co-operating	

R. Evans, Major
for Lieut Colonel
Commanding Bn Rifle Brigade

Army Form C. 2118.

WAR DIARY
or
INTELLIGENCE SUMMARY.
(Erase heading not required.)

Instructions regarding War Diaries and Intelligence Summaries are contained in F.S. Regs., Part II. and the Staff Manual respectively. Title pages will be prepared in manuscript.

Place	Date	Hour	Summary of Events and Information	Remarks and references to Appendices
MONT ST. ELOI	31st July - 1st Aug 1918		Coys. under Coy Commanders for Training. Advance and rearguard actions. Silent Patrols. 3 Other Ranks joined for duty. Battalion Camp shelled night July 31st-August 1st and on morning Aug 1st. Casualties Killed 4 Died of wds 1 Wounded 6 Wd at duty 1 1 Horse killed.	
OTTAWA CAMP	Aug 2nd		Brigade Field Day. Cancelled at 12 noon on account of rain. Battn. moved up to PADDOCK SWITCH at night to test arrangements for Reserve Bde.	
	" 3rd		Coys. under Coy. Commander for Training. Sheet 44 A S.W.	
MAP 44A S.W.	" 4th		Divine Service. C. of E. 10.30 a.m.	
VIMY	" 5th		Battalion moved into support in VIMY VILLAGE relieving 2nd. Devon Regt. Battn. H.Q. at S.23.d.5.8. on forward slope of VIMY RIDGE. C. Coy. in VIMY VILLAGE. A and B Coys in Railway embankment S.E. of village and in BROWN Line trench just E. of embankment. D Coy. with 185 Tunnelling Co. R.E. on ARRAS - SOUCHEZ Road.	
	" 6th		3 Coys. working on front line trench between T.10.c.0.8 and T.16.b.5.2. D Coy. working under 185 Tunnelling Coy. R.E.	
	" 7th		Coys. working as per yesterday. Casualties 2 O.R. wd. shell fire 1 " accidentally wounded.	
	" 8th		Coys working as per yesterday.	
	" 9th		" " " " "	
	" 10th		" " " " "	
	" 11th		" " " " "	

F.T.O.

Army Form C. 2118.

WAR DIARY
or
INTELLIGENCE SUMMARY.
(Erase heading not required.)

Instructions regarding War Diaries and Intelligence Summaries are contained in F.S. Regs. Part II. and the Staff Manual respectively. Title pages will be prepared in manuscript.

Place	Date	Hour	Summary of Events and Information	Remarks and references to Appendices
	Aug 12th 1918		Battalion relieved 2nd. Royal Berks Regt. in left Sub-sector. Dispositions. North to South, D, C, B, A Coys. Each Coy. 2 platoons in main line of defence, 2 in front line of which two sections are pushed forward to observation posts in front of front line. Battalion H.Q. at T.25.b.5.9. Casualties 1 O.R. wounded (at duty) 1 " " (self-infl.)	
	" 13th		Battalion provided covering party of one Coy. for 2nd. Royal Berks Regt. digging new trench between QUEBEC and VESTA TILE (cf. Aug. 6th.) 1 O.R. wd shell fire.	
	" 14th		Covering parties as for yesterday.	
	" 15th		Covering parties as for yesterday. Retaliation asked for for shelling of A Coy's area from 1 - 2 p.m. and provided by 4.5 hows. on hostile battery. 1 O.R. killed while on patrol down ACHEVILLE ROAD.	
	" 16th		Covering parties as for yesterday. A Coy. area shelled 8.0 a.m. 1 O.R. killed.	
	" 17th		Covering party as for yesterday. Also 1 Coy. wiring new trench.	
	" 18th		As for yesterday.	
	" 19th		Covering and wiring parties as for yesterday. Dispositions changed. C Coy. hold whole of Battalion front with 2 platoons garrisonning observation posts and 2 platoons in front line. Remainder of Battn. in main line of defence (BLACK LINE).	
	" 20th		Covering and wiring parties as for yesterday. 15 O.R. joined for duty.	
	" 21st		Battalion relieved in Left Subsection by 2nd. Royal Berks Regt. and took over Right Sub-sector from 2nd East Lancs Regt. Dispositions. C Coy. holding front line and observation posts as in Left Sub-sector. Other Coys. in main defence line - from North to South - D, B, A. 2/Lt. Hon. T.C. Plunkett joined for duty and posted to B. Coy. P.T.O.	

Sheet 44ᴬ S.W. VIMY

Army Form C. 2118.

WAR DIARY
or
INTELLIGENCE SUMMARY.
(Erase heading not required.)

Instructions regarding War Diaries and Intelligence Summaries are contained in F.S. Regs., Part II. and the Staff Manual respectively. Title pages will be prepared in manuscript.

Place	Date	Hour	Summary of Events and Information	Remarks and references to Appendices
	Aug 22nd 1918.		D Coy. relieved C Coy. in front line. Working parties. 1 platoon working on main line of defence, 2 sections " light railway, 1½ " New dug-outs in Railway embankment S.E. of VIMY under 185 Tunnelling Coy. R.E.	
	" 23rd		Working parties as for yesterday. A. Coy's area heavily gassed with Yellow Cross shell (about 1,500 rounds). Casualties 3 Officers 63 Other ranks. A Coy. withdrawn to an area round Battalion H.Q. and sentries posted at limits of infected area.	
	" 24th		B Coy. relieved D Coy. in front line. Working parties as for yesterday. B Coy's area slightly gassed. 1 O.R. wounded accidentally.	
	" 25th		Working parties as for yesterday. 1 O.R. wounded.	
	" 26th		Working parties as for yesterday. C Coy. relieved B Coy. in front line. Battalion on right pushed forward posts into ARLEUX LOOP NORTH about T.29.c.9.0. (Sheet 44a S.W.) Battalion was ordered to push forward patrols to ascertain if enemy had retired. About 11.0 p.m. S.O.S. signal was sent up from one of the right flank forward posts. Our artillery support was extremely weak — enemy did not attack, so patrols were sent out as ordered and posts established at T.29.b.1.0. T.29.a.9.4. and T.29.b.1.9.	
	" 27th		Battalion relieved by 7th Somerset Light Infantry, and went out without any orders as what was going to take place. Enemy shelled communication trenches during relief, causing casualties to incoming unit and killing two and wounding two O.R. of D.Coy. Battalion moved by companies in lorries from CANADIAN MEMORIAL on LENS-ARRAS Road (A.11.a.9.9. Sheet 51B N.W.). to WOOD CAMP, ECURIE.(Sheet 51 B N.W. about A.27.b.9.9.) P.T.O.	

VIMY – OPPY SECTOR

WAR DIARY
or
INTELLIGENCE SUMMARY.
(Erase heading not required.)

Army Form C. 2118.

Place	Date	Hour	Summary of Events and Information	Remarks and references to Appendices
OPPY SECTOR	Aug. 27-28th 1918		On arrival Battalion had a hot meal and was then ordered up into support. Battn H.Q. at B.27.c.7.1. Coys in trenches in B.27.b. B.28.a & c and H.3.a. Relief started 4.0 p.m. 27th Aug. and Battalion was established in new positions about 5.0 a.m. 28th.	
	28th.		Brigade had moved from North flank of Division to South flank and now became right Bde. No work was done this day.	
	29th.		Front line Battn. pushed forward strong patrols to clear up situation in and around GAVRELLE (Sheet 51 B N.W.) C Coy. was ordered forward and placed at disposal of 2nd. Royal Berks Regt. to support and carry for them. In addition Battalion found working parties as follows.— 2 platoons making dumps of S.A.A. and bombs for forward Battalion. 1 Coy. deepening TYNE ALLEY (Sheet 51 B N.W. d.23.central.	
	30th		Battalion found working parties as follows.— 2 platoons forming dumps for forward Battalions. 1 Coy. working on TYNE ALLEY. 3 platoons carrying T.M. ammunition to forward guns. 1 platoon carrying R.E. material for Right Forward Battalions.	
OPPY SECTOR	31st		Battalion found working parties as follows.— 2 platoons forming dumps for forward Battalions. 1 Coy. working on NAVAL TRENCH (sheet 51B N.W. B.30.) 1½ Platoons carry T.M. ammunition to forward guns. C Coy. withdrawn from 2nd Royal Berks. Battalion bathed at ECURIE.	

1st September 1918.

Comdg. 2nd. Battalion The Rifle Brigade.

Lieutenant-Colonel

SECRET.   COPY

2nd. Battalion The Rifle Brigade Operation Orders

Ref. Map. LA TARGETTE.

1. The Battalion will be relieved by the 2nd. Royal Berkshire
   Regt. on the morning of 21st. After relief the Battalion will
   relieve the 2nd. E. Lancashire Regt. in the Right sub-section.

2. C Coy Rif.Bde. will be relieved by A Coy R.Berks Regt.
   D   "   "   "   "   "   "   B   "   "   "
   B   "   "   "   "   "   "   C   "   "   "
   A   "   "   "   "   "   "   D   "   "   "

3. **GUIDES.** 1 Guide per platoon and H.Q. will meet the incoming
   unit as follows.-
   C Coys guides will be at the junction of TOAST & TOMMY
                           Trenches (T.21.b.60.75.) at 9.45 a.m.
   D   "   "   "   be at junction of PEGGY & CANADA SUPPORT
                                     (T.20.a.8.8.) at 9.45 a.m.
   B   "   "   "   "   "   "   ditto.   at 10.30 a.m.

   A   "   "   "   "   "   "   ditto.   at 12 noon.

4. Immediately Coys. are relieved they will move down the BLACK
   LINE to their new positions. GUIDES will meet them at junction
   of TOAST AND CANADA TRENCHES (T.21.d.1.8.)

5. Stores will not be moved, but will be handed over as they stand
   Tools will be collected and dumped at Coy. H.Q. Defence Schemes
   of the area and work programmes will be handed over.

6. The bicycles sent up to B and A Coys. will be sent back in empty
   ration limbers tonight. 1 N.C.O. and 1 O.R. from the Transport
   will report to O.C. D Coy. at 9.0 a.m. 21st inst. to take over
   the empty water tins of B and D Coys. These men will remain with
   the tins until dark, when they will load them on to the
   returning ration train.

7. Relief complete will be notified to the present Battalion H.Q.
   by wiring the word "FIRST".

8. Coys. will inform relieving Coys. of any guards and detached
   posts which they supply in order that they may be relieved.
   - - - - - - - - - - - -

9. The dispositions of the 2nd East Lancashire Regt. is as follows.
   Advanced Coy. - "A" Coy.
   BLACK LINE Coys. from Right to Left - "B"Coy "C"Coy "D" Coy.

10. Relief takes place as follows -
    C Coy. Rif Bde. relieves A Coy. E.Lancs.
    A   "   "   "   "   "   B   "   "
    B   "   "   "   "   "   C   "   "
    D   "   "   "   "   "   D   "   "

11. GUIDES from the East Lancs.Regt. at rate of 1 per platoon & H.Q.
    will meet Coys. at junction of TOAST AND CANADA (T.21.d.1.8.)
    at the following times D Coy. 11.0 a.m. B. Coy 11.45 a.m. A.Coy.1.15
    O.C. C Coy. is making arrangements regarding the relief   p.m.
    direct with O.C. "A" Coy. E. Lancs Regt.

12. **RATIONS** are brought up as follows- They arrive at MORRISON DUMP
    (T.26.c.8.4.) by light railway about 9.45 p.m. From here they are
    pushed on trucks to VANCOUVER DUMP (T.28.a.4.5.) From here they
    are drawn by Companies. The Transport are finding the men to push
    the trucks up each night from MORRISON to VANCOUVER DUMP.

13. **COOKHOUSES** for Coys. are as follows -
    Advanced and Right Coys. about T.28.a.50.15.
    Centre and Left Coys.   about T.22.c.7.2.
    Advanced Coys. food is carried forward in containers.

14. **WATER.** Each Coy. will have 45 tins of water sent up each night.
    Battalion H.Q. 15 tins. These tins are filled at MORRISON DUMP
    and pushed up to VANCOUVER DUMP on trolleys. 45 empty tins will

                                                              P. T. O.

sent back each night by Coys. for filling for the next night. Coys. must fetch the water from VANCOUVER DUMP. The Centre Coy. will detail a party each night to carry the Advanced Coys. water to their Coy. H.Q. From here the advanced Company will carry it.

The advanced Company will send two guides each evening to report to O.C. Centre Coy. to accompany and guide the water carrying party.

O.C. Coys. should arrange with their C.Q.M.Sgt. _tonight_ how much water will be required to be left at the cookhouses for cooking purposes.

C.Q.M.Sgts. should give any necessary instructions to the ration and water parties each night.

15. Defence Schemes of the area, work programmes etc. will be taken over.

16. O.C. Coys. will forward by 12 noon 22nd inst. the proformas showing material taken over, particular attention being made to note the state of S.O.S. rockets, S.A.A., and bombs.

17. Trench kits and Messes will be moved under Company arrangements.

18. 5 Pack Mules will report to the present Battalion H.Q. after dark to remove Orderly Room and H.Q. material and Battalion Reserve L.G. Boxes.

19. O.C. Right Coy. will detail 1 N.C.O and two men as a guard for MORRISON DUMP. These men will draw their rations from Battalion Headquarters. Any other guards or detached posts will also be taken over by each Coy. as necessary. These guards and posts will be reported to Battalion H.Q.

20. SALVAGE will be sent each night to MORRISON DUMP on the returning empty trolleys.

21. In event of ATTACK (a) before 1st relief is complete, Coys. will remain where they are and take orders from O.C. 2nd. Rifle Brigade (b) before 2nd relief is complete Coys. will take orders from O.C. 2nd East Lancs.

22. Relief complete will be wired by word "SECOND".

23. ACKNOWLEDGE.

Capt and a/Adjutant.

```
Copy No. 1  Officer Commanding    Copy No. 7  Quartermaster
 "    "  2  Adjutant                "    "  8  Transport Officer
 "    "  3  O.C. A Coy.             "    "  9  O.C. E.Lancashire R.
 "    "  4   "   B  "               "    " 10    "   R.Berkshire  R.
 "    "  5   "   C  "               "    " 11  25th Inf. Brigade.
 "    "  6   "   D  "               "    " 12  File.
```

SECRET   O.R.No.424

Headquarters,
        25th. Infantry Brigade

        Attached please find copy of War Diary for the
month of September 1918.

                                        Lieut.Col.,
                                        Commanding,
5-10-1918   2nd.Bn. The Rifle Brigade

Army Form C. 2118

WAR DIARY
or
INTELLIGENCE SUMMARY
(Erase heading not required.)

2 Regt Bn
Vol 41

Instructions regarding War Diaries and Intelligence Summaries are contained in F.S. Regs., Part II. and the Staff Manual respectively. Title Pages will be prepared in manuscript.

Place	Date	Hour	Summary of Events and Information	Remarks and references to Appendices
	1/9/18		The Battalion relieved 2nd. Bn. Royal Berks. Regt. in left subsector of Brigade front. Relief complete 11.35.pm. and Battalion disposed as follows.- Battn.H.Q. at B.27.b.8.7. B & C Companies holding main line of defence from B.23.a.0.9½ S.E. along BOW SUPPORT, TYNE ALLEY, NAVAL TRENCH to B.30.a.6.7. A & D Companies holding front line along VISCOUNT ST, BLUE ALLEY, RAILWAY TRENCH to C.19.c.3.1. with section observation posts in CADORNA TRENCH and CECIL SUPPORT. 24th Inf. Brigade on the North and 2nd E.Lancs. Regt. on South of Battalion. Our Artillery showed considerable activity, the enemy very little.	51.S.W.W
	2/9/18		Our Artillery active with harrassing fire. Enemy quiet. At dawn, patrols were pushed forward to CHAMPAGNE TRENCH and CECIL TRENCH but saw no enemy. At night, B & C Coys strengthened wire in front of TYNE ALLEY.	
	3/9/18		At dawn, patrols were pushed forward towards CHEESECAKE TRENCH. Hostile machine gun was located at about C.19.b.05.15. C Company relieved A Company in left part of front line- B Company relieved D Company in right part of front line.	51.S.W.
	4/9/18		Patrols pushed up CHARLES to CECIL TRENCH, saw no enemy. Casualties.- 1 O.R. accidentally killed.	
	5/9/18		Small party of the enemy attempted to enter our lines at C.19.c.40.80. about 2 am., 2 men got into trench but got away again without casualties. Our casualties.- 1 O.R. died of wounds, 2 O.R. wounded. No identification obtained. No artillery barrage to cover raid, though enemy were in CHAMPAGNE & CHEESECAKE trenches and were bombing up CHARLES TR., apparently under the impression that we held it. The Commanding Officer went away on C.O's Course and Major A.E.Wass M.C. took command of Battalion. At night, A Company took over the whole of Outpost and BLUE LINES from B & C Coys, who withdrew to BLACK LINE. 2/Lt. A.HENDERSON and 1 O.R. wounded by a bomb thrown by one of our own during relief.	51.S.W
	6/9/18		At night, a platoon of C Coy. was caught in a hurricane burst which included gas shells. Casualties.- 3 O.R.	

1875 Wt. W593/826 1,000,000 4/15 J.B.C.&A. A.D.S.S./Forms/C. 2118.

Army Form C. 2118

WAR DIARY
or
INTELLIGENCE SUMMARY
(Erase heading not required.)

Instructions regarding War Diaries and Intelligence Summaries are contained in F. S. Regs., Part II. and the Staff Manual respectively. Title Pages will be prepared in manuscript.

Place	Date	Hour	Summary of Events and Information	Remarks and references to Appendices
	7/9/18		Smoke bombs were thrown from our front line, to assist a Raid of 24th Brigade on our left. Operation successful. Several prisoners and a machine gun being captured, with no casualties to raiding party. At night, D Company relieved A Company in front line.	
	8/9/18		Quiet day. Weather changed and rain fell. Trenches bad, especially in Outpost Line. Battalion Transport chosen to represent Division in Corps Transport Efficiency Inspection. 7 O.R. joined for duty.	
	9/9/18		Wet. B Company relieved D Company in Outpost line and took over from E.Lancs. another post at C.25.a.90.95.	S/M
	10/9/18		Daylight patrols pushed forward to CHAMPAGNE & CRUMPET Trenches, and found them un-occupied. At night, futher patrols were pushed out and by dawn on 11th posts were established in CHEESECAKE & CRUMPET Trenches.	
	11/9/18		C Company relieved B Company in Outpost line. Heavier shelling of Outpost line. A Company withdrawn to Camp behind ECURIE.	
	12/9/18		Patrols reported CHESTNUT TRENCH free of enemy. 4 O.R's joined for duty.	
	13/9/18		D Company relieved C Company in Outpost line and attempted to establish a post at junction of CUP & CHEDDAR Trenches. Enemy were holding trench strongly and we failed to establish a post. Casualties.- 1 O.R. killed. 5 O.R's joined for duty.	
	14/9/18		Battalion relieved by 2nd. Battn. E.Lancs Regt. and moved back by bus to ECURIE WOOD Camp (A.21.d.) Battalion established in Camp 5.5. a.m. on the 15th.	
	15/9/18		Rest- Cleaning up and refitting. B.&.C. Coys. bathed.	

Army Form C. 2118

WAR DIARY
or
INTELLIGENCE SUMMARY

(Erase heading not required.)

Instructions regarding War Diaries and Intelligence Summaries are contained in F. S. Regs., Part II. and the Staff Manual respectively. Title Pages will be prepared in manuscript.

Place	Date	Hour	Summary of Events and Information	Remarks and references to Appendices
	16/9/18		Cleaning up & refitting. A.D. & H.Q. Coys. bathed. Inter-Section Shooting Competition.	
	17/9/18		Platoon training. 7 O.R's joined for duty.	
	18/9/18		Platoon training. 7 O.R's joined for duty. Lt.(A/Capt) L.W.MARTINNANT MC. rejoined from Staff of XXII Corps School.	
	19/9/18		Platoon training. 2/Lt. M.E. GLADSTONE joined for duty.	
	20/9/18		Battalion inspected by Divisional Commander at MONT ST. ELOY. 2/O.R's joined for duty.	
	21/9/18		Brigade did night attack, advancing about 500 yards. Battalion moved into support, Battn. H.Q. at B.27.c.55.05. (Sheet 51b.N.W.) 1 Company in KILKERRAN Trench in support to 2nd. E.Lancs Regt. 3 Companies W. & S.W. of GAVRELLE in support to 2nd. R.Berks. Regt. Captain C.E.SQUIRE MC joined for duty.	51 b S.W.
	22/9/18		Trenches bad through rain. 2nd. R.Berks made an attack at midnight 22nd/23rd to capture WHINE TRENCH. A Company moved forward to position just S. of GAVRELLE SUPPORT (WILLIE Trench) D Company moved to A Coys. position in CIVIL AVENUE.	
	23/9/18		Battalion relieved 2nd. Bn. Royal Berks. Regt. Dispositions.- A & D Coys. in WHINE and CHEAPSIDE- 1 Coy. in GAVRELLE SUPPORT - 1 Coy. in COD. CRAB CRAWL- Battn H.Q. at B.30.c.69.28. Casualties.- 2/Lts J.A.S. JACKSON and E.J.WITHERDAN wounded. 2 O.R's killed and 15 O.R's wounded.	51 b N.W.
	24/9/18		Lt.Colonel R.H.LEYLAND killed by a shell while going round the line at about 5.15.a.m. Captain C.E.SQUIRE MC took command of Battalion. Dispositions changed.- 1 Coy. (A.Coy) in front line and 2 platoons of C Coy - 1 Coy.(D.Coy) in CHICKEN RESERVE, CIVIL TRENCH AVENUE and CORK SUPPORT- B Coy. and remainder of C Coy in MARINE and NAVAL TRENCHES - Battn. H.Q. at B.28.c.5.4.	

WAR DIARY
or
INTELLIGENCE SUMMARY

(Erase heading not required.)

Army Form C. 2118

Place	Date	Hour	Summary of Events and Information	Remarks references to Appendices
	25/9/18		Quiet. 1 O.R. wounded. 2 O.R's joined for duty.	
	26/9/18		Lieut.Colonel R.H.LEYLAND buried at ROCLINCOURT (full report attached) Battn. carried up dummy targets to positions in front of WHINE and GAVRELLE SUPPORT NORTH 3 O.R's joined for duty.	57.8 NW
	27/9/18		Chinese attack carried out by raising dummy targets and barrage fire in conjunction with a larger operation further South. R.A.F. reported FRESNES ROUVROY line unoccupied. Patrols pushed out down WIND Trench and GAVRELLE Road reported enemy posts at C.27.a.85.45. and about C.20.d.5.4.	
	28/9/18		Patrols pushed down GAVRELLE Road and WIND Trench: were stopped by enemy fire from about same places as yesterday. 1 O.R. joined for duty.	
	29/9/18		Patrols pushed down down GAVRELLE-FRESNES Road stopped by a party of about 10 Germans. 1 O.R. wounded in this patrol. Captain E.R.B. DRUMMOND - 2/Lt. H.A. BARKER - 2/Lt. A.J.SLUMAN MC. - 2/Lt. E.A.S. COSBY and 2/Lt. D.P.JONES joined for duty.	
	30/9/18		Very heavy rainstorms. Work almost impossible and trenches very bad. 1 O.R. wounded.	

4-10-18.

Lieutenant-Colonel
Commanding 2nd. Battalion The Rifle Brigade

SECRET   2nd. Battalion The Rifle Brigade ORDER No. 121   Copy No. 9

Reference Map 51 B.NW 1/20.000
         OPPY   1/10.000

1. In conjunction with troops on the right and left, 25th Inf.Bde. will move forward the Observation line to the following line, WHINE - CHEAPSIDE - GAVRELLE SUPPORT - CHUTNEY - CURRY - CHESTNUT - CHEDDAR - CANNIBAL. The advance will be carried out after dark.

2. The advance will be carried out by R.Berks. Regt. on the right, E.Lancs Regt. on the left. The Battalion will be in reserve, and will be responsible for the defence of the BLACK LINE now held by the R.Berks. and E. Lancs.

3. Companies will be disposed as follows - 3 Companies in the BLACK LINE from Southern Brigade Boundary to the BAILLEUL GAVRELLE Road inclusive. "A" Company on right, "B" Company centre, "C" Company, Left. "D" Company will be in KILKERRAN TRENCH at B. 23.c? Battn. H.Q. and Aid Post will be at B. 27. c. 5. 0.

4. Boundaries are as follows:-

   Southern Brigade Boundary: I.b.0.7. to C. 26. d. 90. 45.
   Northern   "   "   Grid Line between C. 13. & C. 19.
   Inter Battn.   "   "   C.25.a.3.9 to C.21.c.0.0.

5. The 3 Coys, in the BLACK LINE will be responsible for its defence as soon as the relief of the BERKS REGT. is completed. D Coy. will reinforce the BLACK LINE immediately, now held by the E. Lancs Regt., in event of hostile counter-attack, or on receipt of orders from O.C. 2nd East Lancs Regt. As soon as this Coy. is in position, an officer and a runner will be sent to Battalion H.Q, E. Lancs Regt, and report to the Adjutant exact location of this Coy.

6. PRISONERS POST consisting of 2 Rifle sections of C Coy. under Lieut. Nettleton will be established at the junction of MARINE TRENCH with BAILLEUL-GAVRELLE Road, and will be escorted from there to 24th Brigade H.Q. at B.20.b.1.3. Numbers of prisoners coming in will be immediately reported to Battalion H.Q. by telephone or runner. O.C. C Coy. will be prepared to find prisoner escorts as required by Lieut. Nettleton.

7. Details for relief have already been issued in Battalion Order No. 120. Completion of relief will be reported to Battn. Headquarters by wiring the word "WEST", or by runner.

8. ZERO hour will be notified later.

9. ACKNOWLEDGE.

21st September, 1918.   Capt. and Adjutant.

Copy No. 1   Commanding Officer.
        2   Adjutant.
      3-6   O.C. Coys.
        7   O.C. H.Q.
        8   Headquarters, 25th Infantry Brigade.
        9   O.C. 2nd East Lancs.
       10   O.C. 2nd Royal Berks.
       11   Intelligence Officer.
       12   Signalling Officer.

25th Bde. 8th Division.

War Diary.

2nd Bn. The Rifle Brigade.

October 1918.

Army Form C. 2118.

WAR DIARY
or
INTELLIGENCE SUMMARY.
(Erase heading not required.)

Instructions regarding War Diaries and Intelligence Summaries are contained in F.S. Regs., Part II. and the Staff Manual respectively. Title pages will be prepared in manuscript.

Place	Date	Hour	Summary of Events and Information	Remarks and references to Appendices
	1-10-18		Battalion relieved by 2nd. Bn. E.Lancs. Regt. and then relieved 1/4th Seaforth Highrs in the next Sector south. Orders for move received 1630 on afternoon of the 1st and move occupied all night. Dispositions when move completed.- Battn.H.Q. I.1.c.6.0. (Sheet 51B.N.W.) -B.Coy in front line WHACK TRENCH - C.Coy WOOL, LEG, ARM Trenches. A.Coy. CORK SUPPORT, CURSE SUPPORT, CONRAD, CAB, THE NOSE.-D.Coy. CHICKEN RESERVE - CHALK RESERVE. Casualties .Other ranks.- 2 killed 2 wounded.	
	2-10-18.		Shelling of B Coy H.Q. retaliation asked for. Enemy reported blowing up buildings and making craters in the roads, and divisions to our North moving forward. Patrols pushed forward down COUNT and WAVE Trenches reported enemy in HOLLOW COPSE and the FRESNES-ROUVROY Line. Gas shelling round ARM and LEG trenches.	
	3-10-18.		Continual patrols up WIND and WAVE to see if enemy had retired, but posts found in usual positions in FRESNES-ROUVROY Line. Gas shelling round WIBBLE, ARM and LEG trenches. Lt.Col. Hon. R.Brand D.S.O. took over command of the Battalion. Casualties.-3 Officers. 44 Other ranks.	
	4-10-18.		Patrols as for yesterday. Many fires and explosions observed behind enemy lines.	
	5-10-18.		Patrols out, but enemy still holding line on our front. Battalion exchanged sectors with 2nd. R.Berks. Regt., 2nd. R.Berks. R. took over FAMBOX Sector, 2nd. Rifle Bde. took over GAVRELLE area again.	
	6-10-18.		Battalion holding line- Orders received to attack FRESNES-ROUVROY Line in conjunction with all units of 23rd Brigade and 2nd R.Berks.Regt on left. Bn. H.Q. moved forward to WIBBLE. Major J.K.V.Brown (Att.E.Lancs) took over temporary Command vice Lt.Col. Hon. R.Brand D.S.O. promoted Brigadier General. Companies detailed for operation tomorrow- "A" Company in front line B.&.C. Coys in Support in WHACK trench- D.Coy. in reserve in WIBBLE- Major Brown was in command for operations but did not actually assume command of Battalion until next day.	
	7-10-18.		At.0050 attack by units above named commenced- all objectives gained- By evening whole FRESNES-ROUVROY line was in our possession from SCARFE to GAVRELLE-FRESNES Road. Lt.Col. Hon. R.Brand D.S.O. took over command of 25th Inf. Bde. at 0800, leaving Major Brown in command of the Battalion-Casualties.-1 Off. wounded. P.T.O.	

Army Form C. 2118

WAR DIARY
or
INTELLIGENCE SUMMARY
(Erase heading not required.)

Instructions regarding War Diaries and Intelligence Summaries are contained in F.S. Regs., Part II. and the Staff Manual respectively. Title Pages will be prepared in manuscript.

Place	Date	Hour	Summary of Events and Information	Remarks and references to Appendices
	7-10-18.		In the evening 2nd. E.Lancs Moved up to reserve taking over Bn. H.Q. at I.1.c.6.0.	
	8-10-18.		Success of previous day exploited. Battalion pushed forward to MAUVILLE FARM. Early morning patrols had occupied RAILWAY COPSE By evening enemy had withdrawn to QUEANT-DROCOURT line. Battalion occupied FRESNES village but were ordered to withdraw from it. This village was subsequently occupied by 2nd.Devons Regt. In the evening the Battalion was relieved by the 2nd. E.Lancs Regt. and was transported by lorries to ECURIE WOOD CAMP and went into Reserve. Relief occupied a long time and was not complete until 0530 in the morning of the 9th.	
	9-10-18.		Battalion at ECURIE WOOD CAMP, resting and bathing. Major J.B.G. Taylor MC joined the Battalion as Second-in-Command and took over command vice Major J.K.V.Brown.	
	10-10-18.		Battalion at Ecurie Wood in Reserve at one hour's notice to move. resting and refitting. Battalion warned to be ready to move at a minutes notice after 0700.	
	11-10-18.		Battalion warned to stand by ready to move up the line. Orders received to move by lorry at 0900. Battalion moved off about 1100 by lorry via ARRAS to GAVRELLE. Thence Battalion marched to FRESNES where dinners were taken. Battalion then moved to DROCOURT-QUEANT line at 1600 occupying trenches. C.&.D.Coys in enemy 2nd.line and A.&.B Coys. in enemy 1st line.(C.12.b. Sheet 51 B.).) Dugouts found prepared for demolition and were placed out of bounds to avoid accidents. Battalion billeted in trench shelters for the night.	
	12-10-18.		Battalion standing by. 2nd. R.Berks.Regt. in front pushing on to ESQUERCHIN and CUINCY. At 1500 hours orders received to move forward to RAILWAY Embankment. in QUIERY-LA-MOTTE which was reached at 1700. Battalion at this time billeted here for the night. Some shelling. One water cart damaged. Casualties Nil. Battalion at this time was in Brigade Reserve.	
	13-10-18.		Battalion standing by at QUIERY all day. Enemy reported holding CANAL at DOUAI	

Army Form C. 2118.

WAR DIARY
or
INTELLIGENCE SUMMARY.
(Erase heading not required.)

Instructions regarding War Diaries and Intelligence Summaries are contained in F.S. Regs. Part II. and the Staff Manual respectively. Title pages will be prepared in manuscript.

Place	Date	Hour	Summary of Events and Information	Remarks and references to Appendices
	14-10-18.		Battalion still standing by. Training. O.C.Coys. reconnoitring country ahead. All ranks enjoyed a good supply of vegetables from deserted countryside.	
	15-10-18.		Battalion relieved 2nd. R.Berks.Regt. in front line. Dispositions 2 Companies (C.&D.) in front "A" in support "B" in reserve. Front line approx. in front of DOUAI Prison. Headquarters in Chateau in PETIT CUINCY.	
	16-10-18.		Enemy artillery fairly active, particularly in reserve company's area. This Company "B" was accordingly moved forward to cellars in CUINCY. Casualties:- Lt.A.C.Russell severely wounded- 5 O.Rs wounded. Night spent in active patrolling.	
	17-10-18.		Battalion still in front line. Patrols were pushed forward by both front Coys, to CANAL in front of DOUAI All bridges blown up. Very little opposition. At 1500 a patrol of "C" Coy. had crossed CANAL and entered DOUAI, being first troops to enter the town, which was found completely ransacked. The 2nd. Middlesex Regt. also claimed to be the first Allied troops in DOUAI. Much wanton damage was noticed in the town. Pianos thrown into the Canals- furniture broken with axes- Also pipes of the Organ in the Cathedral had been removed- Draft of 13 O.Rs joined for duty.	
	18-10-18.		Battalion pushed on. "D" Coy being the only company in the front line. Advance continued through WAZIERES with very little opposition. "A" Company in support- "C" Company was disposed about area X.14. b.&.d. and X.8.d. (Sheet 44 A.SE) and B Company occupied WAZIERES. Advance continued without opposition until stream running through X.21.b. was reached when a machine gun opened fire from wood in X.22.d. D Company was finally held up on the bank of the SCARPE RIVER- A Company then passed through D Company and crossed the river during the night and made good VRED and CATTELET. Lt.Col. T.H.Eastwood MC. took over command.	
ANHIERS.	19-10-18.		Battalion relieved by 2nd. E.Lancs Regt. and moved into billets in AHIERES "A" Coy. remaining in VRED. Battn H.Q. in LALAING Chateau.	
	20-10-18.		Battalion moved by route march via CATTLET to MARCHIENNES arriving there about 1000 hours, and went in to billets in the town.	

Army Form C. 2118.

WAR DIARY
or
INTELLIGENCE SUMMARY.
(Erase heading not required.)

Instructions regarding War Diaries and Intelligence Summaries are contained in F.S. Regs., Part II. and the Staff Manual respectively. Title pages will be prepared in manuscript.

Place	Date	Hour	Summary of Events and Information	Remarks and references to Appendices
	21-10-18.		B.& C Coys went on road mending for the morning. Rest of day occupied cleaning up. (N.B.) this was the 11th day out of the line, since the Battalion went in on 5th August last in the VIMY Area.	
	22-10-18.		Battalion paraded for Inspection by the Commanding Officer at 1030 hours and then marched to billets in WARLAING.	
	23-10-18.		Battalion cleaning up generally. Commanding Officer inspected billets.	
	24-10-18.		Battalion still cleaning up and refitting. Details rejoined Battalion from Divisional Details Camp.	
	25-10-18.		Battalion Training under Company arrangements. Particular attention being paid to Platoon training under Platoon Commanders.	
	26-10-18.		Battalion inspected by Brigadier General Hon. R.Brand D.S.O.. After Inspection billets of the Battalion were also inspected.	
	27-10-18.		Church Parade. The Band attended for the first time.	
	28-10-18.		Battalion training. Band plays daily to Companies or H.Q.	
	29-10-18.		Battalion Training. Still at WARLAING.	
	30-10-18.		Battalion Training.	
	31-10-18.		Battalion Training. Captain C.R.Stuart- 2/Lt. L.W.J.Pinnock MM and 6 O.Rs MC joined for duty.	

6-11-18.

C R Ladman(?)
Lieutenant Colonel
Comdg. 2nd. Battn. The Rifle.Brigade

Army Form C. 2118.

WAR DIARY

INTELLIGENCE SUMMARY.

(Erase heading not required.)

Instructions regarding War Diaries and Intelligence Summaries are contained in F.S. Regs., Part II. and the Staff Manual respectively. Title pages will be prepared in manuscript.

Place: BAUDOUR - POMMEROEUL - CATTELET

Date	Hour	Summary of Events and Information	Remarks and references to Appendices
1-11-18.		Battalion still at rest. Training.	
2-11-18.		Battalion Training.	
3-11-18.		Church Parade. In the afternoon the Battalion held a Fete for the benefit of the local inhabitants. It proved a great success. All the children were given prizes, hot cocoa and biscuits. After the National Anthems had been played, the Commanding Officer presented the Maires with a framed coloured drawing of the Regimental Badge. Later, the Maire called on the Colonel and presented a bouquet. Orders were received that 8th Division would be withdrawn into Army Reserve.	
4-11-18.		Orders were received to move to CATTELET area. Battalion marched away from WARLAING at 1330 hours and went into billets in the CATTELET Area, arriving about 1600 hours. Battalion H.Q. at No.7. WIESEN STR. MARICHON.	
5-11-18.		Battalion Training in CATTELET Area.	
6-11-18.		Battalion Training as yesterday.	
7-11-18.		Battalion Training. Company Schemes.	
8-11-18.		Company Schemes.	
9-11-18.		Orders received at 0415 hours to march to ST AMAND at 0800 hours where the Battalion arrived at 1230.	
10-11-18.		March to POMMEROEUL via HERGNIES -VIEUX CONDE' - HARCHIES. The Brigade halted for dinners at 1200 hours, the Battalion being drawn up in a field at LORETTE. The march was resumed at 13.30, and Battalion marched into POMMEROEUL at 16.00 hours amidst aclamations of the populace. March casualties - 10. Length of march: approximately 18 miles.	
11-11-18.		Day spent cleaning up. News received at 10.30 that hostilities cease at 11.00 hours.	
12-11-18.		Battalion moved by march route to BAUDOUR.	

Army Form C. 2118

WAR DIARY
or
INTELLIGENCE SUMMARY
(Erase heading not required.)

Instructions regarding War Diaries and Intelligence Summaries are contained in F. S. Regs., Part II. and the Staff Manual respectively. Title Pages will be prepared in manuscript.

Place: RUMES — ESPLECHIN — BAUDOUR.

Date	Hour	Summary of Events and Information	Remarks and references to Appendices
13-11-18		Battalion in billets at BAUDOUR resting and cleaning up. Following Officers joined Battalion to-day:- Lt. G.H.ROBINSON posted to "A" Coy. 2/Lt. P.LOWDER posted to "B" Coy. 2/Lt. R.U.FISHER " "C" "	
14-11-18		Battalion training at BAUDOUR. The following officer joined Battalion today:- 2/Lt. J.D.COLLIE and posted to "D" Coy.	
15-11-18		Battalion training as yesterday.	
16-11-18		Battalion moved by lorry from BAUDOUR to ESPLECHIN via TOURNAI.	
17-11-18		Battalion resting in billets.	
18-11-18		Battalion marched to RUMES and went into billets.	
19-11-18		Battalion Training.	
20-11-18		Battalion Training.	
21-11-18		Battalion Training.	
22-11-18		Battalion still Training.	
23-11-18		Commanding Officer's Parade and rehearsal of a Ceremonial parade for Brigade Inspection. The Corps Commander was present.	
24-11-18		Church Parade.	
25-11-18		Battalion Training. Commanding Officer's Parade.	
26-11-18		Battalion still at RUMES training. G.O.Cs Inspection (Brigade) at FROIDMONT.	
27-11-18		Battalion Training. Route March.	

Army Form C. 2118.

WAR DIARY
or
INTELLIGENCE SUMMARY.
(Erase heading not required.)

Instructions regarding War Diaries and Intelligence Summaries are contained in F. S. Regs., Part II. and the Staff Manual respectively. Title pages will be prepared in manuscript.

Place	Date	Hour	Summary of Events and Information	Remarks and references to Appendices
RUMES	28-11-18.		Battalion training. The Band gave a concert in the evening.	
	29-11-18.		Battalion training. Adjutant's Parade.	
	30-11-18.		Battalion Route march. In the afternoon the Battalion played the 2nd Royal Berkshire Regt. at Association football and lost 1-2. A Concert was held in the evening.	
	2nd Decr. 1918.			

A. Blackett
Lieutenant Colonel
Commanding 2nd Battalion The Rifle Brigade.

Army Form C. 2118.

2 R^fle B^n

WAR DIARY
or
INTELLIGENCE-SUMMARY.
(Erase heading not required.)

Instructions regarding War Diaries and Intelligence Summaries are contained in F. S. Regs., Part II. and the Staff Manual respectively. Title pages will be prepared in manuscript.

Place	Date	Hour	Summary of Events and Information	Remarks and references to Appendices
RUMES	1-12-18		Church Parade 1145 hours.	
	2-12-18		Company Training.	
	3-12-18		Company Training.	
	4-12-18		Battalion was due to parade at FROIDMONT at a Brigade Ceremonial Parade. Owing to the rain the Parade was cancelled.	
	5-12-18.		Company Training.	
	6-12-18.		Company Training. The Band gave a Concert in the xxxxxxx Concert Hall at 1730.	
	7-12-18.		The King visited TOURNAI and the Battalion was marched in, in belt and sidearms to see His Majesty. The Division fell in by Brigades on the Plain D*x*Exercise, and from there marched to the portion of the road to be lined . The King arrived in a car at 1200, and walked down between the troops, after the Divisional General and the Brigadiers had been presented. The Battalion then fell in again on the Plain d'Exercise for cocoa and haversack rations, and then marched back to RUMES.	
	8-12-18		Church Parade at 0945.	
	9-12-18.		Company Training.	
	10-12-18.		Company Training.	
	11-12-18.		Company Training.	
	12-12-18.		Brigade xxxxxxxx Ceremonial Parade again put off owing to rain.	
	13-12-18.		A Football Match was due to be played against the 3rd. Bn. Rifle Brigade, who were at CHERENG but owing to bad weather it had to be cancelled.	
	14-12-18.		Company Training. The Final of the Inter-Platoon Football Competition was played in the afternoon, No. 1 Platoon of A Company winning.	

Army Form C. 2118

WAR DIARY
or
INTELLIGENCE-SUMMARY
(Erase heading not required.)

Instructions regarding War Diaries and Intelligence Summaries are contained in F.S. Regs., Part II. and the Staff Manual respectively. Title Pages will be prepared in manuscript.

Place	Date	Hour	Summary of Events and Information	Remarks and references to Appendices
	15-12-18.		Church Parade at 1145 . A League Football Match against the 1/7th D.L.I. was played in TOURNAI in the afternoon, and was lost 3-2. A Friendly Hockey Match against 25th. Brigade H.Q. was successful for us, winning by 3-2.	
	16-12-18.		The move to ENGHIEN was begun. The Battalion moved from RUMES at 0900 hours and marched to BARRY for one night.	
	17-12-18.		Battalion marched to ATH, where it arrived about 1330. Lt.Colonel G.N.SALMON DSO. joined the Battalion.	
	18-12-18.		Battalion arrived at ENGHIEN at 1230 hours and billeted in the COLLEGE DES AUGUSTIN	
	19-12-18.		Day spent in cleaning up.	
	20-12-18		More cleaning up. Lt.Col. T.R.EASTWOOD MC, left the Battalion to take over command of the 12th. Battalion, and Lt.Col.G.N.SALMON CMG DSO took over command.	
	21-12-18.		Continued cleaning up, settling in , and scrubbing equipment.	
	22-12-18.		Church Parade in the Theatre attached to the College at 1000 hours.	
	23-12-18.		Company Training.	
	24-12-18		Company Training. 2nd. Round of Divisional Football League. Battalion defeated 28th F.Amb. by 5-0.	
	25-12-18.		Battalion attended a Brigade Church Parade at 1030 hours. Dinners were at 1230. The Brigadier went round and received a great reception from the men. There was a Concert at 1730. In the afternoon the Sergeants played the Officers at Football. The Sergeants won 10-1.	
	26-12-18		A "Six-aside" Football Competition was begun. In the evening a Fancy Head-Dress dance was held with great success.	
	27-12-18.		Company Training. A Route March ordered, had to be cancelled owing to rain . The Battalion played the 1st.Worcesters(away) in 3rd Series of Divisional League and won by 2-0	

Place   RUMES------BARRY----------ATH--------ENGHIEN-------

1875 Wt. W593/826 1,000,000 4/15 J.B.C. & A. A.D.S.S./Forms/C.2118.

Army Form C. 2118.

WAR DIARY
or
INTELLIGENCE-SUMMARY.

(Erase heading not required.)

Instructions regarding War Diaries and Intelligence Summaries are contained in F. S. Regs., Part II. and the Staff Manual respectively. Title pages will be prepared in manuscript.

Place	Date	Hour	Summary of Events and Information	Remarks and references to Appendices
----ENGHIEN----	28-12-18.		Companies at the disposal of O.C.Companies- Cleaning equipment. R.S.Ms Parade cancelled owing to rain.	
	29-12-18.		Brigade Church Parade. Rifle Inspection by Brigade Armourer. Iron rations withdrawn and consumed.	
	30-12-18.		Company Training. Adjutant's Parade cancelled owing to rain. Inspection of rifles by Brigade Armourer.	
	31-12-18.		Companies at disposal of O.C.Companies. The Battalion played 8th D.A.C. in 4th. Series of Divisional League. A Dance for half the Battalion was held in the evening	

A. Sellar. Lieutenant Colonel.
Comdg. 2nd. Bn. The Rifle Brigade.

WAR DIARY
—or—
INTELLIGENCE SUMMARY.

(Erase heading not required.)

Army Form C. 2118.

Jan - Mar 1919   2 Rifle Bde

Instructions regarding War Diaries and Intelligence Summaries are contained in F.S. Regs., Part II. and the Staff Manual respectively. Title pages will be prepared in manuscript.

Place	Date	Hour	Summary of Events and Information	Remarks and references to Appendices
	1-1-19		Company Training. A Dance was held in the evening in the Canteen.	
	2-1-19		Company Training. A Whist Drive was held in the evening in which 76 other ranks took part.	
	3-1-19		Battalion Route March at 1000 hours.	
	4-1-19		Company Training. The Battalion played 2nd. Bn. West Yorkshire Regt in 5th. Series of 8th. Divl. Football League and won 1-0. Band Concert at 1800 hours.	
	5-1-19		Brigade Church Parade at 1100 hours.	
	6-1-19		Company Training. Lt.Colonel G.N.SALMON CMG.DSO. took over Command of 25th. Infantry Brigade during the absence of Brigadier General Hon. R.BRAND DSO on leave.	
	7-1-19		Company Training. A Dance was held in the Canteen. The Battalion defeated 8th. Divisional Signals in the 6th. Series of the 8th. Divisional League.	
	8-1-19		Battalion Route March. "Six-aside" Competition continued.	
	9-1-19		Company Training. A Whist Drive was held in the evening. The final of the "six-aside" competition was played, No.11 Platoon defeated No.10 Platoon by 2 points to NIL.	
	10-1-19		Company Training. Battalion Boxing Competition was commenced.	
	11-1-19		Company Training. Boxing Competition concluded. A Dance was held in the Canteen in the evening.	
	12-1-19		Brigade Church Parade in the College Theatre.	
	13-1-19		Company Training.	
	14-1-19		Company Training.	
	15-1-19		Battalion Route March.	

Army Form C. 2118

WAR DIARY
— or —
INTELLIGENCE-SUMMARY
(Erase heading not required.)

Instructions regarding War Diaries and Intelligence Summaries are contained in F.S. Regs., Part II. and the Staff Manual respectively. Title Pages will be prepared in manuscript.

Place	Date	Hour	Summary of Events and Information	Remarks and references to Appendices
	15-1-19	Cont'd	The following memorandum was received from G.O.C. 8th. Division:-	

" It has been brought to my notice that a party of 2nd. Rifle Brigade, when returning from leave at a Base Depot refused to follow the example of a large body of men of other units, who, led away by agitators, disobeyed orders and refused to parade when ordered to entrain for the front.

These soldiers of the Rifle Brigade carried out all orders and set a high standard of soldierly behaviour and discipline.

I desire to congratulate the 2nd. Rifle Brigade on its Esprit de Corps.

I desire also to congratulate the Battalion on the fine spirit which, at all times, has animated all ranks during the time it has been under my command, and which manifests itself now, in its individuals, when away from their Battalion, in the face of great temptations.

I am proud that soldiers of a unit of 8th Division should have set such a splendid example of discipline".

1875 Wt. W593/826 1,000,000 4/15 J.B.C. & A. A.D.S.S./Forms/C. 2118.

Army Form C. 2118.

WAR DIARY
INTELLIGENCE SUMMARY.
(Erase heading not required.)

Instructions regarding War Diaries and Intelligence Summaries are contained in F. S. Regs., Part II. and the Staff Manual respectively. Title pages will be prepared in manuscript.

Place	Date	Hour	Summary of Events and Information	Remarks and references to Appendices
	16-1-19		Company Training. 1914-15 Star worn for first time. Battalion played 25th. F.Amb. in Divisional League. Result- Draw- 1-1.	
	17-1-19		Company Training.	
	18-1-19		Company Training. A party of Riflemen went to MONS by Bus.	
	19-1-19		Brigade Church Parade. A Concert was held in the Canteen at 1730.	
	20-1-19		Company Training. Orders received for a Ceremonial Parade in BRUSSELS next Sunday. Companies practicing for the Parade.	
	21-1-19		Company Training, particularly on BRUSSELS Parade. Battalion Team played 2nd.Bn. Royal Berkshire Regt. in 8th. Divisional League and won 2-0. Major J.B.G.TAYLOR MC took over command while Lt.Colonel SALMON on leave.	
	22-1-19		Companies training and practising for Ceremonial Parade. A Concert was held in the Canteen at 1730 hours.	
	23-1-19		Battalion in conjunction with 2nd. Bn. E. Lancashire Regt. practised the "march past" before the Divisional General and the Brigadier. The 2nd. Bn. Northampton Regt. were accommodated in the College for the night. In the afternoon, the Battalion played the 2nd. Bn. Northampton Regt. in the Divisional League. Result:- a win for us by 1-0.	
	24-1-19		Battalion paraded at 0800 hours on the MONS Road and marched in conjunction with the 24th. Brigade Group towards BRUSSELS, being billetted for the night at LENNICK ST MARTIN.Billets were not good. The following Honours and Awards were published:- MENTIONED IN DESPATCHES Lt.Col. T.R. Eastwood MC.(Lond.Gazette 20-12-18) Lt.Col.G.N.Salmon DSO (Lond.Gazette 28-12-18)	
			Major J.H.Alldridge MC.DCM do	
			Capt.G.H.G.Anderson DSO.MC. do	
			No.1405 Rfn.N.Davey do	
			No.Z/435 " H.Flight do	

Army Form C. 2118.

WAR DIARY
or
INTELLIGENCE SUMMARY.
(Erase heading not required.)

Instructions regarding War Diaries and Intelligence Summaries are contained in F. S. Regs., Part II. and the Staff Manual respectively. Title pages will be prepared in manuscript.

Place	Date	Hour	Summary of Events and Information	Remarks and references to Appendices
	24-1-19		Cont'd. AWARDED "CMG" Lt.Col.G.N.Salmon DSO. AWARDED MERITORIOUS SERVICE MEDAL No.9012 CQMS Gibson R. (Lond.Gazette 1-1-19) 3568 Sgt.W.Marney ------do------	
	25-1-19		Battalion paraded at 0830 and marched to BRUSSELS and were billetted in ST GILEES area.	
	26-1-19		Battalion took part in Ceremonial Parade and marched past the King of Belgium, formation was in "double fours" 8 pack mules and 8 limbers followed the Battalion. After the Parade all ranks were granted 24 hours leave in BRUSSELS. Snow fell during the march past and during the previous night.	
	27-1-19		Battalion on leave in BRUSSELS.	
	28-1-19		Battalion paraded at 0830 and marched to LENNICK ST MARTIN, and were billetted in same billets.	
	29-1-19		Battalion returned to ENGHIEN arriving about 1430 hours.	
	30-1-19		Practise for Ceremonial Parade.	
	31-1-19		Ceremonial Parade at 1145 in Parc d'ENGHIEN for the presentation of the Croix de Guerre to the 24th. Field Ambulance by General DEGOUTTE. The Battalion and 2nd. Bn. Royal Berkshire Regt. formed 2 sides of the square, and after the ceremony, marched past the General.	
	1-2-1919.			

Major.
Commdg. 2nd. Battalion The Rifle Brigade.

A5834 Wt. W4973/M687 750,000 8/16 D. D. & L. Ltd. Forms/C.2118/13

Army Form C. 2118.

2 Rifle Bgd

J 1832

WAR DIARY
INTELLIGENCE SUMMARY.

(Erase heading not required.)

Instructions regarding War Diaries and Intelligence Summaries are contained in F.S. Regs., Part II. and the Staff Manual respectively. Title pages will be prepared in manuscript.

Place	Date	Hour	Summary of Events and Information	Remarks and references to Appendices
ENGHIEN	1-2-19		General Training. A Special Order of the Day from Lt.Genl.Sir R.H.K.BUTLER KCMG.CB.Commanding III Corps was received as follows"His Majesty the King of the Belgians has asked me to convey to all ranks of the III Corps, and particularly to those who took part in the march through BRUSSELS on January 26th., not only his pleasure at the opprotunity it afforded him and the population of BRUSSELS, for the first time since WATERLOO, but also his personal appreciation of the soldierly bearing and turnout of the troops. I wish also to express my appreciation to the Commanders and Staffs, for the success of their arrangements, and it is with great satisfaction that I repeat King Albert's own expression "As fine a body of troops, as it would be possible to find under arms anywhere".	
	2-2-19		Church Parade at 1100 hours in the Divisional Theatre.	
	3-2-19		General Training. Lts.J.NETTLETON and G.M.ROBINSON demobilized.	
	4-2-19		General Training. A Dance was held in the Canteen at 1730.	
	5-2-19		General Training.	
	6-2-19		General Training. Captain.J.B.KIRKPATRICK & 2/Lt.I.S.WOOD demobilized.	
	7-2-19		General Training.	
	8-2-19		General Training.	
	9-2-19		Church Parade at 1100 hours.Divisional Cross country run won by the Battalion by 2 points. M.PONCET, who has been with the Battalion 5 years, left for duty at 5th.Army H.Q. 2/Lt. J.B.GORDON-DUFF joined from 12th. Battalion for duty.	
	10-2-19		General Training. Lt. J.L.SCOTT demobilized.	
	11-2-19		General Training. A Dance as held at 1730.	
	12-2-19		General Training. Bandmaster S.J.YOUNG, 4 bandsmen and 17 band boys joined from 51st. Battn. for duty, conducted by 2/Lt. R.H.DOYNE.	

Army Form C. 2118.

WAR DIARY
or
INTELLIGENCE SUMMARY.
(Erase heading not required.)

Instructions regarding War Diaries and Intelligence Summaries are contained in F. S. Regs., Part II. and the Staff Manual respectively. Title pages will be prepared in manuscript.

Place	Date	Hour	Summary of Events and Information	Remarks and references to Appendices
ENGHIEN	13-2-19		General Training.	
	14-2-19		General Training.	
	15-2-19		General Training.	
	16-2-19		Church Parade at 1100 hours. A Congratulatory message from H.R.H. the Duke of Connaught(Colonel-in Chief) was published for information: "I have shewn the copy of the letter you received from the O.C. Infantry Base Depot, to the Duke of Connaught, and His Royal Highness has read it with the greatest interest. He considers that those a Riflemen showed the best spirit of the Rifle Brigade, and that their conduct was a splendid example to the rest of the Army. The Colonel in Chief would like you to express his appreciation of their conduct to the men themselves." the Secretary to

The following were awarded the MILITARY MEDAL in the Peace Despatch:-No.Z/333 Sgt. J.Earle No.S/31336 Rfn. A. Bennett. | |
	17-2-19		General Training. Major J.B.G.TAYLOR MC. was admitted to Hospital and Captain C.E.SQUIRE MC took over Command of the Battalion. No.48253 Rfn. S. Carpenter died from pneumonia at the 1st.Australian C.C.S. HAL on 16-2-19.	
	18-2-19		General Training. A Dance was held at 1730. The Band under Bandmaster Young played for the first time.	
	19-2-19		General Training.	
	20-2-19		General Training.	
	21-2-19		General Training. Owing to demobilization it is extremely hard to find requisite number of men for guard duties, each man barely getting 2 nights in bed.	
	22-2-19		General Training. A Band Concert was given in the Canteen at 1745.	
ATH	23-2-19		Church Parade at 1100 hours. The Band played for the Service.The Battalion played the 1/7th DLI	

A5834 Wt.W4973/M687 750,000 8/16 D. D. & L. Ltd. Forms/C.2118/13

Army Form C. 2118.

WAR DIARY
~~INTELLIGENCE~~ SUMMARY.
(Erase heading not required.)

Instructions regarding War Diaries and Intelligence Summaries are contained in F. S. Regs., Part II. and the Staff Manual respectively. Title pages will be prepared in manuscript.

Place	Date	Hour	Summary of Events and Information	Remarks and references to Appendices
ENGHIEN	23-2-19		in the Knock Out Competition of League finalists and was beaten 4-1.	
	24-2-19		General Training.	
	25-2-19		General training. The Battalion 6 aside Team played the M.T. Co. and were beaten 4-0. The R.A. Band gave a Concert in the Divisional Theatre at 1430.	
	26-2-19		General Training.	
	27-2-19		General Training. From now onwards the phrase "in the Field" is discontinued and the actual name of the place to be stated on official documents.	
	28-2-19		The Battalion moved out of the College St. Augustine with R. Berks Regt. into the Ecole des Filles in the Town. Battalion played Div. Signals 6 aside team and drew 2 all.	

C. E. Squire Major.
Comdg. 2nd. Battn. The Rifle Brigade.

Army Form C. 2118.

WAR DIARY
or
INTELLIGENCE SUMMARY.
(Erase heading not required.)

Instructions regarding War Diaries and Intelligence Summaries are contained in F.S. Regs., Part II. and the Staff Manual respectively. Title pages will be prepared in manuscript.

Place	Date	Hour	Summary of Events and Information	Remarks and references to Appendices
	1-3-19.		2/Lts.G.W.S.BROWN & E.J.PLANT and a draft of 60 O.R's proceeded to join the 25th. Batt.K.R.R.C. at DUNKIRK.	
	2-3-19.		Played E.Lancs 6 aside Football.Won 8--0.	
	3-3-19.		Church Parade 1100 hours.	
	4-3-19.		Training.	
	4-3-19.		Major Alldridge M.C.D.C.M.,Captns.J.M.West & D.L.Maclean, Lieut.Bulford & 2/Lts.Cosby and Fyers with 19 of the Band Boys visited WATERLOO. A Special Order of the day was issued by Major Gen. SIR WILLIAM HENEKER KCB.DSO.Commanding the Div.(Copy herewith).	
			2/Lt.A.MACNAMARA struck off strength on proceeding to DUNKIRK as T.C.O.	
	5-3-19.		Training.	
	6-3-19.		Training.	
	7-3-19.		Training. Batt.played Div.H.Q. in the 7th. Series,6 a side competition and won 3--1. This was the final game & left the Batt. 2nd.in the Divn. by 3 pol nts.	
			Lt. Col.T.R.EASTWOOD M.C.rejoined the Batt. from commanding the 1 8th.Batt. & too k over command.	
	8-3-19.		Training.	
	9-3-19.		Church Par ade 1100 hours. The Band played in the Square at 1530,but was forced to stop owing to rain.	
	10-3-19.		Training.	
	11-3-19.		Training. The Band paraded as strong as po ssible for inspection by the C.O. at 1030.	

A5834 Wt.W4973/M687 750,000 8/16 D. D. & L. Ltd Forms/C.2118/13.

Army Form C. 2118.

WAR DIARY
or
INTELLIGENCE SUMMARY.
(Erase heading not required.)

Instructions regarding War Diaries and Intelligence Summaries are contained in F. S. Regs., Part II. and the Staff Manual respectively. Title pages will be prepared in manuscript.

Place	Date	Hour	Summary of Events and Information	Remarks and references to Appendices
ENGHIEN	12-3-19.		Capt. C.R.STUART with 31 O.R's proceeded to join 25th.Bn.K.R.R.C.	
			2/Lts.R.A.MacGEORGE and Hon.T.C.PLUNKET were struck off strength on being confirmed as ADC's to G.O.C.5th.Corps(Lt.Gen.Sir Cameron SHUTE KCB,DSO) & G.O.C.8th.Div (Major Gen.Sir WILLIAM HENEKER KCB ,DSO) respectively.	
	13-3-19.		Parades.	
	14-3-19.		Parades.	
	15-3-19.		18 O.R's proceeded to join 25th.K.R.R.C.	
	16-3-19.		Church Parade 1100. Owing to the smallness of numbers and a fatigue which was found of 16 O.R. there were no men to parade.	
ATH	17-3-19.		Batt.moved to ATH. The men were quartered in the Barracks and the Officers and Orderly Room in billets.	
	18-3-19.		Cleaning up.	
	19-3-19.		The Batt.paraded as strong as possible for inspection by the C.O.	
	20-3-19.		Parades.	
	21-3-19.		Parades.	
	22-3-19.		Parades.	
	23-3-19.		Church Parade 1030.	
	24-3-19.		Parades.	
	25-3-19.		2/Lt.J.WHEELER conducted a draft of 20 O.R's to join 25th.K.R.R.C.	

Army Form C. 2118.

WAR DIARY
or
INTELLIGENCE SUMMARY.
(*Erase heading not required.*)

Instructions regarding War Diaries and Intelligence
Summaries are contained in F. S. Regs., Part II.
and the Staff Manual respectively. Title pages
will be prepared in manuscript.

Place	Date	Hour	Summary of Events and Information	Remarks and references to Appendices
ATH	26-3-19.		Lieut.C.E.GOODY,2/Lt.A/Capt.D.L.MACLEAN and 2/Lt.H.W.SHEARCROFT proceeded to join 52 nd Batt. Rifle Bde. on the RHINE.	
	27-3-19.		Parades.	
	28-3-19.		The CADRE paraded for inspection by the C.O.at 1100 hours.	
	29-3-19.		Parades.	
	30-3-19.		Church Parade 1050.	
	31-3-19.		Parades.	
			During the month the Band played for several units who were giving Dances in and around ATH.	

Lieut.Col.
Commanding 2nd.Batt.The Rifle Brigade.

Army Form C. 2118

WAR DIARY
~~INTELLIGENCE SUMMARY~~
(Erase heading not required.)

Instructions regarding War Diaries and Intelligence Summaries are contained in F.S. Regs., Part II. and the Staff Manual respectively. Title Pages will be prepared in manuscript.

2 Rifle Bde

Place	Date	Hour	Summary of Events and Information	Remarks and references to Appendices
ATH	1-4-19.		Parades. The Battalion bathed.	
	2-4-19.		Parades. Everyone was given metal R.B's for the shoulder, the cloth ones being done away with	
	3-4-19.		Parades. Lt.H.H.Darby M.C. proceeded to join 52nd.Batt. Rifle Bde.	
	4-4-19.		A "Strong-as-possible" parade at 1100 hours, after which a Photograph was taken of the Cadre and Band and also a group of those who still remained who came to France with the Batt. in 1914.	
	5-4-19.		Parades. Lieut.B.R.Everett, 2/Lt.V.G.Neve M.M. and 2/Lt.A.L Aithwaite proceeded to join the 52nd. Batt.Rifle Bde.	
	6-4-19.		Church Parade at 1030. In the evening the Band gave a Concert in the Salle des Concerts at 1800 hours which was very successful.	
	7-4-19.		Parades.	
	8-4-19.		Parades. Gen.Hon.R.Brand, Capt.J.M.West & Lt.F.E.A.Fulford visited Passchendaele, finding relics on the ridge of the Battalions last attack in Dec.1917.	
	9-4-19		Parades	
	10-4-19.		Strong as possible parade at 1030, Lieut W.E.Gage and 2/Lt.E.A.S.Cosby proceeded to England for 2 months leave.	
	11-4-19.		Parades.	
	12-4-19.		Parades.	
	13-4-19		Church Parade at 1030 hours.	

1875 Wt. W593/826 1,000,000 4/15 J.B.C. & A. A.D.S.S./Forms/C. 2118.

Army Form C. 2118

WAR DIARY
or
INTELLIGENCE SUMMARY

(Erase heading not required.)

Instructions regarding War Diaries and Intelligence Summaries are contained in F. S. Regs., Part II. and the Staff Manual respectively. Title Pages will be prepared in manuscript.

Place	Date	Hour	Summary of Events and Information	Remarks and references to Appendices
ATH	14-4-19		Parades.	
	15-4-19		Parades. Battn. bathed.	
	16-4-19		Parades.	
	17-4-19		Strong as possible parade at 1030 hours.	
	18-4-19		12 O.R's proceeded to join 173rd. Prisoners of War Co at Ypres.	
	19-4-19		Parades. Lt.L.W.J.Pinnock MM. proceeded to Engl and on 2 month s leave.	
	20-4-19		Parades.	
	21-4-19		Parades. Battn. bathed.	
	22-4-19		Parades	
	23-4-19		Parades	
	24-4-19		Parades.	
	25-4-19		Strong as possible parade at 103 0 hours.	
	26-4-19		Parades.	
	27-4-19		Parades.	
	28-4-19		Parades.	
	29-4-19		Parades. Batt. bathed.	
	30-4-19		Parades.	

The Band played usually once a week in the PA RK.

6-4-19

P. _____
Lieut.Col.
Commdg. 2nd.Batt.The Rifle Bde.

1875 Wt. W593/826 1,000,000 4/15 J.B.C. & A. A.D.S.S./Forms/C. 2118.

Army Form C. 2118.

WAR DIARY
of
INTELLIGENCE SUMMARY.

(Erase heading not required)

Instructions regarding War Diaries and Intelligence Summaries are contained in F. S. Regs., Part II. and the Staff Manual respectively. Title pages will be prepared in manuscript.

Place	Date	Hour	Summary of Events and Information	Remarks and references to Appendices
ATH	MAY 1919		The Battalion remained in ATH, but moved from the Barracks to the ECOLE DES FILLES, near the Station on the 15th.	

Lieut.Col.
Commdg. 2nd.B att. The Rifle Bde.

SPECIAL ORDER OF THE DAY
by
Major-General Sir WILLIAM C.G. HENEKER, K.C.B., D.S.O.,
COMMANDING 8TH DIVISION.
-------oooOooo-------

To my Comrades; Soldiers of the 8th Division.

      The demobilization of the Division has begun and officers and men are beginning to leave and return to England.

      I have no chance now of seeing you all, as I should like to, in order to say "Good bye", so I must adopt this means of conveying to you what I feel on the breaking up of the Division.

      To those of you who are still here, to those of you who have served in the 8th Division and who are now in other Divisions, to the comrades who have returned to civil life, and also to you gallant fellows who are still in hospital, I desire to extend my warm appreciation of your magnificent services and devotion to duty, and my grateful thanks for all you have done to help me during the two years I have had the honour to command the Division.

      The 8th Division was formed in England and brought out to France by Major-General F.J. DAVIES, now Lieut.-General Sir F.J. DAVIES, K.C.B., K.C.M.G., Military Secretary to the Secretary of State for War, War Office.

      The Division landed in France on November 5th, 1914 and was pushed forward at once to hold the line on the LA BASSEE Road East of ESTAIRES. It saw some heavy fighting in 1915, principally in front of the AUBERS RIDGE, at the battle of NEUVE CHAPELLE, at ROUGES BANCS, near FROMELLES, on 9th May, and at BOIS GRENIER on 25th September, 1915.

      In June 1915 General DAVIES was succeeded by Major-General H. HUDSON, now Lieut.-General Sir H. HUDSON, K.C.B., C.I.E., Adjutant-General in India.

      To the powers of organisation and the capacity for command of its first two Divisional Commanders the 8th Division owes a great deal.

      On 1st July, 1916 in the first SOMME battle the Division suffered very severely and maintained its high reputation.

      On 23rd October, 1916 the Division took part in the stiff fighting for ZENITH TRENCH and suffered severe casualties.

      On 8th December, 1916 I took over command from General HUDSON.

      During March and April 1917 the Division took part in the advance to the HINDENBURG LINE, from BOUCHAVESNES to GOUZEAUCOURT, and in various operations inflicted severe losses on the enemy. A magnificent fighting spirit was displayed by all ranks and the very generous appreciation which the Commander-in-Chief, as well as our Army and Corps Commanders, bestowed upon units will never be forgotten by those in the Division.

      During the above two months the Division received two wires of congratulation from the Commander-in-Chief and six from the Army Commander (General Sir HENRY RAWLINSON, Bart) as well as many similar marks of appreciation and help from our Corps Commander (Lieut.-General Sir J.P. du CANE).

      In reserve to the Second Army during the MESSINES RIDGE battle in June, 1917, the Division was not called upon to go into action. Later however it took part in the battles which were fought on 31st July and 16th August East of YPRES, and it

/captured ...

captured HOOGE and the WESTHOEK RIDGE. In this fighting Brigadier-General C. COFFIN, D.S.O., R.E., Commanding 25th Infantry Brigade, and Capt. T.R. COLYER FERGUSSON, 2nd Northampton Regiment gained Victoria Crosses. The latter award was posthumous for he was unfortunately killed in action.

Our casualties had been severe but the Division had covered itself with glory, and the Commander-in-Chief signified his appreciation of the magnificent fighting spirit displayed by coming to inspect us when we came out of the battle. His generous appreciation inspired all ranks.

In March 1918, after a Winter in the PASSCHENDAELE Salient, we were suddenly rushed down to the SOMME and took part in the heavy fighting of the retreat as part of the Fifth Army.

Ordered to hold the line of the SOMME South of PERONNE, the Division, which then consisted of only nine battalions, was given a front of 9 miles. It was attacked by 9 German Divisions - a German Division against each British Division. For twenty four hours it held the line and hurled the Germans back, and it was not until the enemy were forced to put in three fresh Divisions that any impression was made on our gallant battalions, and then only at one spot. Royal Engineers, Pioneers and everyone capable of holding a rifle were thrown into the fight. The line did not break, it only bent, but it was felt that the strain was too much, and at dusk on the second day, after having held in check 12 German Divisions for thirty-six hours, the 8th Division fell back in perfect order to a newly prepared line. The German Divisions had had enough and did not follow us for twelve hours. It was here on the SOMME that Lieut.-Colonel F.C. ROBERTS, D.S.O.,M.C., 1st Worcester Regiment and Capt. A.M. TOYE, M.C., 2nd Middlesex Regiment gained their Victoria Crosses.

Two days later those of you who took part in it will remember with pride the heroic fighting in the ROSIERES-en-SANTERRE position, and how, although holding 3 miles of front, the reserves of the Division were employed North of our line, and counter-attacking with magnificent courage, restored the situation on a further front of 3 miles, thus aiding three other British Divisions which had been in the battle from the beginning and had suffered severely. It was a wonderful week to have come through alive and to look back upon. The Germans, from first to last, put in 18 different Divisions against the 8th Division.

The line became stable at MOREUIL and, relieved by the French, we came out to re-organise and train, but returned to hold the front just East of VILLERS BRETONNEUX towards the latter half of April.

Attacked at daylight on 24th April by 2 German Divisions assisted by Tanks the front line of the Division was wiped out. The Germans captured VILLERS BRETONNEUX and a portion of the high ground which overlooks AMIENS and the Valley of the SOMME. The remainder of the Division held the enemy all day and prevented him from exploiting his initial success. The situation was critical, and had all the high ground been lost AMIENS might have fallen, and the road been opened to ABBEVILLE. Reinforcements were rushed up in the shape of the 13th and 15th Australian Infantry Brigades, and these, under cover of night, aided by 3 battalions of the 8th Division, carried out a magnificent attack and retook VILLERS BRETONNEUX and the important ground. I always feel that this was one of the most

/critical ...

critical times of the war. Had the Germans improved their original positions by a successful attack at VILLERS BRETONNEUX, they might have concentrated great strength in order to try and drive the blow home; defeated here however they transferred their masses to the South and opened a fresh battle ground on the AISNE.

After the battle at VILLERS BRETONNEUX the Division was sent South to hold a portion of the line just North of the AISNE, North West of RHEIMS.

We were sent there for a rest. Going into the line on 13th May we were all but overwhelmed on the 27th by the weight and power of the German attack which was not stayed on the British front until we had been pushed back for some 20 miles. Extraordinary gallantry was displayed here by the young soldiers of the Division, a great many of whom had only recently arrived from England.

While each unit played a magnificent part in the action, the 5th Battery, R.F.A., and 2nd Bn. Devon. Regiment, were specially selected by the G.O.C., Fifth French Army, under whom we were serving, for a "citation" in French Army Orders, for gallantry. The only survivors of the Battery were four Gunners, while the 2nd Devon. Regiment lost in the action the Commanding Officer, 28 other officers and 552 other ranks.

All the gallant units of the Division fought to the last and, as in the words of the "citation", "responded with one accord, and offered their lives in ungrudging sacrifice for the sacred Cause of the Allies".

I feel convinced that nothing finer in war has ever been chronicled than the action of these young soldiers fresh from England who were imbued with a wonderful spirit - a spirit which no words of mine can adequately describe.

Brigadier-General G.W.St.G. GROGAN, C.M.G., D.S.O., Commanding 23rd Infantry Brigade, won the Victoria Cross during this retreat, on the BOULEUSE RIDGE.

Relieved and sent North again to refit and train, we went into the VIMY RIDGE portion of the line.

On 7th October the Division broke the FRESNES-ROUVROY LINE and three days later captured the QUEANT-DROCOURT LINE and so initiated the British advance North of the SCARPE.

It followed up these successes by capturing DOUAI, MARCHIENNES, ST AMAND, and various smaller towns.

For special devotion to duty and the care of the French sick and wounded at ST AMAND, which was being heavily bombarded by the enemy from 22nd to 25th October, 1918, the 24th Field Ambulance was "cited" in the French Orders of the Day issued by "le Marechal Commandant en Chef" of the French Armies of the North and North East.

Finally at 11 a.m. on 11th November, 1918 the outposts of the Division reached almost the exact place just North of MONS from which the British outpost line had fired the first shots of the war some 4 years and 3 months before. A very remarkable fact.

This short record of the doings of the 8th Division shows what a brave part it has taken in the breaking of the German power.

German prisoners we captured frequently told us that we were called a "Death Division", and said how they feared being put into the line facing us. This was always satisfactory to hear and showed that your efforts were duly appreciated by the enemy.

And now I must mention what, to my mind, is one of the chief factors which has helped the Division to maintain its high reputation - this is the spirit of comradeship which has pervaded all ranks.

/True ...

True comradeship is founded on mutual respect and confidence, and without this spirit discipline would not have carried us so far.

Discipline has been severe, but you have recognised the value of it and have helped to maintain it. Confidence and comradeship have followed, and I have often been relieved of anxiety on hearing this note of mutual confidence sound on the eve of an operation.

I trust you will carry this feeling of comradeship away with you. You and I have been comrades together in the 8th Division in the greatest war that has ever been: let us keep this feeling alive in the future, and let us make a resolve to aid one another whenever an opportunity presents itself.

This note of parting brings to our minds our gallant comrades who have given their lives for their country in this war. They are not forgotten. The thought of their sacrifice will tend to cement the bonds of comradeship which already exist amongst us.

In conclusion I give you my most unbounded admiration for your magnificent behaviour and devotion to duty, and I offer each one of you my best wishes for every success in the future.

A long life and happiness to each member of the 8th Division.

Major-General,
Commanding 8th Division.

25th January, 1919.

www.ingramcontent.com/pod-product-compliance
Lightning Source LLC
Chambersburg PA
CBHW081424300426
44108CB00016BA/2299